Charles Dickens and the Image of Woman

Also by David Holbrook

NOVELS

Flesh Wounds
A Play of Passion
Nothing Larger Than Life
Worlds Apart
A Little Athens
Jennifer
The Gold in Father's Heart
Even If They Fail

LITERARY CRITICISM AND PHILOSOPHY

The Quest for Love
Human Hope and the Death Instinct
Sex and Dehumanisation
The Masks of Hate
Dylan Thomas: The Code of Night
Gustav Mahler and the Courage to Be
Sylvia Plath: Poetry and Existence
Lost Bearings in English Poetry
Evolution and the Humanities
The Novel and Authenticity
Further Studies in Philosophical Anthropology
Images of Woman in Literature
The Skeleton in the Wardrobe
Where D. H. Lawrence Was Wrong about Woman

Charles Dickens and the Image of Woman

David Holbrook

NEW YORK UNIVERSITY PRESS
New York and London

NEW YORK UNIVERSITY PRESS
New York and London

Copyright © 1993 by New York University

Library of Congress Cataloging-in-Publication Data
Holbrook, David.
Charles Dickens and the image of woman / David Holbrook.
p.   cm.
Includes bibliographical references (p.   ) and index.
ISBN 0-8147-3483-9 (acid-free paper)
1. Dickens, Charles, 1812-1870—Characters—Women. 2. Women and
literature—Great Britain—History—19th century. I. Title.
PR4592.W6H63 1993   92-33074
823'.8—dc20   CIP

New York University Press Books are printed on acid-free paper,
and their binding materials are chosen for strength and durability.

Manufactured in the United States of America

c   10 9 8 7 6 5 4 3 2 1

To the memory of my mother, who loved Dickens's novels and named me after David Copperfield, whose story she was reading during her pregnancy.

Gratitude is due to Downing College, the Arts Council of Great Britain, and the Leverhulme Trust for help with the writing of this book.

" . . . But Wooman, lovely Wooman," said Mr. Turveydrop, with very disagreeable gallantry, "what a sex you are!"

—*Bleak House*

Contents

Charles Dickens and the Image of Woman

Introduction

In previous studies I have dealt with the image of woman as she haunts the work of creative writers—Sir James Barrie, Shakespeare, C. S. Lewis, George MacDonald, and D. H. Lawrence. With these I found, as I supposed, that insights from psychoanalysis help us to understand the most baffling meanings. In applying these insights I was not trying to reduce the symbolism of art to some economic theory of the psyche, based (like Freud's theory) on instincts, the death instinct or the sexual instinct or whatever, but to apply phenomenological disciplines in the search for understanding.

Since Freud, psychotherapy has passed through several new phases—"object relations" theory, Kleinian investigation of infant fantasies, John Bowlby's work on attachment and loss, D. W. Winnicott's insights into child nurturing, the existentialist therapy of Viktor Frankl, Rollo May, and R. D. Laing—while psychotherapy has been affected by the European phenomenologists and figures like Martin Heidegger. Happily, I have now dealt with all these movements elsewhere, and may offer, I hope, a kind of literary criticism based on them without having to explain myself yet again.

Freud's best insights, as in *The Interpretation of Dreams,* were phenomenological. That is, they had to do with the phenomena of consciousness—

and, of course, unconsciousness. He saw that dreams, symptoms, sexual perversions, and sexual hang-ups had a *meaning*. It is this element in the Freudian tradition that has been deepened and extended by the figures mentioned above. They have shown that our capacity to find the world and to deal with it are formed within the context of the mother's care, in infancy. We all grow within a mother's body and in a sense within her psyche. We retain in our "psychic tissue" (to use Bowlby's term) the particular marks of her makeup, and the experience she had of us and we of her.

We looked into her face, and saw ourselves emerging in her eyes. D. W. Winnicott calls this "creative reflection," and he believed he found in woman a special state that he called "primary maternal preoccupation"— a special state of psychic parturition in woman in the context of which we find ourselves and find the world. At first the mother allows us to believe we are her; but by degrees she "disillusions" us, so that we have to encounter reality.

This is a complex process, involving the way she handles us, which can be false or true (disaster can occur if a baby girl is handled as if she were a boy, or a boy baby looks into his mother's mind to find what kind of "image" she has of him and finds nothing). A mother who fails to provide an adequate "facilitating environment" for the "maturational processes" may leave within the infant's psyche a dark and even hostile figure that may haunt him all his life. Catastrophes in these processes of early nurture can leave a legacy of lifelong torment in which, often, the central problem is that of exorcizing a dark shadow in the psychic world, of a figure of woman who will not let the soul rest until she is dealt with.

Indeed, all of us suffer from this dark figure of woman in the unconscious since we were all once totally dependent on a woman and she was only weak and human. She gave us life, but might she not also have the power to take it away? Could she not be a witch? She belongs in any case to the father, and in the air are many reverberations from the parents' sexuality, which, as infants, we believed to be a powerful kind of eating. The parents could eat one another up, and perhaps eat us. The breast, which means all the presence of the mother that we yearned for, enjoyed, or were denied, is a focus of both our hope and our delight, but also perhaps of our darkest fears as to the consequences of our voracious appetite, in love or hate.

So, woman is our mother, but then also our mate and, as the Jungians believe, in their analysis of symbolism, our grave, in Mother Earth. All that I am saying, of course, I am saying phenomenologically—in terms of the meanings of the psyche; and, obviously, these symbols have to do with our urgent need to pursue the question of the meaning of life. For, again, we learn to play, and learn symbolism, at the mother's breast; and once we have the capacity to symbolize, we use it (as Winnicott said) to explore the questions, what is it to be human? and what is the point of life? In a great artist like Dickens, then, around the figure of woman circle these pursuits, together with the various facets of her being—angel, guide, whore, witch, mother, libidinal sexual partner, and threat of death.

What puzzled me most when I first began to explore the symbolism of woman in Dickens was the association of woman with murder and death. I shall discuss below the strange image of the hanging woman in *Great Expectations*. It is the shadow of Estella's mother, the murderess with the strong wrists, who is Jagger's housekeeper; but it cannot be her ghost, for she is not dead. Miss Havisham's life is stopped at the hour of her aborted marriage, so she is a dead woman of a kind, while Estella herself has no heart and is emotionally dead. In *Oliver Twist* the appalling murder of Nancy is committed by her common-law husband; she is the prostitute type and a gangster's moll, but she is murdered because her maternal heart goes out in sympathy to Oliver, and over this she betrays her lover. Dickens, as we shall see, was obsessed by the murder and read it in public readings against his doctor's advice until it contributed to his death.

Such a compulsive fascination with such a horrific fantasy suggests that the moment had a particular phenomenological meaning for Dickens, and we may, I believe, invoke the primal scene and the fantasy of the combined parents so that the scene takes on aspects of the dangers of the culmination of sensual lust; the threat in it, at the unconscious level, is one of the dangers of sexual intercourse, as the infant finds them, in voracious fantasy.*

Lady Dedlock is a woman whose emotional life is dead, whose natural feelings are locked up by her denial of her earlier passionate encounter with Hawdon. These situations, it should be noted, are linked to the predicament of a deprived child.

Pip in *Great Expectations* is surrounded by hints of murder: we never

*See below (p. 20ff.) a comment on Steven Marcus's belief that the murder of Nancy represents the primal scene.

know what Compeyson or Magwitch has done, but murder is in the air; Orlick makes a murderous assault on Joe Gargery's sister and, later, on Pip.

In *David Copperfield* it is David's mother who, although not exactly murdered, falls in with the (sexual) wiles of Mr. Murdstone, who blights David's sensitive emotional life and so oppresses the young widow he marries that she dies. In *Little Dorrit* the plot circles around the extraordinary figure Rigaud, who when the book opens is in prison for murder. In *Edwin Drood* there is a murder, apparently caused by jealousy over a woman, and in *Our Mutual Friend*, also, there is an attempted murder of Lizzie Hexam's lover by a fanatical rival, Bradley Headstone. Lizzie herself is brought up under the shadow of murder, as her father retrieves corpses from the river and is suspected of collusion in the murder of James Harmon that is central to the novel.

What does this preoccupation with murder, often associated with woman, mean?

It will surely be accepted that many of these imaginative fantasies have a powerful undercurrent that can only be explained in terms of deep unconscious meanings; they are grotesque, far beyond normal reality, and so disturbing that they have a nightmarish quality. At times, as with some of Dostoevsky's most fantastic moments, they have a desperate quality, as though a character is trying to come up against a reality that he or she urgently seeks—or that perhaps (we may say) the author seeks. Such incidents are Orlick's attack on Joe Gargery's sister and on Pip, or Nancy's murder, or Bradley Headstone's assault on Eugene Wrayburn. These resemble, in phenomenological terms, Raskolnikov's attack on the old woman in *Crime and Punishment*, an act that is the epitome of abnormal criminal acts and the inverted logic that prompts them. It is often significant that such acts have to do with woman—and with hate; they belong to the kind of ferocious hate experienced in infant fantasy, toward the breast and mother.

I believe it is therefore valid not only to see in these themes elements of infantile fantasy but also to speak of a need in Dickens to reexperience the intensity of infantile fantasy for psychic purposes of his own. It is these needs that drive his art, since the problem of the meaning of being is linked with the problems of love and hate, as is only too clear from his work; for in his engagement with the extremes of love and hate, he is investigating the ultimate meaning of being, as Shakespeare was in *King Lear*.

Dickens's dealings with hate are startling: Quilp's treatment of his wife, for instance, and his general villainy; Fagin's impulse to corrupt youth, and his way of having doubtful members of his gang hanged; Monks's impulse to lure Oliver into criminality so he will lose his inheritance; Uriah Heep's manipulations; Littimer's operations in the service of his decadent master; and Sir Mulberry Hawk's menace to Kate Nickelby and his violence to Nicholas and Lord Verisopht. We might have taken Bill Sikes as merely a member of the criminal classes, like MacHeath; but his murder of Nancy is an attack on human sympathy itself, performed in a terrible spirit of inverted morality—"Good be thou my Evil"—it is a glimpse of ruthless-ness. Other characters are carried away by hate—Mrs. Clennam, Bradley Headstone, Whackham Squeers, Monks again ("to vent upon it the hatred that I deeply felt, and to spit upon the empty vaunt of that insulting will, by dragging it, if I could, to the very gallows' foot" [Oliver Twist, 397*]), Steerforth's mother and Rosa Dartle; the reader of Dickens's novels is often startled by the intensity of such moments, and there is often in them a quality of aroused blood and fury that we do not find (say) in Samuel Richardson, Jane Austen, Charlotte Brontë or George Eliot, though we do find this desperate quality in Wuthering Heights.

The tendency toward an inverted morality, when hate is acted out with a sense of justification, leading to intense cruelty in some of these episodes such as the murder of Nancy, suggests a schizoid element in Dickens's fantasy. An explanation may be suggested from Kleinian psychology. If we accept the two "positions" of Melanie Klein's scheme of psychic growth, the paranoid-schizoid is the earliest and deepest stage of development and belongs to a primitive experience of the fear of love. The voracious hunger of the infant, if it is starved of love, is so tremendous, in terms of psychic fantasy, that it comes to fear love; its need is so great that the infant may fear that its hunger will eat up all the world. An individual who grows up with this fear may be tormented by violent fantasies of attacking and emptying the "other" because of his or her hunger for the love of which he or she has been starved. Fairbairn has made an analysis of the strange logic of the schizoid condition, which often culminates in the conclusions, "evil be thou my good" and "good be thou my evil." To such schizoid individuals, who have been deprived of love, love seems the most dangerous

*Page references throughout are to the New Oxford Illustrated Dickens.

thing in the world, so (by infant logic) it is better to hate. It may be better to give up love and the need for love altogether, and operate according to the rules of hate. These tragic moral reversals often appear in Dickens, as they do in Dostoevsky, and it is these that are perhaps most startling. Oliver finds himself within a world operating on the basis of hate, and the inverted morality of hate impels Monks, while in other novels it drives Bradley Headstone, Steerforth, Dombey, Orlick, Quilp, Uriah Heep, and Squeers, in their various ways. But Dickens's primary preoccupation is not with the schizoid problem.

The next stage in infant development is the depressive stage, which belongs to the fear of hate. To enter this stage represents progress because it manifests the finding of the other person, and Winnicott calls it "the stage of concern." The essence of this stage of growth is a recognition of the consequences of one's own hate on others, and so there is a development of the capacity for guilt. Dicken's novels are full of guilt—epitomized eminently by Cruikshank's illustration of Fagin in the condemned cell. Guilt runs through the novels in many forms. Mrs. Clennam is guilty about cheating little Dorrit of her inheritance. Lady Dedlock is guilty about having a premarital affair and a child by her former lover, Captain Hawdon: she is so guilty that in the end she flies away to die: not even heaven can forgive her. Magwitch is a figure of guilt, as is his wife. Guilt haunts the action of *Our Mutual Friend,* not least because of the mystery of the death of John Harmon, and it haunts the mystery of Edwin Drood. All the characters in *David Copperfield* are haunted by little Emily's guilt, as well as that of Steerforth, her seducer. Guilt is clearly an obsession with Dickens.

In Kleinian psychology, guilt is the motive for reparation, and Melanie Klein finds the basis of all our moral capacities in the *depressive position,* the stage at which, concerned about the effects of our own hate on others, we seek to make reparation, and in symbolic terms to make good the mother and her breast, which in fantasy we may have emptied or destroyed. Reparation, of a symbolic kind, impels many human actions and under-takings, especially of a cultural kind—a theme Andrew Brink has taken up in literary criticism.* Guilt is the dynamic behind depression, and the response to depression is either a manic response—a false attempt to remedy the sense of harm caused by others—or true reparation, which is a genuine

---

*See Brink's *Loss and Symbolic Repair.*

engagement with the suffering caused by concern. There is plenty of both in Dickens, and the difference between manic and true reparation can assist criticism here.

In Dickens we find many episodes that evidently represent reparative activity: there is so much suffering. One of the most obvious themes of manic or false reparation is Magwitch's attempt to make Pip into a gentle-man; it is false because it threatens Pip's own authenticity, since it bears no relation to his own discovery of himself. Pip's attempt to save Miss Havisham is a symbolic act of reparation, as are his attempts to protect Magwitch against re-arrest. Little Dorrit seeks to restore her father to a state of "good father" (the father whom no one has ever known); her capacity to endure humiliations, even from him, is a long process of re-parative endurance. Dickens's dramas of the restoration of affluence are symbolic of reparation, too. There are many developments in which people's fortunes are restored to them—to Betsy Trotwood, to Little Dorrit, to Clennam, to Oliver, to Esther. As we shall see, one central theme in Dickens is *the restoration of the inheritance*—as with Esther, Pip, David Copperfield, and Oliver Twist. And we may say that much of Dicken's work has to do with the restoration to central characters of the psychic inheritance that they should have received, by rights, from the mother, from *woman,* had she lived or been available.

There are also many episodes in which tremendous reparation is made through the ordeal of suffering, as with Eugene Wrayburn's being brought back to life, after suffering brain damage, under the loving ministrations of women—in this case Jenny Wren and Lizzie Hexam herself. Esther is nursed through smallpox, while she in turn nurses Charley, and their mutual love is a dynamic of the healing process. Pip goes through a horrible ordeal in the lime kilns and is rescued by Herbert. But he has another, longer ordeal in which, suffering a severe illness, he is nursed by Joe; in the course of this he undergoes a radical moral transformation, by both realizing his love for Joe and experiencing profound guilt over how he has neglected him. Dick Swiveller is nursed through a dreadful illness by the Marchioness. David Copperfield runs away as a child and undergoes ap-palling privation, to be rescued by Betsy Trotwood, who is herself redeemed in the process, by experiencing love. David Copperfield has to undergo the decline and death of his child-wife Dora, and the gradual discovery of his love for Agnes, who also suffers from her secret love for David.

These vast ordeals of reparation bring changes in the hearts of characters, and they often move us deeply because we watch with bated breath to see whether the reparative effort will be successful. Only if it is successful, we feel, can the protagonist as being survive in any true sense. And often the focus of our concern is the love of a good woman.

Dickens is less convincing when he employs magical means to yield a good outcome because in such episodes we have only manic reparation—as when seemingly infinite riches are available from a John Jarndyce or the Cheeryble Brothers or the Mr. Brownlow who takes up Oliver Twist, or even when the Dorrit fortunes are restored. We certainly find it difficult in the extreme to follow the magical switches around John Rokesmith and Bella Wilfer, all of which seem disastrously to belong to the manic. We do not feel it is real or possible—and, of course, the essence of the manic is that it is a denial of death and harm, and a denial of the exigencies of reality. This magic introduction of good fortune often seems false reparation, though sometimes Dickens can use it to demonstrate that mere riches are no solution to the existential problem—as with Bella Wilfer, who experiences such doubts about herself, or as with little Dorrit in her secret yearning for Arthur Clennam.

But where there is moral suffering (as with Pip's anguish over Magwitch) or suffering in sickness or in the presence of death (as so often in *Our Mutual Friend*), then we do feel satisfaction, for the consequence of the anguish is a deepened awareness of our humanness—and of what is authentic, what is right for us, at the deepest level of being. It is the development of the protagonist through such torment that makes *Great Expectations*, *Our Mutual Friend*, *Little Dorrit*, and *David Copperfield* such great novels—because they convey the progress of an inward sense of authenticity.

Since the impulse toward reparation has to do not only with the mother and the mother's breast, phenomenologically speaking, but also with the origins of love and hate, it tends to center around the problem of woman. Dickens pursues themes of reparation around his women in many diverse ways. Betsy Trotwood is rescued from her harsh bigotry and her denial of love on grounds of partiality and prejudice by David's predicament and his claim on her; she comes to love him, and her own ruin and her dreadful marital legacy involve the reader in a further deepening of his or her sympathy. Her love for Mr. Dick and her care for him despite his being simple is yet another manifestation of the power of love in a woman: "the mother knows" as Winnicott puts it. This useful phrase, despite its oddness, seems a completely convincing one to convey the tacit power woman has to do the right thing intuitively. Mrs. Jellyby, whose charity is so "telescopic," represents a misconception of love, directed at export only, while her own home is sadly neglected, with much consequent suffering. (She, by the way, inspired a later, more complex and subtle dealing with campaigning women in Henry James's *The Bostonians*—Miss Birdseye owing a lot to Mrs. Jellyby.) By comparison, Mrs. Pardiggle's form of charity seems to be based on hate. Dickens's comic women are often wicked and cruel but, like Falstaff, they are often found sympathetic because their weaknesses are those we recognize in ourselves, as is the case with Sarah Gamp, who despite her gruesome pragmatism has such life and vitality, from her brightly patched umbrella to her fantasy authority, Mrs. Harris.

At the other extreme are the women whom Dickens portrays as angels: Rose Maylie, Agnes Wickham; he even says of Rose Maylie that "earth seemed not her element, nor its rough creatures her fit companions." These women are less interesting because of the absence in their lives of the reparative need: they do not have to strive with the usual temptations and torments as Esther, Ada, Lizzie, Betsy Trotwood, Biddy, and the more real women do. Agnes suffers a good deal over her father, but is impossibly unselfish. Perhaps in portraying the child-wife Dora, Dickens managed to gain a more critical perspective on his own capacity to idealize woman. Certainly at times he tends to allow himself to depict women as "angels" who have no problems of ambiguity, of emotional need and conflict. With Little Nell this unreal purity becomes morbid: in the end she can only die, resembling a stone angel on a tomb. Her submissive devotion to duty— the duty of a totally committed daughter—is idealized. Even when her father steals from her, she suffers dumbly and fails to challenge him. This "Euphrasia" motif in Dickens will be examined further below, in relation to Dickens's preferences for a certain kind of man-woman relationship, based on the idealization of the father-daughter complex. Lizzie Hexam, Little Dorrit, and the Little Doll's Dressmaker also have cruel and wicked fathers; and while Dickens seems fascinated by this kind of relationship, he shows himself painfully short of insights into the limitations it imposes on the women themselves: he seems not sufficiently appalled by the exploitation of "duty." As will appear, I feel little Dorrit fails seriously to deal adequately with her father, but loves him too absolutely and submissively, while Dickens approves. The Little Doll's Dressmaker perhaps deals most realistically with her "child" (her father), while Lizzie has Eugene to draw her out of her compromise with her father's cruelty: he offers radical criticism of her submission to her father's domination. There are two aspects of the father-daughter relationship in Dickens we need to examine carefully. One is the Euphrasia theme: the archetypal fantasy of the daughter feeding her father with her breasts through the bars of his prison. The other is the reduction of the woman to a child-wife, as manifest in the father-daughter relationship (Clennam and Little Dorrit, John Jarndyce and Esther, David and Dora). Both may be seen as revealing the limitations of Dickens's view of woman's role, in a way characteristic of his time. There is a tendency in Dickens to escape the exigencies and realities of mature relationship by portraying woman as a submissive household servant, carrying her "little" bunches of keys with her "busy little hands" albeit, of course, in the end, allowing the "ship" to bring her a little baby. But the strange fantasies of murder and death seem to reveal that when it came to a full libidinal sexual relationship with woman, Dickens felt himself to be in a state of danger. One means by which he avoided the fear of sex was to present a man-woman relationship from which the libidinal elements are excluded, as with Tom Pinch's relationship with his sister, or by father-daughter relationships, a tendency in his art that echoes his strange relationship with Georgina.

Dickens seems to have idolized the father-daughter relationship: with Esther Summerson and John Jarndyce this inclination is very strong, and though he transfers Esther's affections to Alan Woodcourt in the end, the transfer is made, one feels, with some reluctance; it is done, it would seem, to satisfy the readers, while Dickens's own sensibility is more inclined to celebrate the benign guardian-ward relationship. He likes to fantasize an all-powerful, generous, patronizing father-daughter relationship, in which recognition of the undercurrents of libidinal, normal sexual inclination is repressed. The father figure enjoys all the delights of wifeliness, but without the disturbances of sexuality:

I held his hand for a little while in mine.

"I saw my ward oftener than she saw me," he added, cheerily making light of it, "and I always knew that she was beloved, useful and happy. She repays me twenty-thousand fold, and twenty more to that, every hour in every day!"

"And oftener still," said I, "she blesses the Guardian who is a Father to her!"

At the word Father, I saw his former trouble come into his face. He subdued it as before, and it was gone in an instant; but, it had been there, and it had come so swiftly upon my words that I felt as if they had given him a shock....

"Take a fatherly good-night, my dear," said he, kissing me on the forehead, "and so to rest. These are late hours for working and thinking. You do that for all of us, all day long, little housekeeper." (*Bleak House*, 237–38)

Dickens likes to use the word "little" for women: "the little creature." And by this he shows his inclination to portray the ideal woman as a dutiful daughter, busying herself with her "little" baskets of keys and her household tasks: Esther reports that, "A maid . . . brought a basket into my room, with two bunches of keys in it, all labelled" (*Bleak House*, 68).

John Jarndyce is a foster father to Esther; by comparison Dr. Strong is a father/husband figure to Annie Strong. We may note how with the latter the libidinal leaps out, as she is tempted by a lover—whose passionate interest is symbolized by the red ribbon he steals from her. Dickens is actually somewhat ambiguous about this temptation, and we cannot help feeling that the marriage of this young girl to an elderly man, despite all the honor he deserves, was a mistake, since it means she can never fulfill herself as a young creature capable of passion.

There are several bad fathers in Dickens: little Nell's grandfather gambles and even steals from her; Madelaine Bray's father is a sick and petulant man who oppresses her and keeps her something of a prisoner; Dombey is a bad father to Florence Dombey, and Mr. Murdstone is a cruel stepfather to David Copperfield. Dorrit behaves monstrously to little Dorrit, exploiting her dutiful nature and criticizing her most generous acts as offensive to him and his social status.

But on the whole Dickens seems to idolize the father status, and we cannot help feeling that there was a pressing need in him to be thought a good father himself, although all the indications are that he was a difficult and sometimes bad one. Attitudes to husbands and fathers, of course, tell us a good deal about a writer's attitudes to women and marriage.

Where marriage is concerned, perhaps Dickens's best insights are developed in his comic themes. His caricature of life after marriage is embodied with gruesome realism in his portrayal of the fate of Bumble the Beadle. In chapter 27 of *Oliver Twist* Bumble is shown examining Mrs. Corney's silver: "Mr. Bumble had re-counted the teaspoons, re-weighed the sugar-tongs, made a close inspection of the milk-pot . . ." (*Oliver Twist*, 196). Returning with a stately walk to the fireplace, he declares, with a grave and determined air, "I'll do it!"

He followed up this remarkable declaration, by shaking his head in a waggish manner for ten minutes, as though he were remonstrating with himself for being such a pleasant dog; and then, he took a view of his legs in profile with much seeming pleasure and interest. (197)

By such touches of bodily presence Dickens manages to convey to us the undercurrents of sexuality that often, in marriage, are turned into hate—as happens so terribly with the Quilps, Jonas Chuzzlewit, the Mantalinis, and the Lammles, for instance.

Mrs. Corney plays up to the Beadle in a hilarious scene of sly and awkward courtship: on her breathless return, Bumble asks what has upset Mrs. Corney.

"Nothing," replied Mrs. Corney. "I am a foolish, excitable weak creatur."
　　"Not weak, ma'am," retorted Mr. Bumble, drawing his chair a little closer. "Are you a weak creatur, Mrs. Corney?"
　　"We are all weak creaturs," said Mrs. Corney, laying down a general principle.
　　"So we are," said the Beadle.
　　Nothing was said, on either side, for a minute or two afterwards. By the expiration of that time, Mr. Bumble had illustrated the position by removing his left arm from the back of Mrs. Corney's chair, where it had previously rested, to Mrs. Corney's apron-string, round which it gradually became entwined. (198)

Mrs. Corney has perquisites as mistress of the workhouse:

"Coals, candles and house—rent free," said Mr. Bumble. "Oh, Mrs. Corney, what a Angel you are!"
　　The lady was not proof against this burst of feeling. She sunk into Mr. Bumble's arms; and that gentleman in his agitation, imprinted a passionate kiss upon her chaste nose. (199)

Declaring him "a irresistable duck," Mrs. Corney agrees to marry Bumble, and they exchange endearments such as "dear," "dove," and "love," and he speaks of her "lovely countenance":

The dove then turned up his coat-collar, and put on his cocked-hat; and, having exchanged a long and affectionate embrace with his future partner, once again braved the cold wind of the night. (200)

The next time we meet the pair, however, things are changed.

A paper fly-cage dangled from the ceiling, to which he occasionally raised his eyes in gloomy thought ... it might be that the insects brought to mind, some painful passage in his own life. (267)

Mr. Bumble is no longer a beadle, but is now master of the workhouse, and reflects woefully that he has been married only two months. He admits later,

"I sold myself . . . for six teaspoons, a pair of sugar-tongs, and a milk pot" (268).

Mrs. Bumble fails to respond to Mr. Bumble's stern look, and asks him whether he is going to sit snoring all day. To decide how he shall behave, declares Mr. Bumble, is his "prerogative." Mrs. Bumble sneers at the word with "ineffable contempt." The prerogative of woman, it seems, is to obey.

Mrs. Bumble, seeing that the decisive moment had now arrived and "that a blow struck for the mastership on one side or other, must necessarily be final and conclusive," drops into a chair with a loud scream and falls into a paroxysm of tears.

The drama develops and the comedy has beneath it the irony drawn into it from the previous exchange. We are all weak creatures—and the impulse that draws the couple together is dependence. But now, after sexual union, the mutual dependence is resented, and the struggle for "mastery" begins. Although Bumble is, like Dogberry, a caricature, the presentation has much psychological truth.

Mrs. Corney that was has tried the tears as less troublesome than manual assault. But now she is prepared to try the other method:

The first proof he experienced of the fact, was conveyed by a hollow sound, immediately succeeded by the sudden flying off of his hat to the opposite side of the room. This preliminary proceeding laying bare his head, the expert lady, clasping him tightly round the throat with one hand, inflicted a shower of blows (dealt with singular vigour and dexterity) upon it with the other. This done, she created a little variety by scratching his face, and tearing his hair; and, having by this time, inflicted as much punishment as she deemed necessary for the offence, she pushed him over a chair, which was luckily well situated for the purpose; and defied him to talk about prerogative again, if he dared. (269–70)

As in our own relational difficulties, we find the conflict only binds us together, in its humiliating way, since it is itself a manifestation of need and attachment. So, Mr. and Mrs. Bumble go together to conspire with Monks in the suppression of the relics of Agnes's existence and his fraud on Oliver—until, exposed in the end, they are prohibited from ever again holding office and join the paupers whom they have previously exploited. Such severe realism about human weakness is perhaps what Dickens is most revered for: yet, as we shall see, in his dealings with woman he is sometimes unable to confront reality, while in some of his vacillations around the theme of what woman can or cannot provide, he penetrates to even deeper areas of truth.

Dickens is far too complex a character to be understood in terms of a single theme throughout his work. But it is perhaps worth dwelling further on the phenomenological significance in his work of the orphan theme— the "orfling," as it is called in *David Copperfield*. It seems to represent a hunger for further "reflection." The orphan often also yearns to find the mother's face: there are significant moments, for instance, when Esther first sees Lady Dedlock, and later when she reveals herself as her mother, as we shall see. We may even, I believe, go further and see how a writer preoccupied with the orphan sense of needing to find better access to an inheritance may tend to find woman as an angel, as Oliver finds Rose Maylie.

The younger lady was in the lovely bloom and springtime of womanhood; at that age, when, if ever angels be for God's good purposes enthroned in mortal forms, they may be, without impiety, supposed to abide in such as hers.

She was not past seventeen. Cast in so slight and exquisite a mould; so mild and gentle; so pure and beautiful; that earth seemed not her element, nor its rough creatures her fit companions. The very intelligence that shone in her deep blue eye, and was stamped upon her noble head, seemed scarcely of her age or of the world; and yet the changing expression of sweetness and good humour, the thousand lights that played about the face, and left no shadow there; above all the smile, the cheerful, happy smile were made for Home, and fireside peace and happiness. (212)

Oliver, of course, is an orphan. He is born in the workhouse, delivered by the parish surgeon, and his mother dies on the third page: he is a parish child. In the end he inherits a property, of which Monks has tried to cheat him, amounting to "little more than three thousand pounds," and is adopted by Mr. Brownlow as his own son. Rose Maylie, also an orphan, is an aunt, the sister of Oliver's own mother, Agnes, who was "weak and erring." In chapter 49 there is a long and elaborate unfolding of the plot between Mr. Brownlow and Monks. Throughout it is made clear that Mr. Brownlow's interest in the case arose because he *saw resemblances in Oliver's face.* The coincidences in the book, of course, are incredible, and it is not necessary for our purposes to unravel the fantastically complex plot. We simply note that the essence of Oliver Twist has to do with his being an orphan, while later he is redeemed by a beautiful angelic woman who is his mother's sister (or, we might say, her substitute or reincarnation). The theme of the rediscovered *face* is one we shall look at later: in *Oliver Twist* and *Bleak House* the recognition of a face through a portrait is significant, for example.

Pip, too, is an orphan; everyone who has read Dickens recalls the sad and slightly comical account he gives of the grave of his mother and the series of defunct siblings.

I give Pirrip as my father's family name, on the authority of his tombstone. . . . As I never saw my father or my mother, . . . my first fancies regarding what they were like, were unreasonably derived from their tombstones. The shape of the letters on my father's gave me an odd idea that he was a square, stout, dark man, with curly black hair. From the character and turn of the inscription, "*Also Georgina Wife of the above,*" I drew a childish conclusion that my mother was freckled and sickly. To five little stone lozenges, each about a foot and a half long, which were arranged in a neat row beside their grave, and were sacred to the memory of five little brothers of mine—who gave up trying to get a living exceedingly early in that universal struggle—I am indebted for a belief that they had all been born on their backs with their hands in their trouser pockets, and had never taken them out in this state of existence. (*Great Expectations*, 1)

Both *Great Expectations* and *Oliver Twist* consist of a child growing up with a series of substitute parents—as does David Copperfield, of course, who is also an orphan—his mother having remarried to a wicked stepfather, Murdstone, who treats him so cruelly that he runs away to find a substitute mother in the forbidding but sympathetic Betsy Trotwood. Esther is a kind of orphan, and she has a guardian for father; later she finds her real mother in circumstances in which the acknowledgement cannot be openly made. The orphan theme in *Bleak House* yields the beautiful story of little Charley, which we shall examine.

Little Dorrit is not an orphan, but she is disinherited by the wicked manifestations of Mrs. Clennam, and she is orphaned by Dorrit's collapse and death later in the book. Nicolas Nickleby and Kate have lost their father and their ordeals are those of trying to survive. Florence Dombey loses her mother and is rejected by her father, and when she flees she becomes an orphan and is taken in as a daughter by Captain Cuttle. Estella is virtually an orphan, as her father has been transported, and her mother is kept as a household servant by Jaggers. George Rouncewell is virtually an orphan, as he has kept himself away from his mother and brother. Lizzie Hexam is orphaned early in *Our Mutual Friend*. while Caddy Jellaby is

virtually an orphan because of the neglect of her household by her campaigning mother; Peepy feels very much like an orphan child. Jo, the
crossing sweeper, knows "nothink" of his origins, of course, while the
Marchioness in *The Old Curiosity Shop* is an orphan. Dora is orphaned,
while Tattycoram is taken in from a foundling hospital.

Thus throughout Dickens's works there is a preoccupation with the
urgent needs of the deprived infant and child and of the adult who feels,
like Esther, that he or she has never experienced a full portion of rich
reflecting love. Consequently, when we come to Dickens's image of woman,
the question that hangs over her is whether she can provide that reflection,
that capacity to fulfill the needs of being, the role of the (lost) mother.

A Polly Toodles can provide it better than a Miss Murdstone or an
Edith (though Edith's powers are brought out by Florence—only to lead
to intense envy and hatred in Dombey himself). What Polly provides, as
a strong working-class wet-nurse, is the breast, while often, one senses,
the sickly or oppressed mothers have failed to give the experience of the
breast to their infants. So, crucial to an understanding of Dickens's genius
as a writer is an examination of his attitudes to woman. To penetrate
beyond normal considerations of what this means, we have to try to bring
up insights from psychoanalytical theories about the origins of many of our
adult problems in the infant experiences of hunger, fear, hate, and the
reparative impulse—directed at all we mean by "the breast," the focus of
the mother's care and her capacity to reflect us and bring out from us our
sense of our own being, and our grasp of reality.

It is obvious from recent scholarship that many critics share my puzzlement
about Dickens and woman. Michael Slater, in *Dickens and Women*, writes
in a fascinating way of how Dickens used the women in his life as the
basis of his characters—his mother, for instance, for Mrs. Nickleby and
Mrs. Micawber; his sister Fanny for Fanny Dorrit; Lucy Stroughill in some
of his visions of child-sexless-love; Maria Beadnell as Dora and Flora Finch-
ing; Mary as Rose Maylie and Agnes, and so on. And this in turn leads
him to make some very pertinent comments on the general problem of
Dickens's treatment of women.

He reaches the conclusion that Dickens's "nervousness about any manifestation of aggressive female passion (as opposed to passive female devotion) may be linked to his nervousness about his own strong sexual
responsiveness" (356). He "could not include the turbulence and sensuous

delights of sexuality" in the domestic setting, along with childhood and angels. His women tend to be the Fairy or Angel, the Good Sister, or the kitten: the fully adult woman is missing.

Slater shows by his quotations that the most sympathetically portrayed couples tend to be brother and sister—Nicolas Nickleby and Kate, and especially Tom Pinch and Ruth—while his married couples seem more like fathers and daughters rather than husbands and wives. The attraction of the brother and sister union seems to be that it represents a "sexless marriage" (34), while there are aspects of boy and girl relationships that seem to Dickens especially enchanting, as when David Copperfield speaks of loving little Emily "with greater purity and more disinterestedness, than can enter into the best love of a later time of life."

On the one hand, his experience of his real wife, Catherine, seems to have had little influence on his art. Slater says,

the woman he married and lived with for twenty-two years, fathering a large family by her, appears to have had less impact on his deepest imagination and on his art than any of the other women who hold an important place in his emotional history. (102)

Among these other women were Lucy Stroughill, who was the object of an innocent romance of his happy childhood; Fanny, his sister, whose career at the Royal College of Music was encouraged while he was kept on at the blacking factory; Maria Beadnell, who treated him with cold-hearted contempt and was at the same time flirtatious and flippant. Then there were more significant figures who lived in his household: Mary Hogarth, for whom he grieved as a sister and with whom he fantasized a heavenly reunion, yearning that she might turn out to be of his own blood—a household saint in Dickens's mind, whose relationship to the saintly Agnes Wickfield is clear; and Georgina, another sister of his wife, who embodied that capacity that Dickens regarded as so important for woman—the capacity for a good sisterly relationship. And then there was his mistress, Ellen Ternan, his fascination for whom made Dickens hate his wife and accuse her of many failings, including being a bad mother and housekeeper.

It wouldn't do, I think, to accuse Dickens of being so afraid of women that he hated women, though he does portray some deadly women in his novels (Magwitch's wife, Mrs. Gamp, Mrs. Nickleby, Mrs. Clennam, Mrs. Steerforth and Rosa Dartle, Mrs. MacStinger, Mrs. Corney [Mrs. Bumble]). But we must surely take note of Kate, his daughter (Mrs. Perrugini), who declared that "my father did not understand women," "he was not a good man," and "my father was a wicked man—a very wicked man" (Storey, 219). He was known to swear at his wife, and there are occasional glimpses of his strange behavior at home: for instance, on the eve of Kate's wedding he was found sobbing into her wedding dress (Slater, 185). His final treatment of his wife seems determinedly governed by hatred and misrepresentation. He enjoyed putting women in bodily fear, as Slater reports, quoting an occasion on which Dickens recklessly held a woman in the rising tide, in a melodramatic posture, until her new silk dress was ruined (Mrs. Christian, *The English Woman's Domestic Magazine* 10 [1871]: 339, quoted by Slater, 115) and describing how he ruined two of her bonnets by pushing her under waterfalls. His inclination to bully women is hinted at, as when he referred to himself and Catherine as "Bully and Meek," speaks of exerting "despotic conjugal influence" on her, and writes of how he would keep a strict watch over her housekeeping, "concerning which we hold solemn weekly councils when I consider it my bounden duty to break a chair or two, as a frugal demonstration" (Slater, 111). He spoke of his wife's "bashful sensuality," but that the marriage was energetically sexual is plain from the record of ten children and two miscarriages in sixteen years.

But there is also the indicative episode of Dickens's obsession with Mrs. de la Rue, on whom he exercized mesmerism, in which the fact that (as Slater declares) "the power-relationship was ... sexual" was made plain by a story Dickens wrote at the time, in which a woman "vanishes into infamous oblivion with the man whose face threatening her had appeared in a dream" (Slater, 124).

This, then, was the reality of Dickens's life with his wife and other women, in which it is clear that he could not bring together the ideal and the libidinal, and in which he continued to yearn for an impossible ideal. There was something he felt he had never had: "something beyond that place and time." He wrote to Forster, "Why is it, that as with poor David, a sense comes always crushing on me now, when I am in low spirits, as of the one happiness I have missed in life, and one friend and companion I have never made" (679). Like Esther Summerson, Dickens obviously felt "as if something for which there was no name, no distinct idea, were definitely lost to me," as he goes on. To Esther, he restores this "something" in the strange piece of wish-fulfillment by which she is given to Alan Woodcourt by a kind of magic switch, on Mr. Jarndyce's part, in a ploy, of course, that deprives Esther of any authentic choice in the matter—and as if Dickens could not endorse a woman's free choice in sexual love.

To Dickens fully adult sexual love was, at the unconscious level, terribly dangerous. Michael Slater returns again and again to this problem. It was as if Dickens felt that it was sex that made women cold-hearted: Slater points out that, writing about aunts (like Betsy Trotwood), Dickens mar-veled that "the fire of love should not have been quenched in their lonely hearts," but celibacy was likely to make that fire "burn brighter," and even to preserve women from downright cold-heartedness: "women are never *naturally* vain, heartless, and unloving. They are made so" (176). A woman is often made so by marriage. In the marriages of Charity Pecksniff and Jonas Chuzzlewit, and of Mr. and Mrs. Bumble, he shows the rapid change of courtship into violent brutality and the domination of one partner by the other.

Speaking of the fate of the women in Dickens's novels who are punished by being "endowed with passion" (Edith Dombey, Lady Dedlock, and Louisa Gradgrind), Michael Slater repeatedly notes Edith Dombey, Lady Dedlock, Louisa Gradgrind, and Miss Havisham as women who are "en-dowed with passion." But Edith Dombey's flight with Carter is only a piece of simulated abandonment to passion—she repudiates the man who casts himself as her seducer, and reveals that she only went away with him to humiliate Dombey. Miss Havisham has gone mad because her intended fails to turn up at the wedding—she is passion frustrated and unawakened, and turned to hate. Lady Dedlock has of course the secret of her passionate affairs in youth, but little remains of her passionate nature: she has locked it up in her heart. Louisa simply does not know how to deal with a lover. Surely these women are, rather, *threatened* by passion? Slater says, "we can register just how disturbed he was by this quality in the opposite sex: he seems compelled to show it as finally finished or at least neutralized" (265). Slater concludes that he is reflecting a world that "dealt harshly with women who could not conform to socially approved patterns." No doubt he had to satisfy his readers: but we may, I believe, explore the subjective factors beneath his repudiation of sexuality in women.

One interesting observation emerges from Michael Slater's book: Dick-ens's women tend to be described in terms of their faces (and hair) and sometimes their ("neat") feet: but their figures and bosoms are neglected. There is a tendency for the more admired women to be somewhat ethereal—bodiless, angelic figures. Agnes is like a figure in a church window; Esther Summerson has a mysterious period in which she goes temporarily blind, and is preoccupied with having her face disfigured (though it later becomes as mysteriously beautiful again). She seems to feel at times as if her own beauty, indeed her own feminine and lovable self, has been "given" to Ada, and (as Alex Zwerdling points out) there is a revealing slip at one point when, speaking to Charley about not letting Ada into her sick chamber when she has the smallpox, she says, "Charley, if you let her in but once . . . *I shall die.*" Note she does not say "she will die" but "I will die"— so closely does she identify with Ada, and so closely does Dickens identify with her. The "double" theme is a common one in Dickens (cf. the Harmon story, the Cheeryble brothers), while Dickens himself seemed to need to search for a firm identity. So we may, I believe, see the woman deprived of her birthright as an alter ego of Dickens, who searches continually for a sense of self-being capable of loving and being loved, and in this way remaining in touch with childhood, as a deprived child. His obsession with his mother's "warmth" to return him to the blacking factory to contribute to the family's earnings when he yearned for learning and the opportunity to realize his potential must surely hide an earlier and deeper experience of deprivation *at his mother's breast.*

It is such a deprivation, I believe, that explains Dickens's urgent need to fantasize, on the one hand, and his dread of sensual woman, on the other: a dread that makes him find full adult female sexuality associated with death. For Nancy (he wrote somewhere, "the woman is a prostitute") is both his most fully realized sensual woman and also one who has to be killed in a most brutal way, for daring to show pity for Oliver and loyalty to her man. Her death is a fantasy of the brutal primal scene, and Dickens's continual yearning for childish purity in his women is a way of avoiding the murderous dangers of aroused female sexuality.

Here I was delighted to find confirmation of my suspicions in an appendix to Steven Marcus's book, *Dickens: From Pickwick to Dombey*, titled "Who Is Fagin?" Marcus pieces together various aspects of Dickens's childhood experience and picks out, in relation to this, a number of very betraying phrases and paragraphs.

One of the phrases is in a recollection of Dickens, in which he sees himself sitting on his bed, "reading as if for life." This points to the intense need in Dickens for literary fantasy, and to devise his own fantasies, and this may be linked with the whole question of the humiliation and neglect

Dickens felt as a child, when the father was arrested for debt, the mother followed him into the Marshalsea, and Dickens—who remained outside (a "small Cain," he called himself)—had no home to go to. He seemed to feel most his father's indifference at the time to his yearning for education: his father "had utterly lost at this time the idea of educating me at all."

One day Dickens, who was wrapping blacking bottles at the window, where the workers were watched from time to time, saw his father watching him, and "wondered how he could bear it." We have seen the degree to which Dickens resented his mother's "warmth" for keeping him at the humiliating work. Now he felt his father's freedom was a fraud and an outrage. But Steven Marcus believes that this intense memory of being seen in an exposed situation, and of seeing something menacing, is a screen memory of earlier traumatic experiences. And, as he points out, there are many scenes of the kind throughout Dickens's novels.

These are primal scene fantasies, in which, he believes,

the child [is] asleep, or just waking, or forging sleep while observing sexual inter-course between his parents, and, frightened by what he sees or imagines, is either then noticed by the parents or has a fantasy of what could occur if he were noticed. (Marcus, 373)

In the mind of a very small child, says Marcus, "when parents seem like gods, giants and demons," "sexual intercourse is first apprehended as a form of violence, specifically of murder, inflicted by the male upon the female" (375). In this we have a clue to Dickens's fascination with murder (and, one might add, his preoccupation with public hangings for murder, which he felt ought *to be private:* he was obsessed with the corruption he felt to be inherent in thousands of eyes' being turned on this dreadful activity, and he was especially vivid in his description of a murderous *couple* being hanged). But here, too, we may find clues to Dickens's fear of the fully adult sexual woman, and his fear of sexuality altogether, the converse of which is a yearning for "pure" infancy, and for an innocence, in woman, in love, and in his protagonists, that is prelapsarian: that is, one might say, for a state before the dreadful experience of witnessing the primal scene. This also helps us understand why (for example) the relationship between Eugene Wrayburn and Lizzie Hexam has to go through the threat and experience of murder before it can be accepted: it has to be shown (to the self) that one may survive murder in order to endure adult sexuality.

To return to Steven Marcus: he points out the intensity of the writing about *eyes*, in the way Nancy's dead eyes haunt Bill Sikes, and in the way Fagin is exposed to the eyes of the multitude:

Those widely staring eyes, so lustreless and so glassy, that he had better borne to see them than think upon them, appeared in the midst of darkness; light in them-selves, but giving light to nothing. There were but two, but they were everywhere. If he shut out the sight, there came the room with every well-known object . . . each in its accustomed place. The body was in *its* place, and its eyes were as he saw them when he stole away. (*Oliver Twist*, 368; Marcus, 375)

At the end, Sikes is surrounded by "tiers and tiers of faces in every win-dow," by people fighting each other "only for an instant to see the wretch." At last he calls out "the eyes again," loses his balance, and is hanged by the rope he is carrying.

At the end, with Fagin, the court is "paved, from floor to roof, with human faces: he seemed to stand surrounded by a firmament, all bright with gleaming eyes." As Marcus points out, in the end, "Sikes and Fagin, both of them figures who threaten to ruin, castrate and destroy Oliver, are now in Oliver's place," and the reader is enlisted in their terror. Yet it was the most horrifying scene, Sikes's murder of Nancy, that Dickens read in public *until it killed him*. Yet the essence of the murder is that Nancy dies because she stays loyal to Sikes and is seeking to save Oliver: that is, because of her *maternal instincts*.

But Marcus also points to the strange moments in *Oliver Twist* in which Dickens records what Marcus calls a "hypnagogic phenomenon." They do not emerge out of the logic of the story, and contain elements that are never cleared up, as if Dickens felt compelled to write about a mysterious experience he had had. The first is when Oliver is dozing in Fagin's den:

There is a drowsy state, between sleeping and waking, when you dream more in five minutes with your eyes half open . . . (*Oliver Twist*, 58; Marcus, 371)

Fagin calls the boy by name, and he does not answer. He takes jewels out of a small box, including a trinket that seems to have "some very minute inscription on it" that he pores over "long and earnestly." Suddenly, a flash of recognition passes between them:

for the briefest space of time that can possibly be conceived—it was enough to show the old man that he had been observed. He closed the lid of the box with a loud crash; and laying his hand on a bread knife which was on the table, started furiously up. (*Oliver Twist*, 59; Marcus, 371)

The scene ends inconsequentially, but Marcus links it with his diagnosis of the "primal scene" fantasy, Fagin's attention to the trinket being presumably related to a fantasy of the father being engaged in attention to a sexual goal whose meaning remains incomprehensible to an infant, though when observed turns to furious rage against him.

The second hypnagogic episode is of course the mysterious appearance of Fagin and Monks to the sleeping Oliver in the Maylies' house. Oliver is reading.

There is a kind of sleep that steals upon us sometimes, which, while it holds the body prisoner, does not free the mind from a sense of things about it. (*Oliver Twist*, 255; Marcus, 372.)

As Marcus says, Dickens, in these passages, addresses the reader in a "personal, essayist, and almost musing voice," and each episode contains "illogical" or "false" details, in the sense that something mysterious happens that Dickens fails to clear up. The implication is that, in "sticking so close to Oliver" (for which Dickens, at the time of writing, suffered a recurrence of a childhood malady), Dickens is here approaching, willy nilly, those childhood fantasies of the primal scene, as murder, which he associated with the father: he had, says Marcus, "a feeling of identity with his father, even with that father who appeared to him as destroyer and betrayer," which is why Fagin is so human.

With the fantasy of the primal scene we must link, I believe, those intense fantasies of the infant that are directed at the mother's breast: and here, of course, where Dickens is concerned, we can have no evidence of how he was treated by his mother. We know that Polly Toodles is the picture of a totally maternal woman, as she is chosen to be a wet-nurse for little Paul Dombey, and she is presented as a benign and satisfying female presence, as is Peggoty—the Good Provider.

But the general absence of breasts in the forms of Dickens's women, and his obsession with women's faces as those of angels, often giving the promise of another world, suggest that his abhorrence of female sexuality, such as might have been prompted by primal scene experiences, has a deeper cause in some complication of the processes by which a mother introduces her infant to the reality of the world and other people. We need here to go back to the Kleinian theory of the infant being involved, over his feeding, in his fantasy, in a "cannibalistic attack." There is the question of what D. W. Winnicott calls the way mother and child "*live as experience together*":

The mother has a breast and the power to produce milk, and the idea that she would like to be attacked by a hungry baby . . . it is she who produces a situation that may with luck result in the first tie that the infant makes with an external object, an object that is external to the self from the infant's point of view. (Winnicott 1958, 153)

Winnicott urges us to think of the process as if two lines come from opposite directions:

If they overlap there is a moment of *illusion*—a bit of experience which the infant can take as *either* his hallucination *or* a thing belonging to external reality.

There is a great advantage in finding external reality: it affords relief.

Fantasy things work by magic: there are no brakes on fantasy and love and hate cause alarming effects. External reality has brakes on, and can be studied or known, and, in fact, fantasy is only tolerable at full blast when objective reality is appreciated well. The subjective has tremendous value but is so alarming and magical that it cannot be engaged except as a parallel to the objective. (Winnicott 1958, 153)

In the most primitive state, says Winnicott, the object behaves according to magical laws: "it exists when desired, it approaches when approached, it hurts when hurt. Lastly, it vanishes when not wanted": "to not want, as a result of satisfaction, is to annihilate the object." Winnicott here deals with the problem of trying to understand why, with some infants, they are *not satisfied with satisfaction*. This seems to me possibly to lend insight to Dickens's fear and dread of female sexuality: like a patient to whom Winnicott refers, "his chief fear was of satisfaction"—because satisfaction brought an annihilation of the object, a kind of murder. To such a person, woman might be the source of one's being, but also (as to the Jungians) that grave into which one ultimately plunges—because, in her body, toward which one directs the fantasies of aspiration and idealism, lies the power, in providing sexual satisfaction, that would annihilate one's world altogether. A terrifying infant experience of the primal scene would, of course, exacerbate this feeling, not least in a child who had an extraordinary capacity, as Dickens had, for vivid fantasy, and a hunger to find the very source of his being.

So, while Dickens had a deep respect for woman, he also found her associated with dread. In *Dombey and Son,* writing about Polly Toodles, he says that she was a typical example of the ordinary woman, of "a nature that is ever, in the mass, better, truer, higher, nobler, quicker to feel, and much more constant to retain, all tenderness and pity, self-denial and devotion, more than the nature of men." At times this develops into the Euphrasia theme, which we have examined in *Little Dorrit.* "Nature often enshrines gallant and noble hearts in weak bosoms—often, God bless her, in female breasts" Dickens writes of Nell, when she is thinking how des-titute her grandfather would be without her, in *The Old Curiosity Shop.* But these creatures, often angels, can also be frightening, if stirred up.

There is something about a roused woman: especially if she adds to all her other strong passions, the fierce impulses of recklessness and despair: which few men like to provoke. (*Oliver Twist,* 115)

Dickens's engagement with the problem of woman cannot be understood without taking into account the deeper insights of psychoanalysis, as several critics have found. Lawrence Frank, for example, in *Charles Dickens and the Romantic Self,* makes some useful comments on the images of themselves that Dickens's women have, especially Esther Summerson, who, of course, loses her image before finding it again: and he invokes some enlightening ideas from Maurice Merleau-Ponty ("the image of oneself makes possible the knowledge of oneself, [and] makes possible a sort of alienation" Frank, 1984, 247). Another explanation of Esther's reality is that made by Alex Zwerdling in an article, "Esther Summerson Rehabilitated." He finds the treatment of her internal conflicts psychologically plausible, but criticizes the end as depriving her of existential choice.

There is tremendous poetic resonance around some of Dickens's imagery, as in his depiction of Eugene Wrayburn's reflections on the river, just before his attempted murder:

The rippling of the river seemed to cause a correspondent stir in his uneasy re-flections. He would have laid them asleep if he could, but they were in movement, like the stream, and all tending one way with a strong current. As the ripple under the moon broke unexpectedly now and then, and palely flashed in a new shape and with a new sound, so parts of his thoughts started, unbidden from the rest, and revealed their wickedness. (*Our Mutual Friend,* 698)

That is, they are lustful thoughts, and reveal themselves like *corpses* in the river. The thoughts of seduction directed toward Lizzie seem here to have an apocalyptic quality, associated with sexual love, that brings him near to death, and this association of woman and sexual love with death is an enigma in Dickens's work we need to go on pondering, for it reveals a fundamental duplicity in his view of them.

Bleak House: The Dead Baby and the Psychic Inheritance

Bleak House is in one perspective a thriller, a detective story; but its special power to grip us and move us derives from its deeper content, which has to do with a central theme in Dickens—that of inheritance—the inheritance of each being.

It is highly significant, in the symbolism of the novel, that Esther, who is a kind of orphan, gives her handkerchief to Jenny, the poor woman who lives in the brick kilns, to cover her dead baby, and that later, when Esther is thought to be dying, Lady Dedlock brings the handkerchief from the woman. Later, this handkerchief appears as Lady Dedlock reveals herself to Esther as her long-lost mother. Lady Dedlock dies in the costume of the poor woman who lost her baby. She is in the end discovered through leads given by Guster (who is an orphan) and, of course, by Jo, who knows "nothink" about his parents and is also an orphan, yet plays a considerable part in the action.

Lady Dedlock, then, is one who has allowed her emotional life to die in her by renouncing her passionate attachment to Captain Hawdon, by whom she has had a child she has always been told is dead. Esther, her child, brought up by a punitive woman who often told her that her mother was her shame, is deprived of her emotional inheritance, while Lady Dedlock has been denied her motherly role. Parting from Esther for the last time, she says of herself that "the reality is her suffering, in her useless remorse, in her murdering within her breast the only love and truth of which it is capable" (512). The dead baby symbolizes the loss of the (psychic) inheritance that a child should be entitled to, and the death of the mother's true potentialities.

Faces are important in this kind of drama, and if we read the work of Winnicott we discover why. In *Oliver Twist,* Mr. Brownlow's interest in the case arose *because he saw resemblances in Oliver's face,* while in *Bleak House* the resemblance between Lady Dedlock, Lady Dedlock's portrait, and Esther is something that strikes the blundering Guppy. Esther loses her "old face" through smallpox, and has to come to live with a new face, after much suffering.

The mother is not only the face that reflects the emerging self: she is also the inspiring Stella Maris, who lifts us up toward a higher state of being. The orphan, therefore, feels a special loss: not only has he or she not experienced sufficient "creative reflection" to develop his or her sense of an authentic self; he or she also suffers from a deficiency of spiritual inspiration, and so is prone to idealize the image of woman, when a beautiful face presents itself.

Oliver Twist finds this kind of angelic figure in Rose Maylie; Pip, in Estella; and David Copperfield, in Agnes. But of course the price to be paid by this impulse to idealize is to fail to find woman as she really is, as the creature in whom the libidinal and the ideal are combined. As I shall suggest, this coming-to-terms with the reality of woman is perhaps best achieved by Dickens in his portrayal of Lizzie Hexam.

As so often, in applying concepts from psychoanalytical investigation of the earliest processes of psychic life, we have no evidence in the life of the author. We know little or nothing of Dickens's infancy. He was not an orphan, and all we do know about his childhood relationship with his mother is that, when improved circumstances made it possible for him to leave the humiliating work he endured pasting labels on blacking bottles, his mother insulted his soul by determining to keep him at the toil he loathed. This perhaps indicates some deficiency in her capacity to cherish her son, but for the incident to be remembered as significant we may surmise that there were earlier weaknesses in the relationship that made it difficult for Dickens to sustain an image of the good mother without deep misgivings. But there were other problems, of course, that belong to the whole tenor of his time: his readership pressed upon him an idea of woman that he felt bound to give them back in return, despite its falsity. As an acquaintance of Wilkie Collins, who lived with two women to whom he was not married, Dickens knew well enough how people behaved sexually in real life. The awful opprobrium offered in his novels toward illicit relationships and illegitimate births—sins that put his characters beyond even heaven's mercy—was not the predominant criterion in the social milieu in which he lived, though it may have been in bourgeois circles at large. (Mrs. Gaskell's difficulties show that the Chadband-Pardiggle element was powerful enough in society.) Rather, what we are dealing with are ghosts or phantoms of the imagination—and there we encounter tremendous feelings of guilt, dread, murderousness, and outrage that are associated with the figure of woman, and this suggests some unsatisfactory relationship between Dickens and his mother in infancy.

For some reason Dickens associates woman with the dreadful possibility of being deprived of one's emotional inheritance, and so of being blighted or falsified. In the face of this deprivation one has to struggle and suffer intensely and make prodigious efforts at reparation, to find fulfillment in oneself, and to discover meaning in the world. So when it comes to sexual fulfillment with woman, there is a powerful feeling of inhibition, such love seeming to be full of menace, shadowed by death, and unlikely to lead to harmony and richness. So with him there seem to be, at the unconscious level, terrible dangers in the woman as a focus of sexual desire, and surely this is only explicable according to the kind of insights afforded by psychotherapy.

As I have already suggested, the dead baby in *Bleak House* has a powerful symbolism. The baby is a symbol of the sexuality that produced it; but for the Victorians it was also a symbol of innocence, a creature closer to the angels. The morbid attitude of the Victorians to babies in this mode led to some extraordinary excesses. There is a short story by George Mac-Donald, for instance, called "The Gift of the Christ Child," which surely deserves F. R. Leavis's deadliest critical judgment—"embarrassing." In this a little girl called Phosy, whose father does not love her, picks up a very recently dead baby brother, supposing that he is the Christ child; finding her thus, her father is changed by the image of her devotion, and his love then flows for her in the proper way. Could a Victorian really believe that a child could mistake a baby's corpse in that way? That she could believe it was Baby Jesus? That a hardened heart could be susceptible of change by such an experience? Mrs. Frances Hodgson Burnett's *Little Lord Faun-tleroy,* of course, depends for its effect on the reader believing that hard hearts are capable of redemption by the influence of simple childhood grace, and in the novel the account is not to be despised: presumably here the text is that "a little child shall lead them"? The same kind of process, of course, is demonstrated in *A Christmas Carol.*

More realistically, we can see the dead baby in *Bleak House* as the product of sexual sensuality and so, phenomenologically, as a focus of the fantasies of "inner" and "outer" that go with sexual experience. It is a product of the potentialities indicated by menstruation, always a focus of dread (witness the various ways in which, during their periods, women are supposed to be unclean, likely to spoil rites, pollute society, or turn the cheese); it is a product of those mysterious powers in the psyche by which woman creates us (and can be supposed to decreate us). We must try to see the difficulties Dickens had with the libidinal element in woman in connection with his particular attitude to babies and angels.

In applying my modern phenomenological interpretation I am not trying to explain away Dickens's concern with the baby and infant. I am just trying to show how, as in the fantasies of George MacDonald, the Christian mythology allows for the world of the unconscious to be explored. Dickens's moral concern is perhaps more devotedly Christian than we tend to rec-ognize, more conscious of the ethical precepts of Jesus and the New Tes-tament: there are many places in *Bleak House* where the New Testament is implicitly invoked. Dickens's attitude to children, for instance, obviously bears in mind the sayings of Jesus, about "offences to these little ones." Dickens's warm-hearted comparison is also driven by his recognition of Christ's concern for the poor and the outcast. These Christian preoccu-pations culminate in *Bleak House* in the death of Jo: to him, as he dies, "light is coming," the cart of life is shaken all to pieces, and he is "a-gropin'." He repeats the Lord's prayer:

"Art in Heaven—is the light a-comin, sir?"
"It is close at hand. HALLOWED BE THY NAME!"
"Hallowed be—thy—"
The light is come upon the dark benighted way. Dead! Dead, your Majesty. Dead, my lords and gentlemen. Dead, Right Reverends and Wrong Reverends of every order. Dead, men and women, born with Heavenly compassion in your hearts. And dying thus around us every day. (*Bleak House,* 649)

The scene is very moving, despite the elements of Victorian sentimentality in it, because Jo is a comic if wretched orphan who "don't know
nothink," but who all the same is a survivor; he bites Lady Dedlock's
golden sovereign to make sure it is a good one, and is only too glad to eat
Mrs. Snagsby's broken meats. But for our taste such episodes are too
emotionally loaded, as are the episodes of the brick worker's baby's death
and Agnes's quasi-heavenly status, as when she is the bearer of the news
of the death of Dora and looks like an angel. These moments have a heavy
religiose quality that is very much of its time. Yet, of course, we recognize
the difference between Mrs. Pardiggle's approach and Dickens's. All the
same, the question must inevitably arise—how much did Dickens endorse
this kind of fervor? Did he aspire to be a "good man" himself, or just to
be thought one? Or was he merely trying to satisfy his public?

Often in his work there is a kind of reference to the bearing of Christianity that may be deeply sincere, but to these insistences he cannot avoid
giving a morbid Victorian quality. In the course of invoking religion we
seem to be asked to endorse beliefs that are not really true or possible;
certainly, they seem impossible for us to believe, and one wonders whether
the Victorians could really have believed them. Did they really believe
that Lady Dedlock was beyond even God's forgiveness? Or that Little
Dorrit was being Christlike in her perpetual self-abnegation?[1] How could
they believe such things about babies, about women and children and
human beings in general? How could they believe in such innocence, such
lack of recognition of the realities, as in MacDonald's terrible story? But
besides the obvious moral didacticism there is also here a more complex
symbolism around that dead baby. In one sense, it seems to have to do
with angels, with care, the soul, God's mercy and pity. In another sense,
the dead baby is a symbol of a psyche so deprived that it cannot live and
fulfill itself. The deprived baby evokes the problem of the mother who
could not keep it alive, and so we come to the figure of woman, in relation
to feelings about her, and the extent to which she is to be blamed for our
failures to fulfill ourselves. Even as Dickens embarked on public readings
in which he strove to appear to uphold the domestic virtues, he was
suffering the worst anguish of not being able to establish order and harmony
in his own life, was separating from his wife, whom he considered impossible, and was (apparently) keeping a mistress. So the image of woman, in
this dimension, is the focus of a deep existential perplexity; and if we

attend carefully to his work, we find it leads us to a strong current of guilt around these themes and a sense of something dreadful and murderous in the background.

The Victorians, of course, had developed a heavy taboo on sexuality and on the whole reality of woman. This demonstrated an impossible and harmful desire, which we find in Dickens, that woman should be "inno-cent." The sentimentalized baby in their art, live or dead, is a symbol of that innocence—and this means *sexual* innocence, before the Fall. If only the production of babies could be split off from sexuality and the passion that creates them! We may link this unrealistic sentimentality with the fear of libidinal woman.

In the scenes under discussion in *Bleak House,* the greatest play is made with the contrast between the innocent babe, victim of its parents' gross-ness, and the violence between the parents:

She only looked at it as it lay on her lap. We had observed before, that when she looked at it she covered her discoloured eye with her hand, as though she wished to separate any association with noise and violence and ill-treatment, from the poor little child. (108)

The innocent child is thus separated from the sexual energy that generated it, to which the violence belongs.

We may recall the way, discussed above, in which Mrs. Bumble falls into violence only two months after marriage. In *Martin Chuzzlewit* a similar change overtakes Merry Pecksniff when she marries Jonas and becomes subject to his violent domination. This is clearly related to her sexual knowledge of him, and the point is underlined by Sarah Gamp's professional interest in her possible pregnancy, at the time of her wedding. It is as if sexual union inevitably produces antipathy and discord, and marriage hatred. The horrified submissiveness of Mrs. Quilp, in the face of his cruel tyranny, is another of Dickens's portrayals of a dreadful mar-riage, and Quilp's deformity is calculated to make the sexual union of this pair repulsive.

Behind such dealings with sexuality one often detects in Dickens a deep dread, which displays an unconscious fear of sex as a death-threatening activity; and the concomitant is that creative woman has some of that death-threatening power. Later we shall explore this further in examining Dickens's attitudes, and those of his public, to illegitimacy and illicit passion, and so to the dark side of woman—including man's darker attitudes to woman, and Dickens's own somber side.

In *Bleak House* the baby dies, even as Ada bends over it:

Ada, whose gentle heart was moved by its appearance, bent down to touch its little face. As she did so, I saw what happened and drew her back. The child died. (108)

Besides the sexual themes behind babies, of course, there is the inheritance or *birthright* theme. Esther Summerson is a focus of our feelings about babies coming into the world, their birth, raising, and inheritance: birthright (as in the Jarndyce and Jarndyce case) is, one may say, *the* theme in this novel and in many other novels by Dickens. Dickens's Christian feelings about dead babies seem here to be made plain:

Presently I took the light burden from her lap; did what I could to make the baby's rest prettier and gentler; laid it on a shelf, and covered it with my own handkerchief. We tried to comfort the mother, and we whispered to her what Our Saviour said of children. (109)

The Victorians must have been more acquainted than we are with dead children; but it seems to belong to a certain Christian fairy-story attitude to death, as in George MacDonald's story, for Esther to say "to make the baby's rest prettier and gentler." People who deal with actual dead babies must surely feel a deep distress, and even dread; no doubt they arrange the corpse as decently as they can: but never, surely, would the word "prettier" seem appropriate? However, the dead baby is by now virtually an angel, and is used as a contrast to our earthly state, with Christ being evoked in a powerful way, for His attitude to children.

Dickens has another moral purpose here, of course, having to do with the nature of charity: the scene is intended to contrast with the invasion of the brick maker's privacy by Mrs. Jellyby's associate, Mrs. Pardiggle. She represents the wrong kind of evangelism, the kind that patronizes and offends: she cannot cross the gap to the poor. Among the poor there is brutality, ignorance, and suffering. It would be better for them to have the consolations of a true knowledge of Christ's teaching, but this can only be brought home to them by those who are prepared to share their suffering, who are capable of showing love in action. Such people can invoke the words of Jesus at the critical moment—as here, or as when Jo is dying and

Alan Woodcourt makes him repeat the Lord's prayer at the end. Clearly, Dickens believed in the urgent necessity of applying the principles of Christian compassion, and conveying the Gospel to those who were lost without it.

When Mrs. Pardiggle leaves, the difference between her charity and that of Esther and Ada is made plain:

I hope it is not unkind in me to say that she certainly did make, in this, as in everything else, a show that was not conciliatory, of doing charity by wholesale, and of dealing in it to a large extent. (108)

The influence of the (true) Christianity of Ada and Esther, by contrast, has the effect of bringing out the best in the poor.

I thought it very touching to see these two women, coarse and shabby and beaten, so united; to see what they could be to one another; to see how they felt for one another; how the heart of each to each was softened by the hard trials of their lives. I think the best side of such people is almost hidden from us. What the poor are to the poor is little known, excepting to themselves and GOD. (109)

All this is powerfully didactic, but we recognize it as that excellent impulse in Dickens, under the influence of the words of Jesus Christ, to show that the poor will always be with us, that they too were created in the image of God, and that we should try to understand all conditions of people and seek the "good side" in them. His renderings of characters like Mrs. Gamp or Jo, the Artful Dodger or Mr. Weller Senior are in consequence always humanly sympathetic and positive, as is his touching treatment of little orphaned Charley and her siblings.

But in *Bleak House* the theme belongs to that fairy-tale mode of belief in the supernatural world that can make Esther say,

How little I thought, when I raised my handkerchief to look upon the tiny sleeper underneath, and seemed to see a halo shine around the child through Ada's drooping hair as her pity bent her head—how little I thought in whose unquiet bosom that handkerchief would come to lie, after covering the motionless and peaceful breast! I only thought that perhaps the Angel of the child might not be all unconscious of the woman who replaced it with so compassionate a hand. (III)

Did Dickens really believe in "Angels"? Or is he merely making Esther an innocent believer in them? Did his readers believe in angels? I suppose they might well have done, for there is no doubt that they were exceptionally fervent in religious matters, while their devotional beliefs were a matter of intense interest, as the periodical literature of the time shows.

But, for my purposes, such episodes give the clues to Dickens's *unconscious* preoccupations. Esther has an affinity with the dead baby: her mother has always assumed that she died at birth. When she finds out that her child is still living, but is desperately ill, Lady Dedlock obtains that same handkerchief that has covered the dead baby's face. The question of birthright is thus profoundly underlined, symbolically, at the unconscious level. Behind this is the question of the survival of *being*.

Of course, there are wide implications about the moral issues here that cannot be separated from religious belief. If such a child has an "Angel," and the angel can be aware of how adults behave, aware of the moral significance of their acts, then we live in a totally different world from our present (secular) world of general disbelief or unbelief, in which it is impossible to believe in angels. For in a world in which a baby's angel can be aware of pity and compassion, there are eternal verities and universal considerations in our every act; it is still a world in which "Thou God seest me." An irresponsible sexual relationship would then be seen as one that was likely to create babies (with angels) who have a birthright that may be blighted for life (like Esther's). Sexual passion becomes then a matter of the deepest spiritual concern, for what it may create may go on existing even in heaven and may be able to judge earthly creatures. However, as we know, this kind of religious morality applied to the middle classes: there was less concern for the babies farmed out by prostitutes and the demimondaines.

Later, we shall have to go in more detail into the attitudes in this novel toward illegitimacy. There seems to have been a considerable change in attitudes to illegitimacy during the first half of the nineteenth century. In Jane Austen there is often some discussion of "natural" children; but there is no horrified and prudish dismay about the matter: take, for instance, her presentation of Harriet Smith in *Emma*. It is interesting to ponder the implications of her remark when Harriet's (merchant) parentage is revealed: "The stain of illegitimacy, *unbleached by nobility or wealth*, would have been a stain indeed." But there is no sense of sin and horror about the illegitimacy itself. No one would talk to Harriet Smith as her godmother talks (in chapter 3) to Esther. Dickens seems to need to accede to his audience's opprobrium, for not only do the stepmothers inflict guilt on the illegitimate infants they raise (like Miss Barbary and Miss Clennam); but the women themselves feel they are beyond forgiveness.

One recurring theme is that of the baby that is born of some illicit passion and is then handed over to a near relation, who raises the children in the severest possible manner, as if to punish the infant for the sin of its parents. This has been the fate of Arthur Clennam in *Little Dorrit,* as well as of Esther. It is obvious that Dickens does not approve of such vengeful infliction of punishment of the sins of the mothers on the children (Agnes, Oliver Twist's mother, is pardoned as "weak and erring"), but it seems that his audience enjoyed the frisson of guilt all the same, and he never attempts assertively to exonerate those who fall into the wickedness of illicit passion—or, at least, they can never expect to be received in the company of decent people. The men, like Edward Leeford, do come in for some blame, or are degenerating, like Captain Hawdon.

Let us for a moment, however, turn away from the questions of social *moeurs* and morals over illegitimacy in order to look further at the uncon-scious themes of birthright associated with it. The handkerchief that Esther uses to cover the dead baby's face reappears in the hands of Lady Dedlock in the scene in which she declares herself Esther's mother (book 2, chapter 5), and so for the first time they look at one another.

The mother's face is a powerful archetypal symbol, and the reasons for this are illuminated by Winnicott's notion of "creative reflection": the baby finds itself in the mother's regard. The link between the dead baby and Esther is not only that Esther was once put aside as dead when she was a baby but also that her deprivation of the mother threatens her with *psychic death.* This is a common Dickensian theme: Estella in *Great Ex-pectations* is a woman who suffers from deadness of the emotions, as does Louisa Gradgrind to some extent, while Florence Dombey is threatened with a similar blight by her father's rejection, as she feels her good image of him in her heart die. Dickens is aware of the need for creative reflection and for that imaginative sympathy and play that enable the child to come into its psychic birthright. The handkerchief is a symbolic veil between self and world, akin to the curtain of the bassinette in Berthe Morisot's lovely painting *La Berceuse.*

So the handkerchief that has covered the dead baby's face links the dead baby with the dread of deadness in a psyche that has never sufficiently experienced creative reflection from the mother. When Lady Dedlock comes face to face with the Esther she now knows to be her own child, Esther not only perceives her as completely unbending from her usual "haughty self-restraint" but is also "rendered motionless" by a something in her face that I had pined for and dreamed of when I was a little child; something I had never seen in any face; something I had never seen in hers before. (508)

Later she says,

I looked at her; but I could not see her, I could not hear her, I could not draw my breath (509)

—an experience of the kind a child sometimes has when the mother returns after an absence during which the child has tried to hold her image together in its memory, and failed (see Winnicott, 1958, 309 and elsewhere).

We may remember that earlier Dickens has given Esther an uncanny power to respond to Lady Dedlock's glances:

Shall I ever forget the rapid beating of my heart, occasioned by the look I met, as I stood up! Shall I ever forget the manner in which those handsome proud eyes seemed to spring out of languor, and to hold mine! ...

And, very strangely, there was something quickened within me, associated with the lonely days at my godmother's; yes, away even to the days when I had stood on tiptoe to dress myself at my little glass, after dressing my doll. And this, although I had never seen this Lady's face before in all my life—I was quite sure of it— absolutely certain. (249–50)

Dickens presumably felt this was the operation of "natural love." The reference to the mirror here is significant, for what Esther is shown to be yearning for is what Winnicott called "the mother in her mirror role"— that is, as the responding face in which one finds oneself reflected.

Esther also at this moment hears the mother's voice:

Then, very strangely, I seemed to hear them, not in the reader's voice, but in the well-remembered voice of my godmother.[2] This made me think, did Lady Dedlock's face accidentally resemble my godmother's? It might be that it did, a little; but, the expression was so different, and the stern decision which had worn into my godmother's face, like weather into rocks, was so completely wanting in the face before me, that it could not be that resemblance which had struck me. (250)

She recalls her child self:

And yet I—I, little Esther Summerson, the child who lived a life apart, and on whose birthday there was no rejoicing—seemed to arise before my own eyes, evoked out of the past by some power in this fashionable lady, whom ... I perfectly well knew I had never seen until that hour. (250)

What Esther is yearning for is that *unique* recognition of the existential being that only the mother can give, as she reflects and draws out the potentialities of the self. The need is beautifully expressed by George MacDonald in his fantasy *At the Back of the North Wind:* Diamond tells the North Wind (a kind of fantasy mother) that he does not like the nursery rhyme *Little Bopeep:*

Because it seems to say one's as good as another, or two new ones are better than one that's lost. I've been thinking about it a good deal, and it seems to me that although any one sixpence is as good as any other sixpence, not twenty lambs would do instead of one sheep whose face you knew. Somehow, when once you've looked into anybody's eyes, right deep down into them, I mean, nobody will do for that one any more. Nobody, ever so beautiful or so good, will make up for that one going out of sight. (263–64, Nonesuch Edition)[3]

If we take Dicken's novel at the phenomenological level, then we may see that it is, of course, a terrible thing to deny this reflecting "natural love" to any child. However, Esther seems to have a substantial sense of identity and a rich emotional life and sympathy (compared, say, with Estella in *Great Expectations*); so we may suppose her upbringing has been sufficiently achieved by someone taking the place of a "good mother," however punitive.

This problem is not unconnected with that of the punitive attitude to sexual passion. Esther, we remember, has been told,

"Your mother, Esther, is your disgrace, and you were hers. . . . Unfortunate girl, orphaned and degraded from the first of these evil anniversaries, pray daily that the sins of others be not visited upon your head, according to what is written. Forget your mother, and leave all other people to forget her who will do her unhappy child that greatest kindness. . . .

Submission, self-denial, diligent work, are the preparations for a life begun with such a shadow on it. You are different from other children, Esther, because you were not born, like them, in common sinfulness and wrath. You are set apart." (17)

There are some important points to note here. Dickens intended implicitly to criticize this punitive view; yet odd emphases creep into his way of putting it. The last sentence is revealing: *marriage,* ordinary wedlock, is, it seems, "common sinfulness and wrath," since that is how other legal children are conceived! Esther's dreadful fault would then seem to be that she was born of joyful sexual passion! And, by implication, all of us are born from sinful passion, which is like wrath. "Wrath" presumably refers to the doom cast on Eve when she was cast out from Eden, but its menacing implication also distantly evokes the primal scene—that is, parental sex conceived of as voracious and dangerous, which is how the child conceives of it, from an infantile logic that supposes sex is a kind of eating and, in fantasy, suspects that it is threatening.

Now to return to the symbolism of mother and baby. At the end of *Bleak House* Lady Dedlock changes clothes with Jenny, who is the mother of the dead child. Lady Dedlock has taken possession of Esther's hand-kerchief, which she used to cover the face of this dead baby. When Captain Woodcourt, Mr. Bucket, and Esther eventually find the fugitive Lady Dedlock, she looks like Jenny, because she is dressed in Jenny's clothes (but Jenny, of course, has gone up north in Lady Dedlock's clothes, to put everyone off the scent).

I saw before me, lying on the step, the mother of the dead child ... she lay there, who had so lately spoken of my mother. She lay there, a distressed, unsheltered, senseless creature. (811)

This is a very moving moment. But what it brings home to us is the fact that, at the level of unconscious themes, a dead baby is at the heart of the novel *Bleak House:* that is, the baby Esther, who should have had her birthright but who was presumed dead by Lady Dedlock and who, without a mother's care, would be psychically dead. Lady Dedlock's life is dead, because of the love that is locked in her secret heart. Esther is not psychically dead, because she has been brought up (albeit punitively) by her aunt: that care at least has been a form of love. Yet of course, right to the end, there is a powerful need for love in Esther; and (we may say) she is a projection of Dickens's own need for love. But there is also a sense in which she needs (and experiences) massive fathering love from her guard-ian, in order to bring her fully to life, in the realm of being.

So this novel, like so many of Dickens's novels, is about the need to be loved, about being orphaned or deprived of love: David Copperfield, Pip, Oliver Twist, Esther, Clennam, Paul Dombey, Louisa Gradgrind—all these are brought up in some condition of deprivation, seeking to be fulfilled in the context of love (and often learning through love how to find and how to realize the good and integrity within themselves). This is, we may say, Dickens's "problem," which he turns to good artistic purpose.

There are those who can give love and those who cannot. The worst thing is to deny the capacity for love in oneself: this is Mr. Dombey's sin,

Miss Havisham's error, Estella's predicament, Mr. Murdstone's offense, and the social and philosophical failure of Bounderby and Gradgrind. Little Dorrit pours out love to her father, ruined by the system that incarcerates him in the Marshalsea as a victim of the system. Dickens saw his society as one that generated, encouraged, and falsified those who could not give love as it should be given or who denied love or offended against it, and in this he saw a failure to follow Christ's example and principles. He found here, as Leavis has made plain, a fundamental moral failure, for our moral capacities, as he tries to show in the fable *Hard Times,* depend upon love and upon the experience of those powers that are exercised for love and for nothing else, like play, imagination, and the provision for the "childhood of the mind." In these themes of Dickens there is a powerful and fine moral message: an injunction to the reader to pay attention to the needs of being—to love and imagination and sympathy—rather than to power or possessions.

Lady Dedlock has suffered from the blight of the emotions consequent upon the denial of love:

In truth she is not a hard lady naturally; and the time has been when the sight of the venerable figure suing to her with such strong earnestness would have moved her to great compassion. But so long accustomed to suppress emotion, and keep down reality; so long schooled for her own purposes, in that destructive school which shuts up the natural feelings of the heart, like flies in amber, and spreads one uniform and dreary gloss over the good and the bad, the feeling and the unfeeling, the sensible and the senseless; she had subdued even her wonder until now. (755)

It is an important theme of Dickens's, then, that one should not allow one's feelings to become petrified, since this sphere of the richness of being is the source of one's moral capacities; by inference a society that drew on this richness would be a better one. So, he becomes a true champion of being and makes a radical criticism of bourgeois society.

The themes of deprivation of being because of the failure of inheritance is at the heart of many of Dickens's criticisms of society. This question is dealt with more realistically in another novel about illegitimacy: *Ruth,* by Mrs. Gaskell. It is no wonder, by the way, that Dickens found Mrs. Gaskell sympathetic: her mother died when she was one year old and her novels are about inheritance, too—not least about the heroine who has to draw upon and develop her deepest resources of being in order to cope with a difficult and often menacing world and to realize her integrity. Mrs. Gaskell is more realistic than Dickens about sickness and death, and more painful; in her work bereavement is a truly terrible if positive experience, and she is not afraid to tackle it often, and openly.

But Dickens is realistic enough about society's evils. Our inheritance is often blighted by the chance circumstances of life (what Americans call "happenstance"). But sometimes it is blighted by wilfulness or by being corrupted by ambition, pride, lust, cupidity, avarice, hate; in this we find the Jonsonian quality in the Dickens who gave us Mr. Dombey, William Dorrit, Uriah Heep, Fagin, Mr. Merdle, Mr. Murdstone, Mr. Vholes, Mrs. Clennam. . . . In *Bleak House* the great corrupting external influence is the law and its "wiglomeration": a system that is the servant of property becomes its own justification, and comes to make more and more business for itself until it eats up the great cause in its own costs, thus destroying those who took recourse to it in the first place. The instrument of the individual's quest for his rights may even rob him of his birthright—his freedom, his hope, and eventually his life, as with Richard. This process is also symbolized by the names of Miss Flyte's birds, which are imprisoned all through the progress of the Jarndyce suit, and are only freed when it disintegrates into nothing. The "wiglomeration" represents a great falsification of what is important in life: doing and getting, rather than being. The law seduces people into false egoism rather than selfless love.

All this is fine—and it is written, we may note, in the Christian New Testament: "lay up not for yourself treasure upon earth, where moth and rust doth corrupt." Just as the dead baby's angel was aware of the service done to it by Ada, so there is a heavenly record of devotion to selfless love and duty, in another realm; and in such giving, Christianity tells us, there is meaning (or "salvation").

But yet Dickens cannot do without actual earthly riches. This seems often the manic fly in the pure ointment of his preoccupation with love. "Give up all that thou hast and follow me"—this is often his message for a time, but we know it will not be long before Aunt Trotwood recovers her fortune, or the Cheeryble brothers turn up—or John Jarndyce dips into what appears to be a fathomless pocket. Does this matter? Could there be love, devotion, duty, selflessness—without the money? And the magic?

Later, we shall see why Dickens was obliged, in writing from his own experience, to link the problem of money with self-fulfillment. What Dickens seeks, I believe, may be called *real reparation*. To explain more what this means I shall turn again to Kleinian psychoanalysis. First, however, I want to look over the plot of the novel under discussion.

A close examination of the plot of *Bleak House* reveals many oddities that are not altogether consistent.* What is consistent is the central in-heritance theme. We have to take John Jarndyce, of course, as a *donnée,* as a given part of the drama. He has the money, as Prospero had his magic, and he manipulates the action to make Dickens's point, which is that the money alone does not yield satisfaction; what creates goodness, and estab-lishes meaning, is love. Perhaps behind his social attitudes are those of Jonson and Pope, urging the proper use of riches. In Mrs. Gaskell there is more realism because there is more financial hardship and no benign sponsor in sight; in her more democratic perspective there can be no patronage to solve humanity's social problems. But Dickens's purpose is perhaps differ-ent—belonging to an existentialist preoccupation with the uniqueness of existence.

There is an odd symbolic paradox about *Bleak House:* when we open our edition there is a gloomy engraving of a house with somber trees as frontispiece. It seems this must be Bleak House, but it is not; it is Chesney Wold. Chesney Wold turns out to be bleak, with its rainy weather, its Ghost's Walk, its state rooms and galleries mostly shut up and sheeted up and, of course, the blight of Lady Dedlock's dishonorable secret—her love affair in youth with Captain Hawdon and her illegitimate child, which at first is dead to her.

Bleak House, by contrast, is an establishment that has been redeemed. Tom Jarndyce, before John, let Bleak House fall into rack and ruin because he became involved in the suit with John Jarndyce. Now, however, Bleak House is not bleak at all, for in it lives John Jarndyce, who is the epitome of selfless love and charity. Moreover, Bleak House multiplies: Jarndyce sets up a second Bleak House for Esther and Woodcourt when he renounces the idea of marrying Esther, seeming to realize that his role toward her is that of a father, and that she might transfer her allegiance as housekeeper from him to Alan Woodcourt, who loves her as a potential husband.

---

*See David Holbrook, "Some Plot Inconsistencies in *Bleak House,*" *English,* 39, no. 165 (Autumn 1990): 209.

Whenever he is reminded of painful suffering, or whenever he is reminded of his own generosity, John Jarndyce speaks of the wind being in the East. Bleak House is thus the place where the winds of human suffering and need blow, but where the dangers also lie of being charitable for the wrong reason.

I believe we may say that Bleak House is a focus of *true reparation*. False reparation is manifest in a number of themes in the book. Harold Skimpole is someone to whom give and take have no meaning, and in consequence he turns out to be treacherous—to Jo, to Esther, and, in the end, to John Jarndyce, whom he finally accuses of selfishness after so many years of living on Jarndyce's charity. Harold Skimpole embodies the failure of all reparative processes, and so, beneath the surface of his charming childishness, he is less than human—at times, indeed, dangerously not human at all. He is all manic denial, and since he is incapable of reparation, he is not in the real world at all—almost a kind of psychopath.

Mrs. Jellyby represents manic reparation in a way, too, since her reparation is totally misdirected: for hers is "telescopic charity," capable only of engaging with distant objects, while at home all is neglect. Mrs. Jellyby neglects her husband, her household, and her children, and gives everything to "Africa" (where, in the end, the king of the Borrioboola-Ghanians sells his own people into slavery to buy rum!); and she is associated with Mrs. Pardiggle, whose attempts at reparation are attempts to control others for their own good while remaining indifferent to their true needs and human qualities. This is minatory and authoritarian "charity" ("cringe-or-starve" charity, as today's poor call it), and these characters belong to hate rather than to love.

We may see, I believe, at the center of Dickens's novel the image of the household (his journal was called *Household Words*): the household as the community soul of humanity. The health of this household depends upon the existentialist solution being realized in each unique individual soul, which must grow, must not be falsified, must have its needs to love and be loved met, and must find meaning in life. It must establish *being* in the face of life's *bleakness:* this quest is integral with the health of the household in which it is reared and in which it exists. In contrast, here are the roaming people of the brick works, the inhabitants of Chesney Wold, the people of Bleak House, the inhabitants of Tom All Alone's, and the wanderers about the globe, like Alan Woodcourt and Jo: all these are households or people roaming between households—and the question is whether within the house, and within the house of the soul, things are bleak or not.[4]

The existential question focuses on the *inheritance*: what do we make of our inheritance? If the answer is "Jarndyce and Jarndyce," then we embrace falsification—dust and death. The true process of coming into one's own is by reparation, by giving to others. This is the didactic message of the novel.

Mr. Jarndyce is a father figure, but also a Prospero figure—a figure with whose creative influence Dickens powerfully identifies. We should take his proposal to Esther in this fantasy mode. At the beginning of the book he is nearly sixty, in Esther's estimation, and she is twenty: it is surely inconceivable that they could really marry? His role is to father Esther by his love and help her to fulfillment, as a father does. That he does so, in an age when there was such an animosity toward the illegitimate child, is an assertion of faith in human nature.

Jarndyce says that the east wind blows "When I am deceived or dis-appointed in …." and then stops: he was going to say "human nature." Jarndyce is the embodiment of Dickens's exploration of the problem (which was Shakespeare's) of whether it is possible to have faith in human nature, which is much the same as saying, whether it is possible to have faith in love and its reparative powers.

Jarndyce's mode of acting on the basis of love is continually offset against contrasting modes of false charity, the tyrannical Pardiggle semblance of charity that is really narcissistic and harmful, wherein

charity was assumed, as a regular uniform, by loud professors and speculators in cheap notoriety, vehement in profession, restless and vain in action, servile in the last degree of meanness to the great, adulatory of one another, and intolerable to those who were anxious quietly to help the weak from falling. (204)

The episode where John Jarndyce pursues the fate of Coavinses' man's children—one of the most moving in Dickens—is offered in supreme contrast.

As we have noted, the *orphan* theme is a central one in Dickens. One of the most touching series of passages in Dickens is between orphan and orphan in *Bleak House*—between Esther and Charley. Charley Neckett is the little daughter of the debt collector who works for Coavinses, and who comes to deal with Harold Skimpole. Skimpole is a deadly caricature of the egoist who asserts his childishness as a means to sustain his infant monism: the world, in Skimpole's fantasy, exists for him, and he pretends to a total failure to understand his obligations to the world and money— even as he takes bribes for betrayal.

John Jarndyce acts as father to Skimpole until Skimpole turns maliciously against him. And Dickens is quite serious in contrasting the psychopath-ological egoist who, by failing to engage with the reality of the world in a positive way, leaves a trail of misery and destruction, with the benign realist, Jarndyce, who considers first the needs of the heart in others. The objection to Jarndyce is that (by contrast with the other members with that family name, who are eaten away in a desperate claim on the inher-itance) he seems to have unlimited resources, even to a magical extent. Yet one must also remember that, because of his trust in Esther, to whom he turns over his household affairs in great confidence, he is saved a great deal of expenditure, while he makes no use of his riches to pursue power— only to love.

The debt collector dies, and Skimpole announces that "Coavinses has been arrested by the great Bailiff" (206). He has left "Three children. No mother"—and Skimpole turns happily to the piano.

Jarndyce, however, being a realist of the heart, accepts the human reality of doing something about it. All Dickens's feeling for the orphaned child come into play, and he gives a totally convincing picture of the working-class child in dire straits. The two youngest children are locked in.

In a poor room, with a sloping ceiling, and containing very little furniture, was a mite of a boy, some five or six years old, nursing and hushing a heavy child of eighteen months. There was no fire, though the weather was cold; both children were wrapped in some poor shawls and tippets, as a substitute. (205)

Has Charley locked them up alone?

"Where is Charley now?"
"Out a-washing," said the boy....
... there came into the room a very little girl, childish in figure but shrewd and older-looking in the face—pretty-faced too—wearing a womanly sort of bonnet much too large for her, and drying her bare arms on a womanly sort of apron. Her fingers were white and wrinkled with washing, and the soap-suds were yet smoking which she wiped off her arms. But for this, she might have been a child playing at washing, and imitating a poor working-woman with a quick observation of the truth. (209)

The episode is moving because the child has no time for play—play with the mother being the child's privilege of finding by imagination the reality of the world. She has to plunge into the reality to survive, earning sixpences where she can.

Because her father was a debt collector, she has not found it easy; Mrs. Blinder reports that the response to the children's orphaning has been "not so bad":

"Some people won't employ her, because she was a follerer's child; some people that do employ her, cast it at her; some make a merit of having her to work for them, with that and all her drawbacks upon her and perhaps pay her less and put upon her more. But she's patienter than others would be, and is clever too, and always willing, up to the full mark of her strength and over." (212)

John Jarndyce is deeply moved, both by the child's predicament and by her courage.

"Is it possible," whispered my guardian ... "that this child works for the rest? Look at this! For God's sake look at this!" ...
"Charley, Charley!" said my guardian. "How old are you?"
"Over thirteen, sir," replied the child.
"O! What a great age," said my guardian. "What a great age, Charley!"
I cannot describe the tenderness with which he spoke to her; half playfully, yet all the more compassionately and mournfully. (210)

Jarndyce is drawn into the paternal role. Tom, says Charley, is not afraid of being locked up, is he?

"No-o!" said Tom, stoutly.
"When it comes on dark, the lamps are lighted down in the court, and they show up here quite bright—almost quite bright. Don't they, Tom?" (211)

We are drawn into the child's need to summon up courage and resources in the bitter situation of deprivation—and this is what moves us when Oliver Twist is lost and exploited by criminals, David Copperfield breaks away from home, and Pip is accosted by escaped convicts on the marshes and beaten by Mrs. Gargery. For Charley reality has had too soon a sharp edge:

The little orphan girl had spoken of their father, and their mother, as if all that sorrow were subdued by the necessity of taking courage, and by her childish importance in being able to work, and by her bustling busy way. (211)

The community has helped: Mrs. Blinder has "forgiven" the children the rent; but Mr. Jarndyce is able to do more. Just over a hundred pages later a pretty little girl comes into Esther's room, neatly dressed in mourning, and drops a curtsey. "If you please, miss ... I'm your maid" (334). Tom is at school and Emma is being taken care of by Mrs. Blinder. It has all been done for the love of Esther, and Charley goes around the room "folding up everything she can lay her hands on."

> Presently, Charley came creeping to my side, and said:
> "O don't cry, if you please, miss."
> And I said again, "I can't help it Charley."
> And Charley said again, "No, miss, nor I can't help it." (335).

It is full of sentiment, but not sentimental, for what moves us is the plight of both women—orphaned and having to do what they can to survive. It is a very feminine moment; and so is the passage in which Charley catches smallpox and nearly dies, and those passages that follow in which Charley in turn nurses Esther and tries to prevent her seeing her beauty ravaged by removing all the mirrors. The whole passage is a story of love, in which out of recognition of need, Esther tries to educate Charley, and she in turn tries to serve Esther as best she can, through many vicissitudes of life. In the end Charley ("round-eyed still, and not at all grammatical") marries the local miller, and Tom is apprenticed to the mill.

Esther devotes a parallel degree of love to Caddy, who is also a kind of orphan, and seeks to break away from her unsatisfactory home into her own life. She has a strange little baby that might stand for her inner deprivation:

> such a tiny old-faced mite, with a countenance that seemed to be scarcely anything but a cap-border, and a little lean, long-fingered hand, always clenched under its chin. It would lie in this attitude all day, with its bright specks of eyes open, wondering (as I used to imagine) how it came to be so small and weak. (680)

It has "curious little dark marks under its eyes, like faint remembrances of poor Caddy's inky days" and is "altogether ... quite a piteous little sight."

This poor infant seems almost to be the archetypal figure at the heart of Dickens's novels: the deprived being who spends the rest of his life wondering how, at the hands of the woman who made him, he came to be so small and weak.

Esther I have seen described as a "rather insipid heroine" while G. H.

Lewes found her a monstrous failure: many critics have followed.[5] But I agree with Alex Zwerdling, who, writing in the *Publications of the Modern Language Association,* finds her internal conflicts to be offered in a pain-staking and detailed way, so that they are completely plausible psycholog-ically. She is the epitome of a child brought up with little love—though she is an open, affectionate, and thoroughly responsive person. At the same time, she records how she deals with being traumatized by the ordeal she has suffered, and tries to construct a possible life out of the elements of duty, selflessness, and the hope of a heavenly reward. "She struggles to convince herself that they will do; but they will not. There is a strong intuitive awareness that these elements can only be oppressive if they are not combined with self-realisation." (435) And her hallucinations, her strong attachment to Ada, and her misgivings over Woodcourt belong to her struggle to perceive this. The only problem with Ada is the magic ending, when her guardian relinquishes her suddenly to her lover, which Zwerdling finds totally unconvincing: it robs her of her existential choice. We can, however, see the event arising from Dickens's complex feelings about daughters and fathers. It is as if he chose this magical outcome to overcome the problem of releasing Esther to a full sexual relationship, having, as it were, safeguarded her from this by arranging to marry her to her father figure.

The positive, benign way in which her development is presented must be seen in the light of the fact that she is illegitimate. Alan Woodcourt is an idealized male partner in a sense: he has done a great deal of reparation, and is a good, devout medical man par excellence. But he is also clearly a fully sexual partner, attractive and passionate—perhaps drawn somewhat from the hero of *Persuasion*—while Ada is filled neither with guilt nor shame. It is true that she has (like Ruth) to make a great deal of reparation by "duty" (as "Dame Durden"); but she marries a man who has redeemed himself by helping people survive a shipwreck and by applying himself to a modestly rewarded life as a medical practitioner. So they seem to have a satisfactory married life before them. To redeem a girl with such an inheritance was a remarkable achievement on Dickens's part.

Esther has redeemed the bleakness of Bleak House, and at the end is given another Bleak House by her guardian: this represents the security she has achieved by filling the "body" of the first Bleak House, in coop-eration, of course, with that fount of charity, her guardian, John Jarndyce. He stands in total contrast to the miserable and short-sighted obsession with his own interests of poor Richard, whose existence is eaten away by the lure of the lawsuit (egged on by such as Vholes, whose name, as Leavis suggests, implies some underground vulture, a vicious mole, or ghoul). Richard's preoccupation with his material inheritance kills him: he is parted from Ada, and will not live to see his child. Only a completely disinterested love achieves true reparation: that is the moral of *Bleak House*. Worldly ambition yields only ashes; Lady Dedlock, who has given herself over to respectability and pride, finally prostrates herself at the sordid tomb of her lover, while Richard dies, his mouth filled with blood, while his inheritance is eaten up to pay costs and to nourish a fat legal system.

The sexual message seems to be that love in a meaningful or authentic relationship is more important than anything, and should offer a guide to conduct. "Love" includes charity and offers us the joy we may find in giving to others. A strong parallel theme here is parenthood, whether actual or assumed (like John Jarndyce's).

The relationship in this novel between John Jarndyce and Esther seems yet another version of the Euphrasia myth in Dickens's unconscious, a myth that is so important in *Little Dorrit*. Euphrasia was the daughter of King Evander of Syracuse, and when he was in prison she fed him with her breasts (Dickens refers to this myth in chapter 19 of *Little Dorrit*). By this myth Dickens transforms his idealized woman into an all-providing mother (albeit still a child or daughter) who can offer magical reparation, guaranteeing against death, by her breasts, by her nonlibidinal loving goodness. Esther is this kind of daughter to John Jarndyce at first. We shall look further below at the Euphrasia myth, in relation to Little Dorrit, but here we need to note that it reveals a massive unconscious preoccupation with the need to be given the substance to survive from a source that has itself avoided the devastation of the voracious (sexual) appetite—avoided the ravages of the libidinal—and this may be again related to the question of reparation.

Esther's predicament is underpinned by the theme of Charley the orphan, a series of episodes that have all that depth of feeling that a great artist may have for the predicament of the human creature in immaturity, seeking his or her natural inheritance and encountering the hazards of life. We feel the same emotions for Huckleberry Finn, and Pip, and David Copperfield—and for Leonard Hilton (in Mrs. Gaskell's *Ruth*). The related question of the proper and possible realization of one's inheritance (among other things from one's parents' sexuality) is the existential center of *Bleak*

House. And while *Bleak House* is in some ways something of a thriller, its solutions to the problems of existence emerge from a deep concern with being and authenticity. We follow with much feeling the sorrows of George Rouncewell, for example—another kind of orphan. Ada grows up as a wife afflicted by her husband's mania, and, I believe, Esther Summerson grows to maturity much as Pip does in *Great Expectations,* while the last sufferings of Sir Leicester Dedlock are as moving in a very realistic way as anything in George Eliot.

The creative theme of the novel can thus be seen to have an underlying coherence when viewed in light of the need to love and be loved and, above all, the need for reparation. In discussing the reparative power of love I am, of course, invoking a psychoanalytical concept.

The concept of reparation in psychoanalytical thought stems from Me-lanie Klein. She often wrote in such a way as to make it plain that what she was concerned with was the "cultural" thinking of the baby: the symbolism of its consciousness. That is, she was making a phenomenological analysis of the problems of love and hate.[6] This is clear in the work she wrote with Joan Riviere, *Love, Hate, and Reparation,* at the end of which the authors write

With the capacity for reversing situations in fantasy, and identifying himself with others, a capacity which is a great characteristic of the human mind, a man can distribute to others the help and love of which he himself is in need, and in this way can gain comfort and satisfaction for himself. (116)

Actually, come to think of it, this is what Dickens is doing in *Bleak House:* he himself wants to believe in love and giving—in reparation—in order to feel that there is a meaning in existence. And so he invents a John Jarndyce, with whom he can identify, in "distributing to others the help and love of which he himself is in need," to make reparation.

To the baby, Melanie Klein goes on, the mother is the "original and paramount source of the goodness that he receives from the outer world." It is a painful process for the baby to do without the supreme satisfaction of being fed by her:

If, however, his greed and his resentment are not too great, he is able to detach himself gradually from her and at the same time to gain satisfaction from other sources. (116)

This process, I believe, is delineated in many novels by Dickens in which an original terrible deprivation is gradually made up for by detachment and the gain of satisfaction from other sources: this is Pip's progress, and Esther's, Nicholas Nickleby's, and Arthur Clennam's. The clue to this progress is love, as a means of developing goodness:

This process could be described as retaining the primary goodness as well as re-placing it, and the more successfully it is carried through, the less ground is left in the baby's mind for greed and hatred. (117)

In a book like *Bleak House,* Dickens surrounds his protagonists with greed and hatred. Lady Dedlock has sought power through ambition in the denial of her passion; Tulkinghorne seeks power over others; Vholes represents the huge, predatory power of the law to batten on problems of inheritance and to suck plaintiffs dry—indeed, the whole "wiglomeration" of the Jarn-dyce and Jarndyce Chancery case represents an immense voraciousness that seeks to enlist people's greed in its toils and to reduce them to nothing—to empty them, as Tom Jarndyce blows out his brains. Other forms of greed and hate are more subtle: Mrs. Chadband, Smallweed, Krook, and even Guppy, whose crude egoism goes with a complete inability to sympathize or to be aware of what is going on inside others (Lady Dedlock, Esther). So, despite his contemptuous rejection of bribes, Guppy displays a form of self-interested greed in his desire to possess Esther, who has no feelings for him. In other novels by Dickens, of course, the embod-iments of hate and greed are more obvious. Dombey, Uriah Heep, Quilp, Merdle; but with each, the essential offense is to love, and their activities menace love.

Melanie Klein shows that her concept of reparation, derived from the study of the fantasies of infants, is closely related to the growth of love:

The unconscious feelings of guilt which arise in connection with the fantasied destruction of a loved person play a fundamental part in these processes. We have seen that the baby's feelings of guilt and sorrow, arising from the fantasies of destroying his mother in his greed and hate, set going the drive to heal these imaginary injuries, and to make reparation to her. (117)

The heading to this chapter is "Balance between 'give' and 'take' "—a phrase one could apply directly to the novel *Bleak House,* which is a fantasy of reparation.

Everything in Melanie Klein's psychology, of course, depends upon whether we accept her view that

when the baby feels frustrated at the breast, in his fantasies he attacks this breast; but if he is being gratified by this breast, he loves it and has fantasies of a pleasant kind in relation to it. In his aggressive fantasies he wishes to bite up and to tear up his mother and her breasts, and to destroy her also in other ways. (61)

So rudimentary is the baby's reality sense that he can feel "that he *has really destroyed* the object of his destructive impulses, and is going on destroying it." To escape from the dread and guilt this causes, the infant builds up "fantasies that he is putting the bits together and repairing her." But this does not easily do away with the fear of destroying the object, whom he loves and whom he most needs. Dickens's fear of sexual love, as manifest in his unwillingness to allow it to his characters and in his shrinking from fully libidinal woman, suggests some such problem in his own psyche, and in his massive attempts to exert reparation and love.

Perhaps here I should reiterate the difference between *true* and *manic* reparation. To repair the damaged object, the individual has to acknowl-edge *how much he loves and needs her,* that he does *hate* her, that he dreads dependence on her, and that at the root of the problem lies the fear that he may totally destroy her and so himself: that is, the *fear of death.* There can be a kind of "pretend" or manic attempt at reparation, which tries to love and repair the object without coming to terms with and bearing the pain of acknowledging ambivalence, guilt, despair, and the fear of death— especially the latter—by the manic denial of death. It is this manic denial that lies behind the symbolism of Mrs. Jellyby and especially Horace Skim-pole, and behind all forms of false charity, too, like those of Mrs. Pardiggle and Mr. Chadband. What they represent are activities by which human beings seem to be concerned with "good" but are in fact seriously wide of the mark and never reach the real problems of love, hate and being. ("And how did my wife get that black eye? Why, I giv' it her.")

The struggle is thus complex: but it is not merely a matter of overcoming neurotic traumas or real object loss. *Everyone* suffers from these problems, and the underlying threat is that of an object and a world so destroyed, or a situation so confused by guilt and despair, that all is meaningless.

"Give" and "take" are related to the problem of love: this is clear from Melanie Klein. From my (existentialist) position, I would add that love is a source of a feeling of meaning in life, because the experience of unique being in relation to unique being brings home to one the mystery and singularity of one's own existence. Melanie Klein writes thus about re-paration and guilt:

Feelings of guilt give rise to the fear of being dependent upon this loved person whom the child is afraid of losing, since as soon as aggression wells up he feels he is injuring it. This fear of dependence is an incentive to his detaching himself from her—to his turning to other people and things and thus enlarging his range of interests. (117)

Melanie Klein thus seems to suggest that it is natural and normal in development to give art to the world, to give oneself over more and more to culture and activities in the world. Reparation is a drive in this, not to "repair the object" merely, or to "heal traumas"; it is an element in all normal life (and culture):

Normally, the drive to make reparation can keep at bay the despair arising out of feelings of guilt, and then hope will prevail, in which case the baby's love and his desire to make reparation are unconsciously carried over to the new objects of love and interest. These, as we already know, are in the baby's unconscious mind linked up with the first loved person, whom he rediscovers or recreates through his relation to new people and through constructive interests. Thus making reparation—which is such an essential part of the ability to love—widens in scope, and the child's capacity to accept love and, by various means, to take into himself goodness from the outer world steadily increases. This satisfactory balance between "give" and "take" is the primary condition for future happiness. (117–18)

This casts light on the unconscious themes of *Bleak House*. Dickens, of course, was not a baby growing up but his work perhaps pursues problems left over from infancy. His creative work follows this primary path, as a means to resolve the problem of "give" and "take," and to develop a sense of goodness between himself and the world. He depicts this in Esther's development and in the whole symbolic plot of the novel; we identify with the main characters and experience this reparative process as a path to feeling ourselves meaningfully existing in a meaningful world—a process we all pursue in relation to the image of woman.

Notes

1. See Charlotte Rotkin, *Deception in Little Dorrit*.
2. I believe that the remembered voice of the mother, from before and after birth, is highly significant in our lives, in fantasy, and in relation to sounds and music. The whole dynamic of "being for" and the role of the mother in "creative

reflection" is discussed in the present author's *Sylvia Plath: Poetry and Existence* and elsewhere, including *Images of Woman in Literature*.

3. George MacDonald lost his mother as a small boy and was brought up by a woman relative.

4. The link is made between the "brains," which Tom Jarndyce has blown out because of his psychic confusion over the falsifications of the suit, and Bleak House, which is said at one point to look as if its brains were blown out.

5. For real insipidity we may turn to little Nell. The whole of *The Old Curiosity Shop* is marred by the influence of Victorian melodrama, to which the impossible purity of Nell belongs. There are long exchanges in which characters reveal their villainy while others denounce them. The slavish devotion of Nell and her capacity for forgiveness (even when her father steals from her and deceives her, in his passion for gambling) is too angelic; in one "so fresh from God" it can only lead to a beautiful death, since Little Nell does not engage with the mixed nature of human reality at all. The audience in this mode could enjoy feeling righteous (and feeling that the author was "good") without experiencing any involvement that challenged their own human reality, which they share with the characters.

6. On the general issues here, see Ian D. Suttie, *The Origins of Love and Hate*, and also my *Human Hope and the Death Instinct*.

CHAPTER TWO

Religion, Sin, and Shame

We need now to turn back to the sexual theme, for we cannot discuss love without discussing problems of sexuality, marriage, and procreation, and woman as the focus of these.

What was Dickens's position in relation to the sense of sin and shame that centered on illegitimacy? This problem is of great relevance to *Bleak House* and the later novels.

There seem to be two conflicting attitudes in the texts of religious authority in the Christian tradition. One is that the sins of the fathers shall be visited on the children. The other is revealed in those words that Esther reads from St. John about

how our Saviour stooped down, writing with his finger in the dust, when they brought the sinful woman to him.

"So when they continued asking him, he lifted up himself and said unto them, He that is without sin among you, let him first cast a stone at her!"(19)

Miss Barbary is deeply disturbed by this and rises, putting her hand to her head, crying out, " 'Watch ye therefore! lest coming suddenly he find you sleeping. And what I say unto you, I say unto all, Watch!' " (19)[1]— and she falls down, and dies, with an "immoveable" face. "To the very last, and even afterwards, her frown remained unsoftened" (19). Later,

Miss Barbary's religion is called "distorted." This woman it was who found signs of life in Esther as a baby and took on the infant's upbringing with a stern sense of duty, with no desire or willingness that the baby should live. So punitive is Miss Barbary's attitude to Esther that Esther develops a "terror of herself," and her quest to find herself is involved in shame and disgrace, from which she painfully extricates herself throughout the novel.

Miss Barbary's reaction she assumes to be in obedience to Holy Scripture, "according to what is written": the stern godmother is invoking the stern laws of the Old Testament. And these make it out that the *child* has to pay, in self-denial and diligence, for the sins of the parents.

But the fallen woman has to pay, too. Lady Dedlock cries to Esther, "O my child, my child, I am your wicked and unhappy mother! O try to forgive me!" Esther is glad that the likeness between them has been erased by the scars of her smallpox. But she tells her that, of course, she forgives her, and her heart overflows with "natural love" for her. Her duty was to "bless her and receive her." They embrace, but there can be no real peace to their troubled minds: " 'To bless and receive me,' groaned my mother, 'it is far too late. I must travel my dark road alone' " (510). She must travel from day to day, although she cannot see her way before her "guilty feet": "This is the earthly punishment I have brought upon myself."

"I have a husband, wretched and dishonouring creature that I am!"

These words she uttered with a suppressed cry of despair, more terrible in its sound than any shriek. (510)

What we need to ask is where did the intensity of this anguish come from, this sense of a guilty secret nothing can assuage? It becomes clear at the end that Sir Leicester Dedlock would have forgiven his wife—both her illicit love affair and her giving birth to a child. It is rather Dickens's *audience* that cannot forgive such a lapse, and they could find the grounds of this attitude in the Book of Deuteronomy and St. Paul. A strict religious belief that there was no place for fornicators in the Kingdom of Heaven was the basis for the attitude that there was no place for fornicating women—at least in Victorian middle-class society.

It is difficult for us to imagine how sensitive a subject illegitimacy could be for a writer at that time. And here we may turn to compare *Bleak House* with another novel about a fallen woman. Mrs. Gaskell came to know of a distressing case in which a woman was seduced by her surgeon, and out of this wrote her novel *Ruth,* which was published in 1853. It was greeted by an outcry, not against her sympathetic presentation of the subject, but against the subject being presented in a novel *at all.* Some members of her husband's congregation even burned copies of the book to protest against the very subject being treated sympathetically. Yet Mrs. Gaskell received support and encouragement from (among others) Charles Kingsley and Elizabeth Barrett Browning. Charles Dickens had helped Elizabeth Gaskell over the case from which she made her novel: he helped Mrs. Gaskell to make it possible for the girl in question to emigrate. To die or to emigrate seemed the only solution—for a woman, once she had fallen to seduction, even if she were blameless, and even if the agent of her fall was really to blame (like Steerforth), could never be received in polite society. And the very impulse to help such a creature was itself thought to be very doubtful, as if even heaven would frown on charity in that direction.

We might take a sociological point of view and suggest that the reason for the opprobrium was that the social opportunities open to women were so restricted. As we often see in Jane Austen and Charlotte Brontë, if a gentlewoman did not marry, the only occupations open to her were those of governess and teacher. But these were only available for very respectable women; and, indeed, any lower posts in service for women of lower rank were only open to untarnished females. So there was only one path left for the woman who had been seduced and abandoned with a child, un-marriageable, and beyond being accepted in society: she had to become a prostitute or mistress, if she did not commit suicide or die of shame. To prevent women from falling into such a state, middle-class society had to outlaw the fallen ones and send them to Australia.

But this still does not explain the excited fascination with which the subject is dealt in Dickens—nor, indeed, does it explain his fascination with fallen women (for which kind of woman he set up a home).[2] It explains neither the punitive element in the attitudes of society nor the motives for the attempt to mollify these, which *Bleak House* and *Ruth* surely represent.

Perhaps what is puzzling is the *absoluteness* of the woman's situation, even if we allow for the influence of melodrama in the novel. Lady Dedlock declares that "no affection could come near her, and no human creature could render her any aid"(511). Through the desert that lay before her, she must go alone. In her final parting from Esther she cries of herself, "Forgive her, if you can; and cry to Heaven to forgive her, which it never can!" Why should Lady Dedlock believe that even heaven would not forgive her? Dickens and Mrs. Gaskell are actually caught on the horns of a dilemma: is the breaking of God's laws on sexuality forgiveable or not?

The intense guilt and shame that surround sexual misdemeanors, illegitimacy, and "fallen woman" in the Victorian novel surely has its origins in the intense importance people in the period came to attribute to religion. Religious issues were preeminent, as one can tell from George Eliot's *Scenes from Clerical Life* and other novels, or the novels of Trollope or Mrs. Gaskell. In two novels, *The Warden* and *North and South,* the protagonists make prodigious sacrifices, for themselves and their families, because of questions of religious conscience. In the journals of Victorian England religious issues are debated with passion and at enormous length. Religious questions could dismay and shatter the whole nation, as did questions over Bishop Colenso, Cardinal Newman and the Oxford Movement, and Darwinism.

In the eighteenth-century novel there are, of course, references to "principle," and (as in Jane Austen) this involves Christian principles: in other works, like those of Defoe and Fielding, there is some deference to Christian commandments (such as those that guide sexual conduct or marriage), combined, often in a way of extraordinary duplicity (as in *Roxana*), with a realistic recognition of how human beings actually behave, and sometimes even with an admiring portrayal (again, as in *Roxana*) of how individuals manage to slide around their principles in pursuing their interests, or to adjust them with subtle expediency. In a novel like *Pamela* the most immoral sexual behavior becomes quite acceptable in the hero, once the woman has brought the man to the altar and made a good Christian marriage.

In the background of the Victorian novel we find a formidable adherence to Christian religion, whose precepts on sexuality exerted a powerful influence on people in all walks of life. And what seems dominant in people's thinking about conduct, especially sexual conduct, is the Old Testament and the dire admonitions of St. Paul, such as his letter to the Corinthians:

> Flee fornication. Every sin that a man doeth is without the body; but he that committeth fornication sinneth against his own body.
> What? Know ye not that your body is the temple of the Holy Ghost which is in you, which ye have of God, and ye are not your own?
> For ye are bought with a price: therefore glorify God in your body, and in your spirit, which are God's. (1 Corinthians, 6)

In this kind of exhortation, the theme is that we are bought with a price: Christ died for us, so therefore our souls and bodies are not ours, and we should use them only to glorify God. Our body is the temple of the Holy Ghost: if we sin with our body, we are defiling that temple. In marriage we talk of two people becoming one flesh (which is a version of the union of Christ with His church): if a man fornicates with a harlot he becomes one flesh with her—and so compromises the Holy Spirit, which dwells in the temple of his body and, really, merges God into the sin.

Moreover, we must note that St. Paul writes, "It is good for a man not to touch a woman" (1 Corinthians, 7). This sentence lies at the heart of the Victorian problem with woman and sex, and the whole Christian tradition of blaming Eve for the Fall. No doubt this has lent seeming justification to endless forms of discrimination against woman, but we must remember that it lies behind Christian marriage, which was conducted in the spirit of the pronouncement that it was better to marry than to burn.

The Victorian problem that I am examining, of the guilt and shame associated with sexual lapses, must be seen in the light of such deference to scriptural authority. What Paul conveys is an embodied sense of being bound up in the body with divine presences and truths; moreover, there is a feeling of the inferiority of the flesh: "we are made as the filth of the world." In the words used in the burial service, about the corruptible putting on incorruption, marvelous poetic use is made of this feeling. But in the sexual sphere it embroils the followers of Christian belief in strange constrictures, and a tendency to self-loathing.[3] To give way to "unclean" wantonness was to put oneself in the way of disobedience and so virtually into the camp of other gods, for which there is no forgiveness and only the threat of God's wrath. It was this that deeply affected the attitudes of the intensely religious Victorians.

Dickens obviously believed in the love of charity of Jesus ("let him who is without sin cast the first stone") rather than the atrocious punitiveness of the Old Testament. Yet his own sexual behavior was not altogether exemplary, while he knew many who certainly failed to behave in ways the Victorians believed "proper": Wilkie Collins, for example, who kept two mistresses. Others in that world led extraordinary sexual lives: G. H. Lewes and his wife lived in what seems to have been a kind of sexual commune, with three other couples. Lewes's wife had a child by Thornton Leigh Hunt in 1850; Lewes, his wife, and Hunt lived on good terms together until Lewes entered into an unmarried relationship with George

Eliot. John Chapman had a wife, but also a mistress living in the same house who was governess to his children. He, too, had a relationship with George Eliot, and later with Barbara Leigh Smith, who was to become Madame Bodichon, one of the founders of Girton College. Then he fell in love with an opera singer who boarded in his house, while his diary reveals endless conflict with two or three women, about his promiscuity, while he felt their outrage to be "unreasonable."[4]

There was thus a great gulf between how people behaved, how they regarded the sexual behavior of others, and how they felt such issues should be presented to the public. The public at large, however, faced with people caught up in the consequences of human weakness in sexuality, found themselves faced with the possibility of the most terrible wrath of God falling upon them, and the likelihood of being excluded forever from God's kingdom. For this, more than for anything, for fornication and sins of that lustful kind, they expected God's doom. So, in dealing with a sexual and relational problem, they turned to the ultimate spiritual realities and sought to obey "that which is written" rather than the sense of what was right and most authentic, according to their own hearts—and the consequences were often horrible, unreasonable, and cruel.

It was this religious public for which Dickens and Mrs. Gaskell wrote, and its *moeurs* inevitably affected their dealings with woman and sex. One criterion in Dicken's portrayal of woman is that, at best, they should approximate to angels, giving their whole energy to devotion and duty (Agnes, Little Nell, Little Dorrit), even to fathers who are suffering from alcoholism or gambling mania, who steal from them or threaten them with the forfeiture of their inheritance. The woman-as-angel cannot be reconciled with the real world, its mixedness, its ambivalence in the subjective realm. With Little Nell the attributes of innocent, devoted, long-suffering, pure and selfless angel lead inevitably to a morbid absorption into a setting of tombs and churches, so that inevitably Little Nell must die and virtually merge into something like a stone angel at the end. This is in a phenomenological sense as far as you can get from the libidinal woman.

These aspects of the cultural idea of a woman may be related to the education of women and the behavior expected of them. One element in this pattern stressed by Sir Charles Petrie was the new stability of society. Life for the upper and middle classes was no longer the dangerous and unsettled process of intrigue and strife that it was in the more fluid earlier centuries of rapid social change. A woman who married into the aristocracy or into the mercantile class could expect lifelong security, except for an occasional Merdle catastrophe. Petrie quotes W. F. Neff, in *Victorian Working Women:*

To get ready for the marriage market a girl was trained like a race-horse. Her education consisted of showy accomplishments designed to ensnare young men. The three Rs of this deadly equipment were music, drawing and French administered by a governess at home, or, for girls below the aristocratic and the higher professional ranks, by mistresses in an inferior boarding school. (190)

The sexual codes of the time were devised to hedge this marriage market around with guarantees: "if a woman went in a hansom cab alone with a man who was neither her father nor her husband, nor old enough to be her grandfather, her reputation was irretrievably lost" (Petrie, p 200). This kind of problem is faced by Molly Gibson in *Wives and Daughters* when she comforts Cynthia's lover in the countryside, and is seen alone with him; and by Margaret Thornton (in *North and South*) when she is seen with her exiled brother Frederick at a railway station.

It was assumed that the Victorian male would, on the slightest provocation, take advantage of the Victorian female, if they were alone together (and not engaged). If an engagement was broken off, a girl would suffer opprobrium. Divorce was never mentioned in polite society. As Sir Charles Petrie suggests, the effect of these "safeguards" was that young men sought girls of other classes, which was presumably why universities like Cambridge took such care to check on town girls and landladies' daughters (and to protect undergraduates from the women). Beyond the pale, as several historians have shown, there was the vast system of brothels and organized prostitution, already referred to, to provide outlets for those unable to bear stricter *moeurs*.

But the protected woman, about whose welfare there seemed so much concern—that she should be "pure"—was given little or no training for her role as wife and mother. The intense religious concern, which both Dickens and Mrs. Gaskell reflect, is almost totally concentrated on her avoidance of wantonness, that is, her struggle with the "woman's question"—with not allowing herself to be seduced before marriage. There was an intense concern to protect young women from contact with married women, in case they heard from them of the joys of sexual love (a concern that is delicately satirized in Henry James's novel *The Awkward Age*).

(What they might have heard, may we suspect, is of some of the pains, shocks, and horrors of married life—which in turn might have made them less marketable?)

As we learn from so many novels, as well as from history, the young woman, to whom it was marriage or misery, was more often than not simply not given any kind of training in her practical duties as a wife, as her predecessors in other centuries were. She was untrained in household management and was (as Petrie says) unable to control her servants. David Copperfield's Dora was no exception. She had no idea of the value of money and often squandered what her husband gave her.

But even worse was her total lack of preparation for physical marriage and the sexual life. As we have seen, in Victorian attitudes there was an idealization of marriage as a symbol of spiritual union; the underlying emphasis was taken from St. Paul, who stressed the presence of the Holy Spirit in the body. But this is combined, as in St. Paul, with a sense of the body being filth, and the source of sin, stain, and evil. In many people there must have been a feeling of guilty horror associated with the libidinal and the life of the body, and to this we need to add the problem of fantasy, of the kind of dread associated with bodily hunger that arises in sexual excitement. So in Victorians like George MacDonald one finds a bizarre combination of idealization of love and marriage—of, on the one hand, a feeling about woman as if she were an angel—and on the other in uncon-scious dread of woman as a witch, such as MacDonald writes about in *Phantastes* and *Lilith*. It is not only a madonna/prostitute problem but also a contrast between the Holy Mary feeling and the feeling that libidinal woman may bring mutilation or death; the consequent dread and hostility may be found behind many incidents in Victorian novels. Another complex problem is that the Victorian wife was nearly always pregnant, and there must have been much conflict of feeling about this experience, in both men and women. Many Victorian writers made fantasies out of their uncon-scious feelings about woman's creative power, and their hostility to fem-inine creativity haunted them.

It must have been something like dread of the phantom woman of the unconscious that lay behind Ruskin's impotence and his preference for girls of the prepuberty period. It would seem that the problem for him was the woman's pubic hair, and perhaps her menstruation, because this was a sign of her maturity. In these signs of her creativity the Victorian un-conscious would find the deepest fears of the animal, or "witch," in woman, that surfaces so violently in George MacDonald. Lewis Carroll loved little girls of the prepuberty period, and lost interest in them when they became nubile: his fears of woman are symbolized in his writings. The intense idealization of woman as angel or goddess in such writers as Dickens required a compartmentalization by which the sensual life of woman was split off and denied. Yet many authors like Dickens and MacDonald fathered many children on their wives, while remaining starry-eyed about the "angel" type.

Only now are we beginning to understand the characteristic disabilities of the typical Victorian. The great source of insight here is psychoanalysis. Freud's work is based on a phenomenological analysis of the many hysteric symptoms that spoke, psychosomatically, of the problems that arose from bourgeois marriage at this time, and the fear and guilt that possessed people in consequence.

Imagine the marriage night of a Victorian woman, who would have been trained to catch her husband, and was no doubt full of glowing idealism, but perhaps knew nothing about physical sex. She might have had no knowledge of male sexual organs or the physical processes of sex, arousal, or orgasm. Probably many marriage nights were a kind of rape: the men, who were used to practicing sex on servants or prostitutes, would have only a concern for their own release and no experience of foreplay or concern for their wives' satisfaction, or even a sense of the gentleness or delicacy needed to help a woman to happy satisfaction in the mutual delights of marriage as a partnership. Any impulse to seek, give, or share satisfaction might well, on both sides, be felt to be fraught with guilt, dread, and a kind of blasphemy, even, under the Pauline injunctions, in a devout pair. Of course there must have been many who did enjoy their sexual lives: but all the odds were against any such thing, and there are few embodiments of sexual happiness in Dickens, for example (Biddy, Bella Wilfer?). Often in Dickens and the Victorian novel there has to be terrible suffering before there can be joy (as with Lizzie Hexam and Eugene Wrayburn); there has to be some massive ordeal, by which anticipatory reparation must be made, as a safeguard, before sexual fulfillment can be sought. Hardy, who was still a Victorian, picks up the theme of unfulfillment: Tess of the d'Urbervilles can only find sexual fulfillment when she is virtually doomed to death. In Tennyson and much pre-Raphaelite poetry the woman or women are waiting in some ancient bower or prison (*The Blue Closet*) for the man to come to release them. But, as in *The Blue Closet,* when he does come, he seems to be dead, or death itself. Many novels of the century are about the failure of fulfillment altogether; and one shudders with a kind of dread to think of (say) Edward Casaubon in bed with Dorothea, or Grandcourt in bed with Gwendolen for that matter (to which his treatment of his dogs perhaps gives a clue).

Sir Charles Petrie focuses attention on the word "innocence," and blames the Victorian male:

Innocence was what he demanded from the girls of his class, and they must not only be innocent but also give the outward impression of being innocent. White muslin, typical of virginal purity, clothed many a heroine. (1969, 205–6)

(We may also perhaps point to the white bourgeois wedding dress.) The ideal woman for marriage was one who was demonstrably inferior to the male—ignorant of the world, meek, holding no opinions, helpless, and weak: Dora, a "pretty toy or plaything"; Rosey Mackenzie, "a tremulous, fluttering little linnet"; Amelia Sedley, with "a kind of sweet submission and softness."[5] When they married, the women passed from dependence on their parents into submission to the husband (on Pauline principles). The concept of marriage as a partnership was unknown, while husbands simply did not confide in or consult their wives, on many matters.

This kind of unequal relationship was embodied in the law, under which a woman became legally an infant on marriage and had no right even to her own clothes. Her property became her husband's and she became virtually her husband's chattel. Divorce was expensive, almost impossible, and in any case meant social ostracism.

Instead of dwelling on the word "innocence," again, however, I believe we should use the word "compartmentalization" to bring the Victorian sexual problem into perspective. In Dickens there is an undercurrent of anguished concern with "innocence": consider, for instance, his attitude to Little Emily. This obsession with innocence, however, does not apply to the man. Steerforth has to die to satisfy the moral inclinations of the public, but the difference is in the spiritual implications: woman become "impure" puts herself beyond heaven's forgiveness, as man does not. In this sense, it is a man's world, in which man imprisons woman in his idealizing concept of innocence: once the innocent angel is brought into the house, she is stripped of all her rights and property (until the Married Women's Property Act of 1882).

"Compartmentalization" is the more helpful word, because it draws attention to the unreal way in which the Victorians kept certain aspects of moral behavior separate from one another, as well as certain aspects of reality and certain aspects of consciousness or psychological makeup. The white-muslin-clad purity that could not bear talk of "legs" or that would faint at a kiss (and scream hysterically in childbirth)* was on the other side of a great barrier from the woman who crawled in the mine shaft dragging a truck by a belt that chafed on her pregnant belly until the eighth month (and most of whose babies died in consequence). She of the pure bridal gown was on the other side of the barrier from Kellner's in Leicester Square, where there was a bar with French barmaids, or Kate Hamilton's at the Café Royal in Princes Street. Perhaps the two worlds met when the beau monde and the demimonde rode side by side down the Ladies Mile in Rotten Row. But any woman who wished to maintain her re-spectability and her place in society could not be seen in the gay estab-lishments, though presumably her husband would lose nothing by this (though he might gain something and bring it home to her).

Behind these facades, again, were the sordid realities of baby-farming, the hordes of women driven to prostitution by poverty, the elaborate sexual perversions provided for, and the general poverty and distress of the work-ing people, whose lives were often so terrible that sexual moral problems could hardly be said to exist for them—since they had neither time nor energy nor bodily vitality for such indulgences.

Moreover, by contrast with the pure ideals, even such as the idealized striving of a Ruth, the truth was that the Victorians simply did not live according to their fervently held principles—by the principles that they put forward to the public, as Dickens did, with such a poker-faced "sin-cerity," or that were expressed in the pastoral melodrama.

Yet there was another, much more real struggle going on, and this is manifest in the novels, too. While the Victorian age was locked in some of its social conventions, it was also a revolutionary age. Ruth's redemption by becoming a nurse is significant: she achieves by herself the overcoming of prejudice against her. Throughout the century the status of nursing was raised, and slowly and surely, through such professions, women began to

---

*To the present-day husband who has attended and tried to help in childbirth, it must seem even comic that the first thing they do in Tolstoy novels when labor begins is to "fetch the ikon"!

clamor for professional and business opportunities. Interestingly and re-
markably, especially since we are considering *Ruth*, it was her capacity for
nursing that enabled woman to escape from the impotence to which she
was subjected by a male-dominated society in Victorian England; as Sir
Charles Petrie points out, Florence Nightingale was responsible for more
than medical progress. Jane Eyre, Esther Summerson, and Ruth, in their
roles as teacher, housekeeper, and nurse, are pointing the way to the future
of woman's equality and independence.

Women who take up a nursing role can hardly remain innocent angels.
So, as women sought professional life, the struggle against the ignorance
that went with "innocence" began: the Girls' Public Day School Company
was founded in 1872, and London gave women B.A. degrees in 1878,
Cambridge in 1881. Divorce legislation came in 1858, and the unfair position of women over their property in marriage began to be amended.

By 1901 the position of woman, restricted as it was, had become a great
deal different from what it had been at the beginning of Victoria's reign;
and after 1914–18 the attitude that women's place was in the home was
finally broken.

We have, of course, to do a good deal of study in order to be able to
understand the situation of the Victorian woman. Today we think of
marriage in terms of the mutual choice of a man and a woman to share
their lives, though, of course, questions of property and class still bear on
marriage. In Victorian times, among middle-class people, marriage was very
much bound up with questions of affluence, property, prestige, and family
pride. Behind the pious attitudes to the hallowed sanctity of marriage was
the need to ensure that there was no uncertainty about inheritance. For
that reason, the fidelity of the wife was paramount, while the purpose of
sexual union was procreation. The question of the husband's fidelity was
not so important—and so there was an extraordinary tacit acceptance and
a division between sanctified love at home and heterism abroad. We
glimpse this, certainly, in Tolstoy's novels of the time; in the English novel,
however, new concepts of authenticity were developing in the sphere of
personal relationships.

In the body of laws this inequality in the sexual situation of man and
woman crystallized a situation of cruel unfairness. When John Stuart Mill
looked at the laws of marriage in *The Subjection of Women* (1869), he

concluded that "the wife is the actual bond-servant of her husband, no less so as far as legal obligation goes, than slaves commonly so called."

The woman's situation in law at the time is summed up by Fraser Harrison thus:

Once married, a woman ceased to possess a legal existence: in common with minors and idiots, she had no responsibility under the law. Unless she committed murder or treason, her husband was liable for her crimes. She could not sign a contract, make a will, or cast a role. Prior to 1884, she could be imprisoned for refusing her husband his so-called conjugal rights. "However brutal a tyrant," Mill commented, "she may unfortunately be chained to . . . he can claim from her and enforce the lowest degradation of a human being, that of being the instrument of an animal function contrary to her inclination." Until 1891, she could be legally detained against her wishes by her husband in his house. She could not obtain a divorce, except by a special Act of Parliament.(7)

When we read of Betsy Trotwood's errant husband turning up, we may today feel he was simply a nuisance. The truth was that he had legal power over her, and she had good reason to fear that he was entitled to take over her life and property, and to enforce his rights to her body—or even shut her up in his house.

But as Harrison goes on to point out, it is especially in the sphere of property law that the wife was a slave. As soon as she became engaged, a woman was forbidden to dispose of her possessions without her fiancé's permission. After marriage, all her property, including inheritance and earnings, passed automatically into the ownership of her husband, and he was free in law to do with it anything he liked: if he chose, he could disinherit her. Her children belonged in law to her husband, and even after her husband's death she did not automatically become their legal guardian; a special provision had to be made in her husband's will.

The innocence of the Victorian woman went with ignorance, and here we find further evidence of the astonishing compartmentalization of the Victorian consciousness. Fraser Harrison has an interesting section on what he calls "nasty knowledge," a phrase that he takes from the British Medical Journal of 1894. There was a widespread total ignorance among middle-class women, not only of sexual matters before marriage but even of their own bodies.

Harrison quotes the astonishing story of Marie Stopes, a zoology student and doctor in botany who only realized six months after her marriage that it had never been consummated (she found the clues to sexual reality, apparently, in the British Museum); her book *Married Love* became an immediate bestseller.

Bewilderment and fear, suggests Harrison, were the common experiences of the woman's marriage night, not least because most women were still encapsulated in child fantasies and nursery fairy tales about the origins of babies and other sexual matters.

While motherhood was a sacred task, the Pauline influence, combined with other traditions, meant that the reproductive functions were regarded with disgust. Women were seriously alienated from their own bodies. Not only did the sexual approaches of the male bewilder and frighten the female; she herself was also inhibited about her own sexuality, which she feared and which filled her with shame.

Again, it is hard for us to think ourselves back into such ignorance. As Fraser Harrison points out, it was not until 1832 that the ovum was definitely identified, and not until 1863 that medicine confirmed beyond doubt that menstruation depended upon ovulation. Even so, even medical thinking continued to suppose that menstruation was some manifestation of excess "nutritive force." Where ordinary people were concerned, women associated menstruation with impurity, and many girls were never given any preparation for this startling change in their bodies.

They were encouraged to behave like invalids while they suffered the "curse" or the "flowers" or the "poorly time." The phenomenon in woman was, of course, used as an excuse for preventing women taking to the professions, or active forms of employment, or business—though no doubt servants and women in the mines had to cope as well as they could.

But the taboos over menstruation indicate that for the Victorian woman all that dark animal side of bodily life was something to be hidden and regarded with disgust and shame. Yet as psychoanalysis tells us, sexuality cannot be enjoyed unless we came to terms with the dark aspects of our bodies and our sensual needs. It is hardly surprising that the Victorians had such difficulties, that seldom, for instance, in their novels is there any positive realization of sexual love. What one does find in their culture is an association of woman with death and murder, symbolizing their fear of some dark and terrible force in the female spirit.

Notes

1. *St. Mark,* 13: 35.
2. Dickens's attitude to the women in his home for the fallen was authoritarian and paternalistic: they had to behave, to be reeducated, to follow a strict routine, and to be penitent. Then they were sent out as emigrants to start a new life. One suspects that besides satisfying Dickens's charity, they also provided him with some satisfactions for his need to triumph over and control women.
3. Cf. the hymn, "That o'er its own shortcomings weeps with loathing." There are hints in several hymns that masturbation is a grave sin: *ne polluantur corpore,* etc.
4. See David Holbrook, *Holy Vows: The Extraordinary Menage: John Chapman and George Eliot, London Magazine* 30, nos. 7–8 (Oct.–Nov. 1990): 20.
5. Edith Wharton found a parallel emphasis on woman's "innocence" in upper-middle-class society in New York at the turn of the century: *The Age of Innocence* is a bitterly ironic title.

Little Dorrit; Little Doormat

Little Dorrit which was published in 1856, is another novel about inheritance with illegitimacy in the background. Once again, an illegitimate infant is brought up by a harsh mother substitute who inflicts on the child a fierce and punitive religious vengeance the justification for which is supposed to be in the Old Testament. Dickens wishes to champion the approach of the New.

It is also about father-daughter relationships, and about love and duty. F. R. Leavis saw it as the greatest of Dickens's novels, but I have serious doubts about it, which I want to pursue, invoking for my purposes concepts from philosophical anthropology that have to do with love and good relationships, such as I have tried to apply above.

In this, again, I shall be asking what *Little Dorrit* is "about" in terms of its symbolic meaning, or its meaning as poetic drama, including unconscious meaning.

Since the book is so large, and since its complex plot creaks so much, I feel it would be useful first to give the story of the plot as straightforwardly as I can. In this I shall follow closely the account given by John Holloway in the Penguin Edition, for which we must all be grateful.

The crux of the matter here, too, has to do with inheritance. Mrs. Clennam, who is not Arthur's mother even though she brought him up, has cheated Little Dorrit out of a thousand guineas.* This "secret" lies at the heart of the intensely complex plot, which stretches from London to China and Marseilles and involves the mysterious Rigaud-Blandois and John Baptist. We may also note, once again, the symbol of the mysterious decaying house, which shudders and trembles. Mistress Affery thinks it is a ghost of someone who has been wronged there, but it is really some kind of subsidence or structural decay that conveniently brings down the build-ing on the head of Rigaud-Blandois in the final denouement, just as Mrs. Clennam and Little Dorrit are rushing back to the house to prevent the villain blackmailing Mrs. Clennam over the suppressed codicil to a will. Again, we have the typical Victorian melodrama theme of an unrealized inheritance and various forms of skullduggery connected with it. Mrs. Clennam's motives, however, are not impelled by cupidity but by the desire to punish "evil-doing"—or so she claims.

The situation with which the novel deals has been brought about by a Mr. Gilbert Clennam, who is dead when the book opens and whose will is at the center of the plot.

He had put forward his orphaned nephew as a husband for the Mrs. Clennam of the story. This orphaned nephew is Arthur's father—but Mrs. Clennam is not his mother. For, after her marriage, Mrs. Clennam finds that her husband has already gone through a form of marriage with another woman, who has borne him this son, Arthur.

Mrs. Clennam is, like Esther Summerson's aunt, a woman devoted to the vengeful religion of the Old Testament, and she demands that Arthur be given into her custody, to be brought up sternly: "knowing that the transgressions of the parents are visited on their offspring, and that there was an angry mark upon him at his birth" (*Little Dorrit,* 791). She has set out to "work out his release in bondage and hardship," for his good.

She has claimed to be allowed to bring up the child in this way, threat-ening to expose her husband if he does not allow it, and to make sure that the uncle will cut him off financially. Mrs. Clennam gets her way: the real mother has gone mad and died, and the father has gone abroad and later died, too.

The uncle, Gilbert Clennam, has meanwhile come to learn about Ar-

---

*In our terms (in 1992), say, fifty thousand dollars. See "What Was Mr. Darcy Worth?" by the present author, *Cambridge Review,* December 1984.

thur's real mother: he has heard only that she was a girl his nephew had loved but then abandoned in order to marry the woman his uncle had chosen for him. He hears that the real mother has gone mad and died. In remorse, and as a kind of recompense, he adds a codicil to his will, and it is around this codicil that the plot pivots.

The codicil leaves a thousand guineas to the youngest daughter of the man who at one time acted as patron to Arthur's true mother—or, if that man had no daughter, to his brother's younger daughter. This patron was Frederick Dorrit: he helped the girl to become a professional singer. But Frederick had no daughter, and so the legacy is due to his brother William's youngest daughter, Little Dorrit.

Arthur's father had dictated this codicil to Mrs. Clennam, and it had been witnessed by herself and Jeremiah Flintwinch. But she has concealed the document, hiding it in a place that she alone knew. At last she grows paralyzed and cannot get to where it was hidden.

When Arthur is coming home, Mrs. Clennam becomes anxious that he might find the paper, so she reveals the hiding place to Flintwinch and tells him to destroy the will. Instead he gives it, with other papers, in an iron box, to his own brother Ephraim, who is at that time staying in the house (book 1, chapter 4, "Mrs. Flintwinch has a dream"). His motives are not clear, except perhaps that he wants to exert power over Mrs. Clennam; after the collapse of the house, of course, he is in retirement in Amsterdam as Mynheer von Flyntevynge.

Rigaud-Blandois, who is a fugitive from justice in Marseilles, where he had been imprisoned on suspicion of killing his wife, comes into the story as a drinking companion of Ephraim Flintwinch (who is also a debt defaulter). When Ephraim dies of a fit, Rigaud-Blandois gets hold of the iron box and the suppressed codicil and so is in a position to blackmail Mrs. Clennam.

When Arthur, on his return from China, has a suspicion that there is some shadow on his father's dealings in the past, he is right—only the duplicity is his mother's (who is not his mother) rather than his father's. His father's watch contains the initials of the motto ("Do not forget," D.N.F.), and this is intended as a reminder of the disregarded codicil; Mrs. Clennam interprets it as a reminder of the evil-doing for which she has been exacting revenge.

All this elaborate plot was invented by Dickens to devise, once more, an inheritance that threatens to blight the lives of the protagonists. Little

Dorrit, who slaves at needlework in obscurity for the haughty Mrs. Clennam, has been cheated by her out of a legacy that would have given her independence. Arthur's sensibility has been "disappointed since the dawn of its perceptions": another blighted inheritance.

He has not yet given up all his hopeful yearnings. But the hard-featured qualities of his home (which really is a Bleak House) goes with the dead face of his mother:

She and his father had been at variance from his earliest remembrance. To sit speechless himself in the midst of rigid silence, *glancing in dread from one face to the other* had been the peacefullest occupation of his childhood. (33; my italics)

Now, his mother lies "on a black bier-like sofa . . . propped up behind with one great angular black bolster, like the block at a state execution in the good old times" (33).

Mrs. Clennam is placed clearly as an adherent of the religion of the Old Testament:

She then put on the spectacles and read certain passages aloud from a book—sternly, fiercely, wrathfully—praying that her enemies (she made them by her tone and manner expressly hers) might be put to the edge of the sword, consumed by fire, smitten by plagues and leprosy, that their bones might be ground to dust, and that they might be utterly exterminated. As she read on, years seemed to fall away from her son like the imaginings of a dream, and all the old dark horrors of his usual preparations for the sleep of an innocent child to overshadow him. (35)

So this novel again explores the theme of the effects of a stern upbringing on a child, as with the Gradgrind children, Estella, Esther Summerson, and David Copperfield, seen in the light of the teachings of Christ.

The contrast between Old Testament religion and the Christ-following religion of the New is made plain at the end of the book, when Mrs. Clennam at last confesses to Little Dorrit about the codicil and the legacy. Little Dorrit forgives her. Mrs. Clennam tries to vindicate herself: she would prefer to be known to Little Dorrit, rather than to the "son of my enemy who wronged me."

"For, she did wrong me! She not only sinned grievously against the Lord, but she wronged me. What Arthur's father was to me, she made him. From our marriage day I was his dread, and that she made me. I was the scourge of both, and that is referable to her." (790)

Dickens is slightly equivocal over this matter. Has Mrs. Clennam's mode of bringing up Arthur been beneficial or not? She tells Little Dorrit,

"I kept over him as a child, in the days of his first remembrance, my restraining and correcting hand. I was stern with him, knowing that the transgressions of the parents are visited on their offspring, and that there was an angry mark on him at his birth. I have sat with him and his father, seeing the weakness of his father yearning to unbend to him; and forcing it back, that the child might work out his release in bondage and hardship. I have seen him, with his mother's face, looking up at me in awe from his little books, and trying to soften me with his mother's ways that hardened me." (791)

Arthur, however, does not have to strive hard to overcome this legacy, as Little Dorrit has to strive to overcome hers, in order to fulfill himself.

Mrs. Clennam is surely, by all implications of the plot, a wicked woman: a cheat, cruelly punitive, vicious, and destructive. Moreover, her hypocrisy is intense, in that she seeks to portray her criminal and inhuman acts as motivated by religion:

"For his good. Not for the satisfaction of my injury. What was I, and what was the worth of that, before the curse of Heaven! I have seen that child grow up; not to be pious in a chosen way (his mother's offence lay too heavy on him for that), but still to be just and upright, and to be submissive to me. He never loved me, as I once hoped he might, but, he always respected me, and ordered himself dutifully to me. He does to this hour. With an empty place in his heart that he has never known the meaning of, he has turned away from me, and gone his separate road; but even that he has done considerately and with deference." (791)

From our point of view, nothing could be more terrible than the punitive and vengeful way she has brought up this child. She evidently deceives herself about her jealousy of his mother's sexuality and the evil nature of her own motives. Who is she to be respected, and to demand "duty," whose whole life has been built around hate and the denial of the volition and rights of others? Yet Dickens does not altogether dissociate himself from her evaluations of Arthur's respect and dutifulness: and this it seems to me is a serious fault in *Little Dorrit*. While offering to condemn the religious moral approach of the Old Testament devotees, the novel cher-ishes at the same time the submission, respect, and sense of duty these old precepts inspired, both in Arthur and Amy.

Mrs. Clennam admits to Little Dorrit, whom she has cheated, that she has relished her hold over her: "You have been in fear of me, but you have supposed to me have been doing you a kindness." But rather than humiliate herself in remorse, she seeks to enlist Little Dorrit, because she loves Arthur, in protecting her from Arthur's wrath by concealing her offense.

"Let me never feel, while I am still alive, that I die before his face, and utterly perish away from him, like one consumed by lightning and swallowed by an earthquake." (791)

Little Dorrit, who is always shrinking about something or other, shrinks away, and Mrs. Clennam cries, "Even now, I see you shrink from me, as if I had been cruel." (792). "As if": when we consider Little Dorrit's predicament at worst, there can be little doubt about Mrs. Clennam's horrible cruelty, since she has been a witness, at first hand, of her struggles and toil. Little Dorrit may recoil from Mrs. Clennam's state of mind, but there are other straight responses to cruelty and meanness, besides the punitive. Mrs. Clennam is allowed too much by way of self-vindication, and Little Dorrit makes Dickens's point:

"I have done," said Mrs. Clennam, "what it was given me to do. I have set myself against evil; not against good. I have been an instrument of severity against sin. Have not mere sinners like myself been commissioned to lay it low in all time!"

"In all time?" repeated Little Dorrit.

"Even if my own wrong had prevailed with me, and my own vengeance had moved me, could I have found no justification? None in the old days when the innocent perished with the guilty, a thousand to one? When the wrath of the hater of the unrighteous was not slaked even in blood, and yet found favour?"

"O, Mrs. Clennam, Mrs. Clennam," said Little Dorrit, "angry feelings and unforgiving deeds are no comfort and no guide to you and me. My life has been passed in this poor prison, and my teaching has been very defective; but, let me implore you to remember later and better days. Be guided only by the healer of the sick, the raiser of the dead, the friend of all who were afflicted and forlorn, the patient Master who shed tears of compassion for our infirmities. We cannot but be right if we put all the rest away, and do everything in remembrance of Him. There is no vengeance and no infliction of suffering in this life, I am sure." (792)

So, Little Dorrit, silhouetted against "the softened light of the window," like Agnes, is an angel. But that is the trouble with her: as an embodiment of Christ's forgiveness she is too much inclined to condone and so to forfeit her own authenticity: she becomes an idealized all-pardoning submissive.

The passage makes clear again Dickens's stand in favor of Christ's forgiveness, as against an approach to sin based on Deuteronomy (though he is here, I believe, writing in generally biblical language rather than quoting actual scripture). To Mrs. Clennam's request, "Little Dorrit yielded willingly"—but as they approach the house, the edifice falls.

We suppose the point is that, to be truly Christian, one must extend compassion not only to sinners but also to those who have misguidedly castigated and punished sinners, assuming self-righteously their right to do so. Yet why is Mrs. Clennam presented in such a sympathetic light or, at least, a forgivable light? Why does Little Dorrit connive at her deceiving Arthur further, when his life throughout the book has been commendably devoted to unraveling the matter of the shadow that he feels to be on his father's life—while the woman he believes to be his mother is the major barrier to this path to atonement? Has Mrs. Clennam fully made restitution to Little Dorrit? An assurance on that point would be worth pages of (melodramatic) equivocal explanations by this wicked woman on the subject of her being called to judge other sinners. On the next page she is going to collapse into a state of dumb paralysis from which she never recovers; but where does she offer any expression of regret or true contrition for her deeds? She seems, after all, to have reduced Arthur to the state of lesser living for all of his days. Of him Dickens says at one point, "It was the momentary yielding of a nature that had been disappointed from the dawn of its perceptions" (32; my italics).

I am not of course asking for a torrent of self-flagellating recriminations. Nor am I asking for Mrs. Clennam to be thrashed like Wackford Squeers. It is the question of right response that I am concerned with: essentially, Little Dorrit's responses. Of course, some of Dickens's reactions to evil are as false as anything can be—they sometimes involve the reader in sadistic responses, as when the cruel schoolmaster (Squeers) is cruelly dealt with, or in satisfaction at seeing the brutal murderer (Sykes) being hanged by his own noose. There are, however, responses, such as Micawber's to Uriah Heep or Pip's to Magwitch, in which we share "useful hate"—the expression of a human repugnance, a proper expression of disquiet and rejection, and an insistence on the realities of what has happened—albeit together with understanding. It is these elements that are missing here, and this, I believe, is a serious defect in the novel.

John Holloway, in his introduction to the Penguin Edition, says that we must approach *Little Dorrit* as a fiction, and

a fiction sets before its readers not only generalized truths about life, but also, and indeed more characteristically, a more visionary dimension of life: possibilities and potentialities.... (27)

In the end, Arthur Clennam and Little Dorrit find one another, as true love partners, despite all the vicissitudes of fate that have tossed them here and there, and despite the unpromising inheritance of each. In the moral of the book, money, riches, ambition, security, power over others, public influence—all these are shown to mean nothing to the existential quest of the two leading protagonists. But in the end, "vision" is hardly the word, since both man and woman are so drab and colorless: what have they to offer toward our sense of "life's possibilities and potentialities"? They are, it is true, full of a serious sense of duty and responsibilities, full of moral scruple: they are concerned not to hurt the feelings of others, not to impinge on others or to exert authority over others. They turn the other cheek, accept their faults, and represent the meek that inherit the earth. They are, one might say, true followers of Christ, in these respects.

To portray such a love, with its devotions to duty, might seem a triumph. But in the upshot, it is not only uninspiring; it also lacks an essential vitality that lays its own claims on life. The protagonists are not selfish enough: that is, they do not stake out a sufficient claim for their own self-realization and fulfillment. They are, like Little Dorrit in her dealings with the repulsive and deceitful Mrs. Clennam, too full of compunction, too willing to be submissive to the impositions of others. As we shall see, this is especially true of the central relationship between Amy and her father.

It is as if Dickens forgot that there are other alternatives to the brutal authoritarianism of the Old Testament, on the one hand, and to the universal forgiveness of Christ, on the other. For there is also the right to exert one's own moral independence, holding at arm's length the attempts of others to intrude into one's life, to undermine it, or to smother it; and there is one's right to live one's life not for others but for one's own sake. In these respects Little Dorrit and Arthur fail, and so one ends the book with a depressing sense of their effacement. The relationship between Arthur and Amy has too much the air of a chastened father-daughter relationship, from which all libidinal elements have been excluded, and in which the main dynamic, if it can be called that, is a dutiful relegation of the world.

What is it that is wrong? I believe it is a failure to cherish ambivalence. We know from psychoanalytical theory that our moral dynamics—our capacity to be good—are related to the problem of ambivalence: our admixture of love and hate. No one can escape this problem, and all of us experience envy, jealousy, the impulse to wound and even to destroy—in unconscious fantasy if not in any apprehended mode susceptible to volition.

There can be no moral development until we accept, in ourselves and others, capacities to be mean, spiteful, envious, or destructive, as well as capacities to be generous, selfless, loving, and cherishing. The trouble with Little Dorrit is that she is too good: she is always "the least, the quietest, and weakest of Heaven's creatures" (96). She always does her duty and shrinks from any recognition of her pains: she is lowly and Christlike. Dickens exclaims, "Shall we speak of the inspiration of a poet or a priest and not of the heart impelled by love and self-devotion to the lowliest way of life?" (71). Undoubtedly, Dickens's description of Little Dorrit's origins, her birth and upbringing in the Marshalsea Prison, is moving: consider, for example, the account of her early relationship with the Turnkey.

But Little Dorrit is also very much the Victorian woman, belonging to the type discussed above with reference to Sir Charles Petrie. I have defended Esther Summerson against the charge of insipidity: she often displays insight and energy, and deals well with difficult situations, such as when she chooses to isolate herself upon contracting smallpox, or when Lady Dedlock reveals herself as her mother—though, like all women in Victorian novels, she is over-given to weeping and swooning, and she is defined by her little basket of household keys. But while one cannot but respect Little Dorrit for the efforts she makes to maintain respect and decency and to sustain her family by her work, under the most unpropitious circumstances, she is too unworldly by half—too *innocent.* And innocence, as we have seen, was the cherished quality in the Victorian woman that inhibited her capacity to be effective and free.

Moreover, the purity and innocence is polarized toward a father figure. Dickens has a strong tendency to idealize the father-daughter relationship. In *Bleak House* it would have taken a huge effort on his part to show Esther transferring her affections from the much older partner John Jarndyce, a father to her, to Alan Woodcourt, her real lover—so he takes resort to magic. The whole environment of the Bleak House father-home has to be created anew so that Esther is transferred to a fairy-tale father-created household, in the preparation of which Woodcourt is involved at every stage. Esther is thus deprived of significant choice. Behind this problem lies one of *control,* and we have to say, I believe, that the dutiful daughter in both books is woman under very careful *magical* control. The father-daughter relationship is sexless, and thus has none of the dangers of free sexuality. Esther is carefully transferred to Woodcourt in this way. In a parallel way, Little Dorrit turns from being a submissive child-wife-daughter to her own father toward another father figure, Arthur Clennam, who earlier in the book speaks of her as "poor-child" and "little creature," and who regards himself as being past passion, like an old father. ("Done with that part of life" [334].)

Arthur is early on much impressed with Little Dorrit's demeanor toward her father. "Her look at her father, half-admiring him and proud of him, half-ashamed for him, all devoted and loving, went to his inmost heart" (82). Dickens places this action in the context of such painful and humiliating circumstances that we find it hard not to excuse Mr. Dorrit, and are brought to feel that it would be unthinkable or, if thinkable, then uncharitable to condemn him. Little Dorrit says,

"Not that he has anything to be ashamed of for himself, or that I have anything to be ashamed of for him. He only requires to be understood. I only ask for him that his life may be fairly remembered.... He is very much respected.... He is far more thought of than the Marshal is...." If ever pride were innocent, it was innocent in Little Dorrit when she grew boastful of her father. (97)

Page by page, we are brought to acquiesce in the idealization of Little Dorrit, so much so that we would feel caddish questioning her view of her father and her own all-pardoning submissiveness to him. This is not to deny, of course, the acknowledgment that he requires *understanding*— but that understanding should include some placing, some response that might draw out authenticity in him.

For the truth is that however much one might understand him, Dorrit *is* something to be ashamed of, and he ought to be ashamed of himself. Little Dorrit is aware of this, of course, but seeks to hide it, and will certainly not confront it. The "respect" he has attained is a false one: he has gained it by a masquerade—and by extorting "presentations" from people by cadging. It has become customary to make gifts of money to William Dorrit, and he exacts these with all the fawning devices of a beggar. That he is ashamed of the practice becomes clear when later, after his release, John Chivery tries to give him a bundle of cigars, and so reminds him of prison: to accept gifts was a humiliation, because he lowered himself to cringe and solicit. Dickens is aware of this, and makes Little Dorrit aware of it; but he cannot find any way in which Old Dorrit can be given back some self-respect in this respect, and probably here he was working on his image of his own father. In Micawber the father is comically caricatured; in Magwitch he is seen with pity; in William Dorrit the bitterness is deeper, and the man more corrupt—but his cruelties go unchallenged by those who love him. Of course, one might say that this is a kind of corruption any penal institution inflicts on its inhabitants, but all the same, it is a shameful practice. It falsifies his human integrity.

Later, of course, Dorrit becomes quite falsified in a different way by his riches, and is cruel and mean to his family and friends—but again Little Dorrit never condemns him. She realizes that there are dangers in release for such a man, who has been "inside" for so long.

"I have often thought that if such a change could come, it might be anything but a service to him now. People might not think so well of him outside as they do there. He might not be so gently dealt with, as he is there. He might not be so fit himself for the life outside, as he is for that."

Here for the first time she could not restrain her tears from falling; and the little thin hands he had watched when they were so busy, trembled as they clasped each other. (98–99)

Her insights into her father's possible problems with his freedom are intelligent and insightful: they are real. But, of course, being a Victorian woman, she suffers badly from coming out of her "innocence" even that far: her tears fall, her "little" hands tremble (ah, such "busy" little hands!). Little Dorrit is continually trembling, shrinking, turning white, and weeping; she is, in many ways, except for her efficiency in some respects, like Dora: that is, she is a doll, or something between a doll and an angel, and at the same time a doormat. Yet Dickens raves about this very submissiveness:

What affection in her words, what compassion in her suppressed tears, what a great soul of fidelity within her, how true the light that shed false brightness round him! (97)

(She has just said that Dorrit's manners are said to be "a true gentleman's" and that "he is not to be blamed for being in need, poor love. Who could be in prison for a quarter of a century, and be prosperous!")

She knows that there is a (good) father she has never seen, and she yearns for him, but she does nothing to find him, as by standing up to him. The fault seems to suggest some impotence in Dickens in the face of his own maddening father.

Dickens sees that the light she throws over Dorrit is "false." But where Dickens is wrong is in accepting that the casting of false brightness is acceptable, as love and devotion. Little Dorrit connives at the old man's false pride; she compounds his absurd gentility:

"It would be a new distress to him even to know that I earn a little money, and that Fanny earns a little money. He is so anxious about us, you see, feeling helplessly shut up there. Such a good, good father!" (99)

Love and fidelity are fine things; but, again, they require the acknowledg-ment of weaknesses. It is not anxious concern about his daughters that prompts Dorrit to keep himself unaware of his daughters' scrapings; it is his own egoism and false pride. He does not feel helplessly shut up; He enjoys being a kind of prison baron—but does little or nothing for the welfare of those who grant him such false deference. He is *not* a good father, and it is not the best exercise of love and fidelity to fall into such false idealizations. It is not love to put up with such offenses to love, in absolute devotion. This is not to say he deserved such treatment as Lear had from Goneril and Regan; but a speech like Cordelia's first one might have been in order.

I have discussed the nature of falsifying institutions in *Bleak House*—the Court of Chancery itself, and the whole complex of Chesney Wold. The debtor's prison is such a falsifying institution in this novel, and is mirrored in the symbolism of the book by Merdle's empire. Merdle's name clearly derives from the French word for the substance that Freud declared to represent "inner contents": *merde alors!* Merdle's false gold generates only false social relationships and identities* (Dickens is marvelous on the pretensions of Mrs. Merdle, who is "the Bosom.") The Marshalsea holds those who have nothing or less than nothing; they are imprisoned because they are minus quantities. They have no identities, yet even here Dorrit creates himself a role or identity of sorts. Little Dorrit represents love and fidelity generating Christlike meanings in this negative environment. It is not, I think, as John Holloway puts it, a question of stripping away "sur-faces" but of finding what is there "within," established by love, devotion, *reparation.*

But reparation cannot be achieved; substance and meaning cannot be established on the basis of "false light" and without the realistic recognition of the mixed nature of human nature in the other. For the creative writer, this means developing the ability to find the ambivalence in himself.

---

*I believe it is possible that Dickens picked up the name, in association with ill-gotten gains, from the cloacal language about "merds" of Ben Jonson's *Alchemist,* with all its unconscious symbolism.

Strangely enough, the Marshalsea itself also seems to put a limit on this process. Little Dorrit makes a strange remark: "I think it would be almost cowardly and cruel not to have some little attachment for it, after all this." To whom would it be "cruel" if she were not to love the prison? Why would it be "cowardly"?

Strangely enough, having so much of the action inside the Marshalsea puts a form of false security around the relationship between Little Dorrit and her father, and the situation strangely limits the realism. It is quite the opposite in *Pickwick Papers*. When Mr. Pickwick goes to prison, a somber note takes over the book, and its range extends into a wider perspective on human suffering. The odd thing about the Marshalsea is that it places a limitation of a sentimental kind on Little Dorrit's appreciation of her father, on her love and fidelity—provides an excuse for her compliance.

There are times when it would have been better for Little Dorrit to stand up to her father and to resist him. In saying this, of course, I am asking for a different book. But surely her love and devotion would have been more convincing if Little Dorrit had not been so consistently without fault? We excuse her because we say, "Oh, but her poor old father has been in prison for a quarter of a century" or "But she herself was born in the Marshalsea." The Marshalsea itself thus seems to become a rather special protective kind of home, and spontaneous action within it is limited by an inhibiting pity that has a sneaking *love* for the Marshalsea itself. In this setting, too, Little Dorrit herself is limited by her role, and (again) by her "innocence."

It needs to be emphasized, as a psychotherapist might well emphasize to a patient, that love is not the uncritical acceptance of the other, nor is fidelity total submission. Nor is it selflessness: "She was not accustomed to think of herself, or to trouble any one with her emotions" (99).

I turn for a moment to the attraction that F. R. Leavis evidently felt for Little Dorrit. Leavis believed that selflessness was a virtue, often elsewhere accusing others (like Bertrand Russell and Othello) of being "imprisoned in the ego." He obviously rallied strongly to a Little Dorrit who "would not trouble anyone with her emotions." But then she is also sexless, submissive, totally loyal, innocent, quiet, and wholly under control: everything, that is, that no real woman is—and that certainly one's own inner phantom woman of the unconscious is not.

At the Heart of the Marshalsea

One of the crucial scenes in *Little Dorrit* is that between Little Dorrit and her father in chapter 19, book 1. The chapter provides a clue to the symbolism of the Marshalsea: like the Court of Chancery and the Jarndyce case, it is the embodiment of a structure that falsifies the true self. We find similar structures elsewhere: Pip, for instance, is caught up in one, a false inheritance, Estella is caught up in the strange fabric of Miss Havisham's establishment; Dombey is caught up in his business house; Gradgrind, in his educational system; Bounderby, in his melancholy elephants, the machines, and his own egoism.

What is the true identity? The final paragraphs of chapter 19 are puzzling: what does Little Dorrit mean when she cries out, "No, no, I have never seen him in my life!" Who is "he"? The answer is in the previous paragraph: "she . . . wondered did he look now at all as he had looked when he was prosperous and happy," "as he had so touched her by imagining that he might look once more in that awful time" (231). The word "awful" is puzzling, until we realize this refers to his earlier remarks about his own death. He has declared that his children have never seen him as he really is: "my children will have never seen me" (227). There is no record of his prosperous self: "If I had but a picture of myself in those days, though it was ever so ill done, you would be proud of it, you would be proud of it"

83

(227). They will only see this true face, perhaps, in his death (which is the "awful time"): "Unless my face, when I am dead, subsides into the long departed look—they say such things happen, I don't know—my children will have never seen me" (227). It is this theme, presumably, that makes John Holloway talk about "surfaces" and the way they are penetrated in this novel. But the essential theme is, rather, the quest for true self-being from within, existentially, in the condition of being-unto-death.

The intensity of feeling in this chapter, "The Father of the Marshalsea in two or three relations," again suggests, that the father-daughter relationship was of great significance to Dickens: as I have pointed out, it is of significance also in *Dombey and Son* and *Bleak House*. When Mr. Dombey strikes Florence, he menaces the image of himself that she holds in her heart, which she is trying to sustain in love. In *Bleak House,* Esther's real father is a ruined man, addicted to opium, living in a garret as a copyist of law documents; he commits suicide and is buried in a squalid corner of unconsecrated ground. She has to make enormous efforts of duty and love to her surrogate father, who is a rich fountain of love, before she can move over, as it were, into an adult love relationship, and find the proper image of man to which to relate.

This preoccupation raises the whole question of what the father-daughter relationship symbolizes in literature—in (say) T. S. Eliot's poem *Marina,* Shakespeare's *Pericles;* Shakespeare's *Lear,* Mrs. Gaskell's *Wives and Daughters.* In discussing Shakespeare's *Pericles* I have suggested that the daughter symbolizes belief in the creative feminine principle: "the hope, the new ships"—that is, this symbolism has to do with one's relationship (if one is a man) to one's own female dynamic. It also has to do, of course, with one's relationships to woman in life, one's wife and daughters, and to one's own authenticity of being, since being belongs to the feminine mode.

The situations in which such a theme is explored are those of "the world"—the world of economic harshness and drive in Dombey; the world in which there are pirates, brothels, and storms in *Pericles,* the world that can be wrecked by one's arrogance and self-deception in *Lear.* The recurrent theme is that of authentic being: what Cordelia's love eventually brings home to Lear is that sense of absolute authenticity that enables him to triumph over all concern with what the world does to them:

> The good years shall devour them, flesh and fell,
> Ere they shall make us weep

Dickens must have had *Lear* in mind in writing *Little Dorrit;* and it is this theme, insofar as it is Learish, that made the book so interesting to F. R. Leavis, I believe. But there is another mythical theme of great significance in Dickens's mind, indicated by this slightly coy reference:

There was a classical daughter once—perhaps—who ministered to her father in his prison as her mother had ministered to her. Little Dorrit, though of the unheroic modern stock, and mere English, did much more, in comforting her father's wasted heart upon her innocent breast, and turning it to a fountain of love and fidelity that never ran dry or waned, through all his years of famine. (229)

As John Holloway tells us in his notes to the Penguin edition, this refers to Euphrasia: "Euphrasia, daughter of King Evander of Syracuse, whom she fed when he was in prison with the milk of her breasts" (905). This is a most important mythical reference, as it indicates that Dickens is thinking of Little Dorrit as "good breast," and that his theme is reparation, in the Kleinian sense. The coyness of his reference may also be interpreted. Saying that Euphrasia ministered to her father as her mother ministered to her actually gives an indirect clue to the powerful sexual feeling underlying Dickens's preoccupation with the "daughter" theme: the unconscious preoccupation is with the daughter "ministering" to the father *as the mother ministered to him,* and the image of a daughter giving suck to her father is an intensely erotic, if incestuous, image. But the theme is also deeper than sexual, for it suggests the daughter giving love and meaning to the father (perhaps as the mother did not), and this must arouse suspicions that Dickens himself felt the possibilities of the creative influence of love and meaning from his own daughter, in ways that he had not known from his wife—a longing for feminine sustenance such as an infant should obtain from the mother. After all, there is enough about deprivation, especially deprivation of inheritance, in Dickens's work to suggest this. I have suggested above that reparation may be an attempt to cure the self, and we may see Dickens's own massive "giving out" and his preoccupation with giving out, loving, healing, *making good,* as an impulse that has its roots in his own deprivation at the breast. The image of a daughter feeding her father in the way her mother ministered to her had an enormous appeal to him. So, in his life, he tended to have, even in his household, a devoted, "pure" sister figure, a nonsexual, nonlibidinal partner (Mary, Georgina).

But also, of course, the impulse toward the daughter is fraught with guilt. So Dickens goes on to desexualize the image. Little Dorrit is of "unheroic modern stock" and is "mere English," yet she does "much more." Hers is not to be a physical nourishment; she comforts her father's heart "*upon her innocent breast.*" The English Victorian woman can do more because of her *innocence*—that word again. Because she is not (like a foreign Greek woman) involved in sensuality, she can transcend her breast into true reparation, "turning it to a fountain of love and fidelity that never ran dry or waned, through all his years of famine" (229). Little Dorrit is thus eminently "Little Mother": she is an idealized fountain of motherly love that pardons all, and never rejects or withdraws, whatever the bitter circumstances. At first reading, I took the "it" to be his wasted heart, but that cannot be so: it is her innocent breast that is turned to a fountain, for one could hardly accept that Dorrit's heart becomes a fountain of love and fidelity. He is treacherous to her, as when he betrays to Chivery that Little Dorrit is on the bridge, when he tries to blackmail her into accepting young Chivery's advances for his own comfort, and so on. His own love is often confused by his totally false standards of social prestige and status. Yet the odd ambiguity reveals Dickens's wish, his idolization that makes him wish, that the father can benefit from the equivalent of a mother love in his daughter, this love having the additional attraction of being "innocent"—that is, without the complications of the libidinal, of the full sexual relationship with a woman.

Unfortunately, to endorse the kind of love and fidelity embodied in Little Dorrit is to endorse an unreality—and an injustice. Dorrit's view of himself we shall examine in a moment, but it includes the false view of him that Little Dorrit wants to accept: "She was too content to see him with a luster round his head." That is, as Dickens knows and shows he knows, she wants to see him as a saint or even as a Christlike figure, but the truth is that he is anything but that. Dickens sees that she is mistaken, but he gives her none—or far too little—of Pip's revulsion at the falsifying effect on himself of a "love" like Magwitch's that is caught up in its own false fantasies. Little Dorrit's error is in becoming too embroiled, because of her "innocence," in a false assumption: that while a woman's love can be all-forgiving, and an endless fountain of fidelity, the man is entitled to infringe fidelity and to insult that love with impunity. This would only be acceptable if the man were an infant. Since he is an adult and a father, not all the horrors of quarter of a century in the debtors' prison can excuse the offenses to his daughter's being that he commits. This is not to say that she ought not to go on loving him—members of a family often do go on loving one another, despite outrages, which are forgiven—but what we are examining is the author's portrayal of this complex, and in Dickens's portrayal there is a serious lack of realism and justice: Little Dorrit is honored too much as totally submissive, while Dorrit is pardoned too easily for being a selfish old brute.

Of course, there is a sense in which love is absolute: certainly, with children one never withdraws one's love, however badly they behave. Yet this love need not be all-tolerating, and it is true love that must at times (as through the bad patches of adolescent hostility) move into painful positions of confrontation or resistance, for fidelity's sake, for the sake of love. Love can even be painfully critical, as it is with Mr. Knightley, who castigates Emma and makes her weep with remorse.

If we examine the beginning of chapter 19, we find that Dickens had no doubt about the character of William Dorrit: his rendering of his "jail-rot" is done with profundity and wit. He is also critical of Amy's idolization of her father, but he goes over too easily into an idealization of her idolization, endorsing the absoluteness of her "innocent" love, which is utterly submissive. In being so submissive Little Dorrit forfeits credibility as an adult and becomes sentimental; we are invited into the author's unreality, his tendency to find the ideal woman "angelic," which also means sexless and without independence of spirit (Estella is by contrast full of spirit, despite her emotional coldness, and so are Bella Wilfer, Lizzie Hexam, Biddy, Nancy, and Betsy Trotwood).

Dickens, as we have seen, is interested in the way in which individuals may be corrupted and brought to forfeit their "true self-being" by some kind of system or complex in which they are ensnared or that they inherit: the Dombey empire, the Merdle empire, the Jarndyce case, the Marshalsea, the utilitarian calculus. The cure for this falsification is love. We may even reduce this to "hard hearts" versus "love": Dickens is pursuing Lear's question, "Is there any cause in nature that makes these hard hearts?"

But, of course, thinking of the analogy with *King Lear,* such an opposition is most effective when the love refuses to compromise with false exploitation of love, and tries (as with the Fool and Kent) to bring love out of falsification and inauthenticity, even at the risk of the protester's life. The Fool and Kent so love Lear, and are so devoted to the principle of his kingship, that they put their own safety and well-being in danger by criticizing him for his false postures.

Little Dorrit, in her devotion, is shown accepting deprivation as she spends her night out at her "party" in the cold night, though this seems to come about because of her own carelessness about closing time in the prison, and a rather absurd shyness about discussing the problem with Clennam. But that, of course, is just how your "innocent" Victorian woman would behave. Her suffering at her street "party" is not a conse-quence of any sacrifice or act of duty, though Dickens probably had in mind some kind of reduction to "bare necessity" such as Lear suffers in *King Lear.*

But Little Dorrit differs in ways related to the differences between the ages: one cannot imagine Cordelia being called "Little Cordelia" (though Lear is tender to her in a childlike way in the last act), nor can one imagine Little Dorrit arriving with an army to save her father. She lacks both Cordelia's dogged determination not to be falsified and Cordelia's an-guished discrimination against her father—discrimination that refuses to compromise. Those who shrink from encountering Lear's reality opt for sycophantic hypocrisy and combine this with rejection and dire cruelty, as do Goneril and Regan. By contrast, Cordelia's is a manifestation of a love that accepts ambivalence. Like Kent, Cordelia wants to *love* Lear and oblige him to be *true Lear:* she is a determined realist. To her sisters she says,

> I know you what you are....
> Love well our father;
> To your professed bosoms, I commit him:
> But yet, alas, stood I within his grace,
> I would prefer him to a better place.

Little Dorrit lacks Cordelia's sagacity, her critical power, and her de-termined authenticity. She is well aware of her father's degradation, and quite properly lovingly forgives him; but where she fails is in not refusing to accept his manipulations. She secretly bears, tremblingly, his offenses to her, as when he betrays her to the turnkey's unwelcome attentions—when she should, for his sake and hers, for love's sake, deal with him in this respect. Similarly, later she bears, without reproof, his criticisms of her behavior when she will not live up to a socialite life. It is not enough that she should refuse to be falsified in this respect; she should have made it plain to him why she would not falsify, and why he was wrong in so trying to falsify her, on a parallel with Cordelia's "I cannot heave my heart unto my mouth"

Incidentally, I am indicating in what way Shakespeare made Dickens possible; and (as Q. D. Leavis has pointed out*) the greatest achievements of the English novel would not have been possible without Shakespeare. At the same time I am indicating weaknesses in the Victorian sensibility, right at the core of the problem of "being" to which both Shakespeare and Dickens addressed themselves, and this indicates the great difference between the ages. The Euphrasia myth had an influence on Dickens that is as weakening as the Electra myth proved a source of strength for Shakespeare. Moreover, the Euphrasia myth has an incestuous content that is dismissed by the heavy use of the concept of "innocence": in the Victorian consciousness woman was an innocent breast, a source of solace and nourishment, but one whose own erotic spirit was denied—so that when the Victorian male, like Ruskin, saw the woman's pubic hair, expressive of her animal and libidinal needs, and her creativity, he became impotent out of fear and dread. Yet he wanted to be at her breast, imbiding grace. Little Dorrit (Little Mother) is thus a way of avoiding many aspects of reality: sexless, she provokes no guilt; without Cordelia's spirit, she prompts no problems of equality and mutual regard; always trembling and turning pale, she evokes the impulse to protect, and so control. And in consequence, she cannot really restore authenticity of being in the world of hard hearts; she can only encourage a fantasy that the world would be a better place if we were all children, obedient and submissive (or certainly if all *women* were so).

But to return to the beginning of chapter 19: here, in a comparison of Frederick and William Dorrit, Dickens shows himself quite clear as to William's petty snobbery, his fantasy that sustains him through his long incarceration and the depth of his jail-rot—yet he makes of it a Jonsonian comedy that reverberates out into a general satire on human nature.

The brothers William and Frederick Dorrit walk up and down the College-yard,

of course on the aristocratic or Pump side, for the Father made it a point of his state to be chary of going among his children on the Poor side, except on Sunday mornings, Christmas Days and other occasions of ceremony, in the observance whereof he was very punctual, and at which times he laid his hands upon the heads of their infants, and blessed those young Insolvents with a benignity that was highly edifying. (221)

*See Leavis 1983.

One calls it "Jonsonian," but it is in fact centrally "English" in a much wider way: it could be compared with Chaucer on the Reve, Shakespeare on Dogberry—

> I am a wise fellow; and, which is more, an officer; and, which is more, a householder; and, which is more, as pretty a piece of flesh as any is in Messina; and one that knows the law, go to; and a rich fellow enough, go to; and a fellow that hath had losses

—and Pope on Sir Balaam, "the aristocratic or Pump side" having exactly the same caricature effect as "And, lo, two puddings smok'd upon the board."

The comedy is deepened by the contrast between the one brother, who is "free" but has let himself go, and the other brother, who is imprisoned but builds a structure for himself as father of the Marshalsea. To his brother he says,

> "If you could be persuaded to smarten yourself up a little, Frederick—"
> "Do you think your habits are as precise and methodical as—shall I say as mine are? ... I doubt if you take air and exercise enough, Frederick. Here is the parade, always at your service." (222)

He has the supporting structure of the institution, and he has the devotion of his daughter (whose attention is the equivalent of the domestic services of a wife):

> "I have impressed upon Amy during many years, that I must have my meals (for instance) punctually. Amy has grown up in a sense of the importance of these arrangements, and you know what a good girl she is." (223)

As we read this we are amused, bitterly, by this man's capacity to extol his regular life—which is achieved by the submission of Little Dorrit to the status of a domestic slave—and we feel William Dorrit is a hypocrite and domestic tyrant. Yet his daughter's love is, all the same, to be measured by the extent to which she dutifully and uncomplainingly serves the tyr' anny and is, moreover, unwilling either to allow others to criticize it or to criticize him in her own heart—let alone defy or reprimand him about it.

Dorrit goes on:

> "I wish I could rouse you, my good Frederick; you want to be roused."
> "Yes, William, yes. No doubt," returned the other....

"But I am not like you."
... "Oh! You might be like me, my dear Frederick; you might be, if you chose." (223)

Yet, as we very soon see, William's keeping himself "roused" is a ploy to avoid the deep despair and depression any real recognition of his actual state would bring. Because of this, he is impatient of distress in others, while attributing to himself certain "qualities"—moral qualities—that his brother does not have, but that he has, to endure the "College." And these qualities include the ability to see in his "testimonials" a sign of the goodness of human nature and the fine spirit animating the Collegians as a community, seeing in them "at the same time no degradation to himself, and no depreciation of his claims as a gentleman" (225). There follows a moving paragraph in which Dickens shows himself aware of the complex mixture of misery, hope, shabbiness, and dignity to be found in the Marshalsea (his own father was once taken up for debt and imprisoned there):

Such was the homily with which he improved and pointed the occasion to the company in the lodge, before turning into the sallow yard again, and going with his own poor shabby dignity past the Collegian in the dressing-gown who had no coat, and past the Collegian in the sea-side slippers who had no shoes, and past the stout greengrocer Collegian in the corduroy knee-breeches who had no cares, and past the lean clerk Collegian in buttonless black who had no hopes, up his own poor shabby staircase, to his own poor shabby room. (225)

It is like a tiny thumbnail sketch of a group of Canterbury pilgrims: note the vivid exactness of such touches as the dressing gown, the seaside slippers, the corduroy knee breeches, and the *buttonless* black. Here indeed the seediness is real, and by contrast the claim to "moral qualities" is shown to be the impulse to believe a lie.

In the shabby room is Little Dorrit: but while the way she has laid ready for him "his old grey gown" is movingly expressive of her devotion, the image is spoiled by the religiose touch:

His daughter put her little prayer-book in her pocket—had she been praying for all prisoners and captives!—and rose to welcome him. (225)

It spoils because it gives Amy's subsequent challenge to his pretense of "moral qualities" a pious air, more appropriate to Pecksniff, Chadband, or the converted Uriah Heep. There is now a "touch of shame" in the air, and it seems to be prompted by a pious admonition from Amy, unspoken of course, combined with that kind of totally forbearing forgiveness that has even a minatory quality:

As she stood behind him, leaning over his chair so lovingly, she looked with downcast eyes at the fire. An uneasiness stole over him that was like a touch of shame: and when he spoke, as he presently did, it was in an unconnected and embarrassed manner. (225–26)

And we have moved from the deep human comedy of *Much Ado,* or Jonson or Pope, into Victorian melodrama, even to the gestures:

While he spoke, he was opening and shutting his hands like valves; so conscious all the time of this touch of shame, that he shrunk before his own knowledge of his meaning. (226)

His meaning ("if I was to lose the support and recognition of Chivery and his brother officers, I might starve to death here") is that he is prepared to sacrifice her feelings for his own petty prestige and comfort.

If only, instead of bending her head in mute, pious remonstrance that betrays no remonstrance, Little Dorrit had said, firmly, "Father, I think it was mean of you, to let the Chiverys know I was on the bridge, because you are aware I do not welcome his attentions. I do not think my refusal of his approaches would mean in the end that you would lose their respect, and as for talk of starving, you know that is nonsense." A more independent and spirited girl, of the Elizabethan age or of the present day, might add, "And I do not see that groveling to turnkeys benefits either your dignity or my self-respect." In response to either remark, there might have been a painful scene, but the reader would not have lost his respect for either character—and the air would have been cleared in a way it is never cleared in *Little Dorrit.* Nor would this have meant any less love. Consider, for example, the extremely painful way in which Elizabeth confronts Darcy, without losing the reader's self-respect or doing irreparable harm to their relationship—or, again, the way Mr. Knightley upbraids Emma.

But Dickens believes in the endless masochism of Little Dorrit: and so, in truth, we have an even more painful spectacle, that of Dorrit gradually being forced, by Little Dorrit's sanctimonious silence, into something like a breakdown.

"What does it matter whether I eat or starve? What does it matter whether such a blighted life as mine comes to an end, now, next week, or next year? What am

I worth to any one? A poor prisoner, fed on alms and broken victuals; a squalid, disgraced wretch!"

"Father, father!" As he rose, she went on her knees to him, and held up her hands to him. (227)

He goes on "looking haggardly about," and we are well into the Victorian highly moral stage scene:

"O despise me, despise me! Look away from me, don't listen to me, stop me, blush for me, cry for me—Even you, Amy! Do it, do it! I do it to myself! I am hardened now, I have sunk too low to care long even for that."

"Dear father, loved father, darling of my heart!" She was clinging to him with her arms, and she got him to drop into his chair again, and caught at the raised arm, and tried to put it round her neck. "Let it lie there, father. Look at me, father, kiss me father! Only think of me, father, for one little moment!"

Still he went on in the same wild way, though it was gradually breaking down into a miserable whining. (228)

It is a deplorable scene: but in a sense Dickens has brought it on himself, just as the characters have brought it on themselves by their own false relationship. The gestures are stage histrionics; the repetitions and excla^mations are those of the particularly stylized modes of the melodrama of the time—as is Amy's prayerbook and Dorrit's empty self-criticism, which sinks into maudlin self-pity.

What we might feel is that the episode would have been so much better had Little Dorrit some of the qualities of Betsy Trotwood, who evidently experiences deep emotions but is able to deal with distressing circumstances in a mode of realism in which genuine love is at work: Betsy uses Mr. Dick to distance herself and to stimulate herself to action rather than words. This is comic, but one of the hallmarks of melodrama is a total absence of all comedy and irony. And with this absence of wit there goes a suspension of intelligence and of emotional realism.

We can believe in Dorrit's "jail-rot" and his attempts to sustain some sense of self-respect in jail: we can believe he would fall into temporary breakdowns. But as we follow his confused ramblings we become aware of an underlying purpose in the author having to do with idealizing the father-daughter relationship in a certain way:

Still he went on in the same wild way, though it was gradually breaking down into a miserable whining.

"And yet I have some respect here. I have made some stand against it. I am not quite trodden down. Go out and ask who is the chief person in the place.

They'll tell you it's your father. Go out and ask who is never trifled with and who is always treated with some delicacy. They'll say your father. Go out and ask what funeral here (it must be here, I know it can be nowhere else) will make more talk, and perhaps more grief, than any that has ever gone out of the gate. They'll say your father's. Well then. Amy! Amy! Is your father so universally despised? Is there nothing to redeem him? Will you have nothing to remember him by, but his ruin and decay? Will you be able to have no affection for him when he is gone, poor castaway, gone?"

He burst into tears of maudlin pity for himself, and at length suffered her to embrace him, and take charge of him, let his grey head rest against her cheek, and bewailed his wretchedness. Presently he changed the subject of his lamentation, and clasping his hands about her as she embraced him, cried, O Amy, his motherless, forlorn child! O the days that he had seen her careful and laborious for him! (228)

There are moments when the outburst is convincing: it begins convincingly, and we applaud the intention, which is conveyed succinctly:

Thus, now boasting, now despairing, in either fit a captive with the jail-rot upon him, and the impurity of his prison worn into the grain of his soul, he revealed his degenerate state to his affectionate child. (228–29)

But there follows the reference to Euphrasia, and we have to say that much of the scene goes soggy—and it is soggy with the language and histrionic modes of Victorian melodrama, which turn it out of the insightful (and Shakespearean) into a fairy tale, into that impossible fantasy world in which the Victorians could believe, wherein the grossest emotions could be indulged and all brought to good by the ministerings of an "innocent" breast: by magic.

So, instead of the loving dealings of "practical people," in which one might imagine an Amy who could exclaim, "For God's sake, father!" we have an awed resolution that is as soggy as the histrionics:

When his tears were dried, and he sobbed in his weakness no longer, and was free from that touch of shame, and had recovered his usual bearing, she prepared the remains of his supper afresh, and, sitting by his side, rejoiced to see him eat and drink. (229)

That is how one deals with and tolerates a child. It is true, of course, that much of the way we deal with difficult old people may derive from how we deal with a child (as Jenny deals with her "child" and as Little Nell deals with her father). But there is too much falsification here, as Dickens presents Little Dorrit totally devoid of irritation—of ambivalence—and

Dorrit himself so easily cured of his "shame" by her attentions, and yet so incapable of love in his egoism:

All this time he had never once thought of *her* dress, her shoes, her need of anything. No other person upon earth, save herself, could have been so unmindful of her wants.

He kissed her many times with, "Bless you my love. Good night, my dear!"

But her gentle breast had been so deeply wounded by what she had seen of him, that she was unwilling to leave him alone. (229–30)

Our response to Little Dorrit is false because she is so totally capable of masochistic submission, however brutally egoistic her father is. Her love, Dickens goes on to say, "had saved him to be even what he was," a hypocrite, even over what he believes he had "done" for Amy (when he has done nothing). The falsity is so intense that it is as if Dickens desperately needed to believe something about love that could not be true.

Chapter 19 is crucial and central to the book. In it Dickens tries to reach into the complexities of this character in his jail-rot, and to place him; and he tries to place Little Dorrit's idolization of him, but yet can approve of her prostration before his grotesque self-image:

"I am in the twenty-third year of my life here," he said, with a catch in his breath that was not so much a sob as an irrepressible sound of self-approval, the momentary outburst of a noble consciousness. "It is all I could do for my children—I have done it. Amy, my love, you are by far the best loved of the three; I have had you principally in my mind—whatever I have done for your sake, my dear child, I have done freely and without murmuring."

Only the wisdom that holds the clue to all hearts and all mysteries, can surely know to what extent a man, especially a man brought down as this man had been, can impose upon himself. Enough, for the present place, that he lay down with wet eyelashes, serene, in a manner majestic, after bestowing his life of degradation as a sort of portion on the devoted child upon whom its miseries had fallen so heavily, and whose love alone had saved him to be even what he was.

That child had no doubts, asked herself no questions, for she was but too content to see him with a lustre round his head. Poor dear, good dear, truest, kindest, dearest, were the only words she had for him as she hushed him to rest. (230–31)

One cannot but suspect something seriously wrong with Dickens in his relationships to his own children, for him to want to fantasize a situation in which a daughter could so totally worship such a horrible and hypocritical father.

For a father is not Christ or God the Father and does not deserve such worship, while a daughter is not a mother to him, as to a baby, who must worship and pardon everything it does. To embody "love" in such terms is to indulge an unreality, and in doing so Dickens shows himself to be embroiled in the Victorian concept of Ideal Woman, that innocent breast-fountain who is totally deprived of all authenticity and freedom, who fails to find fault with her master sufficiently to escape from his tyranny. So *Little Dorrit* is about tyranny—and in its piety falsely recommends the woman's total acceptance of any exploitation, on her knees: "O spare his life! O send him to me!"

When we turn from Little Dorrit's relationship with her father to the one with Arthur, we find a different kind of fantasy. With father William, Little Dorrit is all forgiveness—giving father all the forgiveness Dickens yearned for. With Arthur, Dickens again fantasizes an angel who will restore the inheritance of a deprived child:

"From the unhappy suppression of my youngest days, through the rigid and unloving home that followed them, through my departure, my long exile, my return, my mother's welcome, my intercourse with her since, down to the afternoon of this day with poor Flora," said Arthur Clennam, "what have I found!"

His door was softly opened, and these spoken words startled him and came as if they were an answer:

"Little Dorrit." (165)

To her, he might be God:

"... seeing a light in the window." Not for the first time. No, not for the first time. In Little Dorrit's eyes, the outside of that window had been a distant star on other nights than this. She had toiled out of her way, tired and troubled, to look up at it, and wonder about the grave, brown gentleman from afar off, who had spoken to her as friend and protector. (170)

In wishing this protector well, her prayers are noted in heaven:

Little Dorrit turned at the door to say "God bless you!" She said it very softly, but perhaps she may have been as audible above—who knows!—as a whole cathedral choir. (173)

Arthur wants to take her up protectively in his arms:

So diminutive she looked so fragile and defenceless against the bleak damp weather, flitting along in the shuffling shadow of her charge, that he felt, in his compassion, and in his habit of considering her a child apart from the rest of the rough world, as if he would have been glad to take her up in his arms and carry her to her journey's end. (173)

He offers her food, but she doesn't eat, and, as he "softly put his glass towards her," she is not thirsty either.

Her (secret) love for Clennam is a total devotion. She trembles in utter and abject innocence:

He saw her trembling little form and her downcast face, and the eyes that drooped the moment they were raised to his—he saw them almost with as much concern as tenderness. "My child, your manner is so changed!"
The trembling was now quite beyond her control. Softly withdrawing her hand, and laying it in her other hand, she sat before him with her head bent and her whole form trembling. (380)

It is all a doubtful indulgence—Little Dorrit reduced to a jellylike state (three tremblings in two short paragraphs) and deeply agitated by loving Arthur, Arthur in such a stupid state of unawareness that even the author seems to get irritated by him:

He never thought that she saw in him what no-one else could see. He never thought that in the whole world there were no other eyes that looked upon him with the same light and strength as hers. (381)

To Little Dorrit Arthur unwittingly talks about his relationship with Flora, and how he is past it, is "done with that tender part of life":

"I found that I had climbed the hill, and passed the level ground upon the top, and was descending quickly." If he had known the sharpness of the pain he caused the patient heart, in speaking thus! Yet he was doing it, to ease and serve her. (381)

It is all characteristically Victorian fantasy: the woman cannot speak out, by convention: she must be patient and all-bearing. The concern is not with delicacy so much as with extracting the maximum spurious pity for the suffering of the absurdly innocent. Arthur goes on:

"I found that the day when any such thing would have been graceful in me, or good in me, or hopeful or happy for me, or any one in connection with me, was gone, and would never shine again." (381)

This is, examined coolly, almost as much "maudlin self-pity" as the lamentations of Old Dorrit—and through it one may hear something of the author's own voice, "any one in connection with me" and "never shine again" being phrases that might have come from a letter from Dickens at the time.

But Little Dorrit, as a fantasy angel, is deeply wounded by these laments:

O! If he had known, if he had known! If he could have seen the dagger in his hand, and the cruel wounds it struck in the faithful bleeding breast of this Little Dorrit! (381)

This is the language of very bad, ham melodrama, and, totally without any modifying humor, it unconsciously echoes the true history of Pyramus and Thisbe:

Whereat with blade, with bloody blameful blade,
He boldly broached his boiling bloody breast.

But Dickens cannot stop himself:

He heard the thrill in her voice, he saw her earnest face, he saw her clear true eyes, he saw the quickened bosom that would have joyfully thrown itself before him to receive a mortal wound directed at his breast, with the dying cry, "I love him!" (382)

It is infantile wish-fulfillment fantasy, with a strange touch of sadism: Little Dorrit with her worn shoes and her old frock is both Cinderella and a victim over whom Dickens gloats as she trembles and suffers—the totally controllable submissive woman. So, we progress to the fairy story Little Dorrit herself tells of the princess always spinning hopefully at her wheel. But Arthur says, "Always think of me as quite an old man" (383), and wonders if, among her devotion and duties, she has "an interest in someone else, an interest incompatible with your affection here."

"No, No, No." She shook her head, after each slow repetition of the word, with an air of quiet desolation that he remembered long afterwards. . . . The time came when he remembered it well, long afterwards within those prison walls, within that very room. (383–84)

She is full of thanks, and cries that he is "so good"; from beginning to end, the scene (chapter 32) is all spurious theatricals.

This kind of mawkish melodrama contrasts strikingly with Dickens at his best. Characteristically Victorian, he could at one moment demand of us that we enter into the dimensions of an infantile fairy tale, and at the next moment be penetratingly sophisticated and insightful, deeply critical of his society.

By contrast with the awful melodrama of Arthur and Amy is his marvelous portrayal of Mrs. General. At a time when women needed chap-
erones and girls needed training for the marriage market, genteel button
molders like Mrs. General were indispensable; and it satisfies something
in her, to be such a legislator of gentility:

> In person, Mrs. General, including her skirts which had much to do with it, was
> of a dignified and imposing appearance; ample, rustling, gravely voluminous: always
> upright behind the proprieties. (450)

The wit returns to the writing, and it is a Jonsonian wit, imbued with
a critical edge—and the quality of the language goes with it.

Mrs. General's "skirts," her "ample, rustling presence," endorses the
"proprieties" about which Dickens is here wryly ironic. Dorrit's genteel
pretensions are exposed because we have been accustomed for so long to
see him as an imprisoned pauper. Now he is equally imprisoned within
the falsifications of "the proprieties," and Mrs. General is his jailer. She
is inviolable in her propriety:

> She might have been taken—had been taken—to the top of the Alps and the
> bottom of Herculaneum, without disarranging a fold in her dress, or displacing a
> pin. (450)

The wit is sophisticated: "the Alps" suggests a range of experience to
which the English middle-class propriety is indifferent (compare Harriet
in E. M. Forster's *Where Angels Fear to Tread*); Herculaneum is known
to contain images and relics that speak of a magnificent but barbarous time,
and of libidinal human activities. It is indeed comic and amazing that Mrs.
General remains unruffled by these experiences, her pins staying in place.

> If her countenance and hair had rather a floury appearance, as though from living
> in some transcendently genteel mill, it was rather because she was a chalky creation
> altogether, than because she mended her complexion with violet powder, or had
> turned grey. If her eyes had no expression, it was probably because they had nothing
> to express. If she had few wrinkles, it was because her mind had never traced its
> name or any other inscription on her face. A cool, waxy, blown-out woman, who
> never lighted well. (450)

If the early part of the description is like Jonson's verse, the latter is
more like Shakespeare's: "there is no art / To find the mind's construction
in the face." The description has considerable depth, and is bitingly ob-
servant of a kind of emptiness that belongs to a comfortable kind of in-

sensitivity and denseness. The last sentence is hilarious, making her a kind of extinguished lamp, who has no illumination to offer. Dickens both demolishes her and leaves her a monument to empty forms, and these are profoundly critical of the condition of innocent uselessness to which Victorian society reduced its woman:

> Mrs. General had no opinions. Her way of forming a mind was to prevent it from forming opinions. She had a little circular set of mental grooves or rails, on which she started little trains of other people's opinions, which never overtook one another, and never got anywhere.
>
> ...Mrs. General was not to be told of anything shocking. Accidents, miseries and offences, were never to be mentioned before her. Passion was to go to sleep in the presence of Mrs. General, and blood was to change to milk and water. The little that was left in the world, when all these deductions were made, it was Mrs. General's province to varnish. In that formation process of hers, she dipped the smallest of brushes into the largest of pots, and varnished the surface of every object that came under consideration. The more cracked it was, the more Mrs. General varnished it.
>
> There was varnish in Mrs. General's voice, varnish in Mrs. General's touch, an atmosphere of varnish round Mrs. General's figure. (450–51)

The magnificent passage establishes Mrs. General as a falsifier—a careful creator of inauthenticity, in the denial of life's realities, in the name of what is proper.

Some of the themes of *Little Dorrit* are lumbering, as in the whole Blandois—Flintwinch story about the will and the house and the rest. So, too, is much of the "moral" action: William Dorrit in his pretentiousness is seen in poverty to object to any charitable act in Amy (as over Old Nandy); when the company gets to the Alps, he is seen in riches and freedom to be objecting in the same way to her kindness to Pet, even insulting to Arthur in the process. All this becomes too obvious and somewhat labored.

What are the episodes in *Little Dorrit* that spring from a deeper creative purpose, such as to justify Leavis's reference to Blake?

Perhaps the most important poetic theme is that of the essential continuity of the self, and its essential ("being") needs, which are not satisfied by riches and comfort nor necessarily harmed by privation. The trouble with William Dorrit is that he is a slave to forms, whether poor or rich, and is willing to sacrifice genuine love and relationship to the mere varnishings.

Little Dorrit doggedly persists in sticking to her affections—and it is this Cordelia element in her that we must admire. Her letter to Arthur Clennam from Venice has its weak sentimental moments: would she really write this, for example?

That you remember me only as the little shabby girl you protected with so much tenderness, from whose threadbare dress you have kept away the rain, and whose wet feet you have dried at your fire? (471)

But it also contains some insightful matter on this subject of familiarity:

For instance, when we were among the mountains, I often felt (I hesitate to tell such an idle thing, dear Mr. Clennam, even to you) as if the Marshalsea must be behind that great rock; or as if Mrs. Clennam's room where I have worked so many days, and where I first saw you, must be just beyond that snow.... It is the same with people that I left in England.
     When I go about here in a gondola, I surprise myself looking into other gondolas as if I hoped to see them. (469–70)

Dorrit has revealed the same feeling among the mountains:

"But the space," urged the grey-haired gentleman. "So small, So—ha—very limited." (441)

And Little Dorrit, with her capacity to see things as they really are beneath the surface, pities him:

I often feel the old sad pity—I need not write the word—for him. Changed as he is, and inexpressibly blest ... the old feeling of compassion comes upon me. (470)

But she cannot fling her arms around her father, because Fanny would be angry at such a "show" and Mrs. General would consider it an impropriety. The best underlying theme is thus that of the falsification of the experience of the conscious self, and of what we know to be true about it.
     Mr. Dorrit and Mrs. General, as devotees of the genteel, thus become cruel in their assumption that Amy has "no force of character and self-reliance."
     Fanny has these, but has "too much material"—that is, too many opinions. Fanny is not sufficiently submissive, as a Victorian woman ought to be. In the exchanges between Dorrit and Mrs. General, all Dickens's wit returns:

"I have pointed out to her that the celebrated Mrs. Eustace, the classical tourist, ... compared the Rialto, greatly to its disadvantage, with Westminster and Black-friars bridges...."

"You will find it serviceable, in the formation of a demeanor, if you sometimes say to yourself in company—on entering a room for instance—Papa, potatoes, poultry, prunes and prison, prunes and prism." (475–76)

To the "elegant varnisher," everything is "demeanor"; the anguish of the heart is nothing, because she is empty. But we are deeply distressed by the way in which the object of her faithful and unflushing love colludes with the agents of his deference to the "society" of Mrs. Merdle's bosom:

"I sent for you, in order that I might say—hum—impressively say, in the presence of Mrs. General, to whom we are all so much indebted for obligingly being present among us, on—ha—on this or any other occasion," Mrs. General shut her eyes, "that I—ha hum—am not pleased with you." (477)

Nothing disagreeable should ever be looked at, says Mrs. General: Amy should not study the vagrants. Delivered of this sentiment, she retires, leaving Amy with her father.

There is repressed emotion in her face, and had it been George Eliot writing the chapter, Dorrit might have received something of that kind of attempt to bring truth home to a corrupted mind that love is capable of exerting. But Little Dorrit must be so selfless:

Not for herself. She might feel a little wounded, but her care was not for herself. Her thoughts still turned, as they had always turned, to him. (477–78)

Dickens unfortunately transfers the Victorian ideal of the ever-submissive and self-unsparing wife to the daughter. Yet what Little Dorrit is witnessing is the same corruption in her father as she saw when he was suffering from the jail-rot:

She felt that, in what he had just now said to her, and in his whole bearing towards her, there was the well-known shadow of the Marshalsea wall. It took a new shape, but it was the old sad shadow. She began with sorrowful unwillingness to acknowledge to herself, that she was not strong enough to keep off the fear that no space in the life of man could overcome that quarter of a century behind the prison bars. (478)

This is fine, and is transmuted from Dickens's experience of his own father, and the shadow of himself. But the shadow is also too much allowed to inhibit Little Dorrit's response to her father's cruelty. For it is cruelty and tyranny:

"Amy" he returned, turning short upon her. "You—ha—habitually hurt me." (478)

What this is is understood by every person of "delicacy and sensitiveness" except her. She constantly revives a certain "topic"—and he is off again in one of his orgies of self-pity. Amy says nothing, but touches him gently; and gives him "nothing but love."

This is the only time he speaks to her of the old days. But what he asks for is utterly impossible, and nowhere else is William Dorrit more like Lear. For he is demanding that Amy shall take the kind of "surface" offered by Mrs. General, and attempt by falsification to sweep the old experiences off the face of the earth and obliterate them.

Amy knows this cannot be done, and she cannot disguise her unhappiness in the new grandeur. We recall that she hoped that once he was free, she would see him as he really was. Perhaps, indeed, this is how he really is; but we shall never know, because Little Dorrit never challenges him: she never suggests that, in response to her revelations of her true self and true love, he might try to be true to her, and this is an artistic failure.

How Little Dorrit might have responded is demonstrated by Frederick in the same chapter, after Dorrit has decided to solve the problem of the Gowans on the basis of learning that they are friends of the great Merdle:

"To the winds with the family credit!" cried the old man with great scorn and indignation. "Brother, I protest against pride. I protest against ingratitude. I protest against any one of us here who have known what we have known, and have seen what we have seen, setting up any pretension that puts Amy at a moment's disadvantage, or to the cost of a moment's pain." (485)

Dickens obviously felt that someone should say it—and in the hullabaloo that follows, all Dorrit can say is, "we will—ha—keep this to ourselves." Fanny goes in for violent fits of embracing Amy, and alternately gives her brooches and wishes herself dead. It all points to the inadequacy of the family in the face of their situation and their relationships, but in this confusion, to offer a merely submissive, all-pardoning love, however much based on Christ's dictum, is, in the light of our modern insights from psychotherapy, to compound confusion and tyranny, and it is a serious weakness in Dickens that he so admires this craven faculty in his heroine.

One feels no such objections, however, to Amy's role in the last terrible scenes of her father, in chapter 19 in the second book. Despite one or two melodramatic touches, like Frederick's last outburst ("O God . . . thou seest this daughter of my dear dead brother," etc.), the chapter is remarkable for its breadth of perspective and comic-tragic power. In this chapter, since Dorrit has broken down and is dying, Amy's total devotion is appropriate.

The chapter begins outside the walls of Rome, with Dorrit galloping in a carriage across the Campagna and building castles in the air about marrying Mrs. General—embracing, we might say, respectability at last. Ominously, he meets a funeral procession, and a great cross borne before a priest:

He was an ugly priest by torchlight; of a lowering aspect, with an overhanging brow; and as his eyes met those of Mr. Dorrit, looking bareheaded out of his carriage, his lips, moving as they chaunted, seemed to threaten that important traveller; likewise the action of his hand, which was in fact his manner of returning the traveller's salutation, seemed to come in aid of that menace. (638)

This priest might have been death himself, and throughout *Little Dorrit* the best moments are those when the actions of the characters are seen in relation to the presence of death, whether in poverty or luxury.

Dorrit reaches his destination and goes to find Little Dorrit himself. What he finds is a Frederick who is so cheerful that Amy is telling him he must be growing younger every day; and what Dorrit sees is a brother who is responding to Amy with the kind of love and affection that is capable of being aware of what is happening in the other's life. Dorrit is jealous, but the momentary scene brings out the deadness of his own capacity for love and sympathy. Comically, his jealousy prompts him to accuse Frederick of going downhill, of becoming tired and wandering— and he orders him to bed.

For the first time since leaving the Marshalsea, Little Dorrit is serving Dorrit's meal and pouring his wine, as she used to do in prison. And from time to time he seems to start, as if wondering whether perhaps they are still there. He is anxious and tired, and by subtle touches Dickens conveys to us a grotesque sense of futility in Dorrit's intentions of matrimony, as he hides away the presents for Mrs. General he has bought in Paris. Dickens derives much comedy from what he calls the pruney and prismatic nature of the family banquet. Dorrit tends to go to sleep during the meal.

His courtship of Mrs. General is conducted in language of the most elaborate gentility. Referring to "the favorable opinion Mr. Dorrit has formed of my services," she goes on to say, "I have found, in that only too high opinion, my consolation and recompense."

"Opinion of your services, madam?" said Mr. Dorrit.
"Of," Mrs. General repeated, in an elegantly impressive manner, "my services."
"Of your services alone, dear madam?" said Mr. Dorrit.

"I presume," retorted Mrs. General in her former impressive manner, "of my services alone. For to what else," said Mrs. General, with a slightly interrogative action of her gloves, "could I impute—?"

"To—ha—yourself, Mrs. General. Ha, hum. To yourself and your merits. . . ." (645)

This is enough to oblige the lady to fly into genteel and proper embarrassment. It is high comedy: "on the return of that lady to tea, she had touched herself up with a little powder and pomatum, and was not without moral enhancement likewise" (646), like a figure in a Gilray or Hogarth cartoon (or Pope; "Betty, give this cheek a little red"). However, Dorrit begins to look like death: he gives Mrs. General a "bony kiss" and next day presents himself "in a refulgent condition as to his attire, but looking indefinably shrunken and old" (646).

Suddenly, at the dinner, he goes mad, and imagines himself back in prison. It is a deeply moving moment because "society" itself appears as a prison (and, though we do not know it yet, is indeed condemned to death when Merdle's empire collapses). The company he addresses *become* the inmates of the Marshalsea as he addresses them:

"Ladies and gentleman, the duty—ha—devolves upon me of—hum—welcoming you to the Marshalsea. . . . The space is—ha—limited—limited—the parade might be wider; but you will find it apparently grow larger after a time—a time, ladies and gentlemen. . . ." (647)

So, the Marshalsea is both "society," the company of the rich, and the world, or life; and in consideration of the brevity of the time and space of our life, it would be better to attend to primary matters of love and meaning. "My daughter," cries Dorrit, "Born here!"—and here we feel that since he is a broken man, it is all she can do to cling to him and try to get him away, for his own dear sake. Dorrit, in his old form, suggests "testimonials," and we recognize that this is only what that world does, in its dealings in bourgeois society. Naturally, faced with this painful scene, the Bosom is exceedingly mortified, not least because at the beginning of the dinner "the bosom was in admirable preservation, and on the best terms with itself."

Dorrit sees the staircase of his Roman palace as the stairs of the prison, and Dorrit, like Little Dorrit, can only see the world now in terms of the old times. He does not now know Mrs. General, but as for Amy, "he loved her in his old way."

They were in the jail again, and she tended him, and he had constant need of her, and could not turn without her. (649)

Here, when Dickens says she would have laid down her life to restore him, it makes sense, because Dorrit is now dying; his castles vanish, the reflected marks of the prison vanish, and she sees him at last as he really is:

Quietly, quietly, the face subsided into a far younger likeness of her own than she had ever seen under the grey hair, and sank to rest. (650)

It is a marvelously tragic chapter: and at the end the two brothers lie dead, "far beyond the twilight judgements of this world; high above its mists and obscurities." And, as with Dickens at his best, it urges on us consideration of what, in the face of mortality, the point of life might be.

In this study I am trying to examine Dickens's attitude to woman in general, not least at the unconscious level. But it is also necessary to take into account his own anguish over his relationships with real women. At the height of his success, his relationship with his wife proved deeply unsatisfactory, to say the least. The often-quoted relevant passage is that from his letter to Forster of 5 September 1857:

Poor Catherine and I are not made for each other, and there is no help for it. It is not only that she makes me uneasy and unhappy, but that I make her so too . . . we are strangely ill-assorted for the bond there is between us. (Mackenzie, 292)

Dickens admitted his own part in the problem: "I claim no immunity from blame." His tours, his theatricals, and his readings seem to have been a form of escape from the problems of his marriage. On 11 October 1857, he wrote to Anne Cornelius, their servant, giving her instructions to convert his dressing room at Tavistock House into a bedroom, and to close up the door leading to Catherine's bedroom.* And Dickens was now in the state of being fascinated by Ellen Ternan.

The whole family was aware of this sad state of affairs, and at times Dickens was in a state of distraction. He assumed there was no possibility

---

*Mackenzie, 294.

of an escape from the marriage, and he longed for some magical solution, as the image of the young and lively Ellen intensified in his consciousness.

I am weary of rest and have no satisfaction but fatigue. Realities and idealities are always appearing before me, and I don't like the Realities except when they are unattainable—*then*, I like them of all things. I wish I had been born in the days of ogres and dragon-guarded Castles. I wish an Ogre with seven heads ... had taken the Princess whom I adore—you have no idea how intensely I love her!— to his stronghold.... Nothing would suit me half so well this day, as climbing after her, sword in hand, and either winning her or being killed. (MacKenzie, 295)

The readings and the drama seem to have offered a better relief from this intolerable situation than writing novels, and in this we may also, I believe, find some indication of the fascination Dickens had for melodrama, and the satisfaction it gave him. He himself said at this time, in a talk to the Royal General Theatrical Fund, "Every writer of fiction writes in effect for the stage." (MacKenzie, 296). Dickens began to give professional per-formances on the platform in April, and of course (as the MacKenzies say), many of these were attempts to evoke the family virtues. Yet at the same time he indulged other fancies in the theatrical way: at a Manchester performance of *The Frozen Deep* he had appeared with Ellen Ternan in a farce called *Uncle John* in which he took the part of an elderly man who falls in love with a young ward and makes her lavish presents of jewelry. A bracelet he had bought for Ellen was mistakenly delivered to Catherine; Dickens responded to her expressions of outrage by pointing out that he had sent such tokens to other ladies who had taken part in theatricals (Mackenzie, 298). But now, it seemed, some more radical separation was imperative.

Dickens wrote to Angela Coutts (May 9), "I believe my marriage has been for years and years as miserable a one as ever was made.... I believe that no two people were ever created with such an impossibility of interest, sympathy, confidence, sentiment, tender union of any kind between them, as there is between my wife and me.... Nature has put an insurmountable barrier between us, which never in this world can be thrown down" (MacKenzie, 298). He even accused Catherine of mental unbalance.

Rumors were circulating, and Dickens took resort to lawyers to insist upon disavowals from Mrs. Hogarth, and later Dickens published a disa-vowal in *Household Words* that (say the Mackenzies) sounded like some-thing from a sensational novel. He also wrote a letter to the manager of his public readings, saying of his wife that it would be "better for her to go away and live apart" and speaking of her "mental disorder." He also declared Ellen Ternan "virtuous and spotless": this appeared in the news-paper. Kate Dickens said,

My father was like a madman when my mother left home. This affair brought out all that was worst, all that was weakest in him. He did not care a damn what happened to any of us. Nothing could surpass the misery and unhappiness of our home. (Mackenzie, 305)

Ellen Ternan left the stage. Catherine Dickens seems to have wished, later, to be able to show the world that once Dickens had loved her, as was clear from his letters.

The Mackenzies suggest that the very emotions of childhood that had brilliantly served Dickens's art were wholly inadequate for the demands of marriage. His problems seem to have stemmed from a profound and never-appeased antagonism to his mother, and he carried this resentment over into his marriage. Kate described her mother as a "sweet, kind, peace-loving woman, a lady," but others saw her as a commonplace but not ill-disposed woman. At any rate, she seems to have been quite incapable of coping with Dickens's success and elevation to fame: his fame severed him from her. She had five miscarriages and ten children, but never seems to have enjoyed motherhood. The Macready household saw her as a "whin-ey woman" whose negative state of mind had done much to break the marriage.

On Dickens's part, he was able to bring solutions to bear on his fantasy situations, but his creative efforts brought little relief to the problems of his life, and there his conflicts led to restless anxiety and despair.

Forster describes him as kindly, generous, helpful and well-meaning. He genuinely believed that only such New Testament virtues as love, charity, and forgiveness could change the hearts and minds of men, and he tried to practice what he preached. But the world of fancy and the world of reality remained apart. In life he would "rush at existence without counting the cost": he

had not in himself the resources that such a man, judging from the surface, might be expected to have. . . . There was for him no "city of the mind" against outward ills, for inner consolation and shelter. (MacKenzie, 306)

He lost his temper, bullied his family, suffered from smoldering resentments, and felt that his home might have collapsed were it not that he shored it up by his self-sacrificing efforts: in many ways, that is, he was like William Dorrit.

The relationship between Dickens and Ellen Ternan, and his (Uncle John) fantasy of that relationship obviously, then, lie behind that between Esther and John Jarndyce—and behind Arthur Clennam and Little Dorrit. We can read Arthur's reflections in this light:

> He had come to attach to Little Dorrit an interest so peculiar—an interest that removed her from, while it grew out of, the common and coarse things surrounding her—that he found it disappointing, disagreeable, almost painful, to suppose her in love with young Mr. Chivery in the backyard, or any such person. On the other hand, he reasoned with himself that she was just as good and just as true, in love with him, as not in love with him; and that to make a kind of domesticated fairy of her, on the penalty of isolation of heart from the only people she knew, would be but a weakness of his own fancy, and not a kind one. Still, her youthful and ethereal appearance, her timid manner, the charm of her sensitive voice and eyes, the very many respects in which she had interested him out of her individuality, and the strong difference between herself and those about her, were not in unison, and were determined not to be in unison, with this newly presented idea. (259)

The slightly tortuous prose here seems to indicate something written out of Dickens's own experience: we, I believe, have to ask, well, what of Dickens's "fancy" and Little Dorrit as a "domesticated fairy"? And what of Arthur's patronizing remark, "I have an interest in the little creature" (271). The problem is that we find it very difficult to sympathize with a hero who has an attitude like that to the heroine: it is not propitious for an equal, adult relationship, despite the respect for "such trial and devo-tion—such quiet goodness."

Quoting Forster, the Mackenzies, at the end of their chapter on Dick-ens's failed marriage, say he "found it as hard as an eager and clever child to bear ... frustration." In *Little Dorrit* there is a kind of yearning for a *child* relationship. Little Dorrit early on relinquishes and renounces her love for Clennam, and tells a masochistic fairy tale about a princess pining away, having only the shadow of a passerby in her life. Clennam is on the verge of being attracted to Pet (with her "wonderful eyes"), but he throws away the roses of his libidinal attraction to her, and they seem "pale and unreal." He assumes the part of "a very much older man that had done with that part of life" (334). Pet speaks of her difficulties in leaving her father, and hopes that her parents will come to terms with her marriage to Gowan, and Dickens exclaims,

When were such changes ever made in men's natural relations to one another: when was such reconcilement of ingrain differences ever effected! (336)

—which is an intelligent insight not from the melodramatist, but from the suffering husband. In Clennam and Little Dorrit he yearns for a sexless relationship that does not present such anguish; in a sense, also, in going back to Little Dorrit Clennam is going back to *mother*—a better mother than Dickens himself had experienced.

When we have taken into account Dickens's extraordinary situation, in his marriage and his relationships with women, it is clearer why Little Dorrit has to be so submissive and all-forgiving as a little mother. Dickens (whatever he might admit, as in the above quotation questioning how much men could be altered) wanted to believe the melodrama fantasy. His ideal woman would pardon all those meannesses, disloyalties, cruelties, and madnesses of which he had shown himself capable, while Arthur is his ideal man, reduced to sexless, conscientious care (doubtful only of his mother's secret)—and ingenuous to the extent of having to be told by her other lover, young Chivery, that Little Dorrit loves him. The social world in *Little Dorrit* is marvelously done—Mrs. Merdle and her parrot, Mrs. General, Fanny and the Sparkler, the Marshalsea. But at the heart of the story is an unreal fantasy of a love relationship from which are excluded all those realities of passion, weakness, and ambiguity from which Dickens suffered—from which, indeed, is excluded "life"—and so it is astonishing that F. R. Leavis should find *Little Dorrit* such a central masterpiece that he used her image on the cover of his book on Dickens.

The disadvantages of the modes of Victorian melodrama become clear if we compare with them the quality of Dickens's dramatic writing at its best. This can be both comic and moving at the same time. In the melodramatic scenes in which Little Dorrit is present something spoils them from ever becoming realistic—the presence of a kind of emotional loading, an expectation of magical influences. This has to do with the presence of fantasies of wish fulfillment.

Nothing like this spoils the superb scene between William Dorrit and young John Chivery, in chapter 18 of book 2. Young John has called on Dorrit, intending to give him a bundle of cigars. Dorrit asks him up, and he is smiling and much gratified. But when the attendants withdraw and they are alone, Dorrit turns on him:

"Now, sir," said Mr. Dorrit, turning round upon him and seizing him by the collar when they were safely alone. "What do you mean by this?"

The amazement and horror depicted in the unfortunate John's face—for he had rather expected to be embraced next—were of that powerfully expressive nature, that Mr. Dorrit withdrew his hand and merely glared at him.

"How dare you do this?" said Mr. Dorrit. "How do you presume to come here? How dare you insult me?"

"I insult you, Sir!" cried Young John. "Oh!" (631–32)

It is a typical William Dorrit scene: he cannot bear to be reminded of the humiliations of the Marshalsea, and anyone who reminds him, even affectionately, of those times, he accuses of insulting him. He also knows young John has been fond of Amy, and while he was anxious to expose her to his unwelcome attentions when he was a prisoner, he must now regard it as unthinkable that John should be an appropriate suitor. He may at some level feel shame that he ever assisted John in his advances to Amy. On his part, young John is no doubt aware of Dorrit's feelings about his interest in the daughter now that Dorrit is a rich man. So, the scene is full of complex feelings between these men.

But of course young John is not, like Amy, an idealized character. In such a situation she would only respond in terms of the most muted vulnerability, and would endure her father's cruelty with infinite love and forgiveness. Young John is hurt: he is stunned, and protests in a quite normal way—so, the scene has a realistic robustness that the melodrama scenes do not have.

In consequence, Dorrit himself reacts, and becomes aware of the difficulties of the matter:

John Chivery backed to the door.

"Stop, sir!" cried Mr. Dorrit. "Stop! Sit down. Confound you, sit down!"

John Chivery dropped into the chair nearest the door, and Mr. Dorrit walked up and down the room; rapidly at first; then, more slowly. Once, he went to the window, and stood there with his forehead against the glass. All of a sudden, he turned and said:

"What else did you come for, sir?"

"Nothing else in the world, sir. Oh dear me! Only to say, sir, that I hoped you was well, and only to ask if Miss Amy was well?"

"What's that to you, sir?" retorted Mr. Dorrit. (632)

Mr. Dorrit becomes ashamed, and is seen later to be wiping his eyes, looking tired and ill.

"Young John, I am very sorry to have been hasty with you, but—ha—some re-membrances are not happy remembrances, and—hum—you shouldn't have come."

"I feel that now, sir," returned John Chivery; "but I didn't before, and Heaven knows I meant no harm, sir."

"No. No," said Mr. Dorrit. "I am—hum—sure of that. Ha—Give me your hand, young John, give me your hand."

Young John gave it; but Mr. Dorrit had driven his heart out of it, and nothing could change his face now, from its white, shocked look. (633)

We have the sense of a conflict between real people, and within real people, as we do not when Dorrit is with Little Dorrit in such a scene. We can "hear" the voices and follow the inner experiences of the char-acters. Nothing can relieve the physical shock that young John has received, while Dorrit is really tormented by remorse because John's response is so real and natural. We can see, by comparison with this scene, how in the scenes with Amy, Dorrit is not in dialogue with a real woman but a phantom, a fairy projection. And this is important, for Dickens's purpose here is to show how imprisonment on the one hand and riches on the other can falsify being and relationships. If this is to be enacted convinc-ingly, then there must be painful inner changes and conflicts inside people, while their acts must be shown to have real consequences. There must be moral development—and it is just this that is missing in the scenes between Little Dorrit and her father, because her response is too "pure," too ideal-ized and unreal, while his is in consequence too bland—safeguarded too much from the consequences of his own cruelty and self-deceit.

Here Dorrit and young John break through to reminiscences of the old days that they have shared in their common humanity:

"Oh, indeed!" said Mr. Dorrit.
"Do you—ha hum—go upon the—ha—"
"Lock, sir? Yes, sir."
"Much to do, John?"
"Yes, sir; we're pretty heavy at present. I don't know how it is, but we generally *are* pretty heavy." (633)

Yet, despite the recaptured bonhomie, "nothing while John was there could change John's face to its natural colour and expression or restore John's natural manner" (634).

In the light of a distinction between realistic drama and the melodrama that falsifies, the culmination of the relationship between Little Dorrit and Arthur Clennam must surely be seen as belonging to the false?

It seems to me, by contrast, quite awful. Of course, I take the general point that the discovery of the true self and its destiny and the fulfillment of good relationships are essentially apart from all considerations of money or worldly role. Dickens does his best to make the love between Arthur and Amy a fulfillment, with the image of the posy of flowers in chapter 19 and the description of the countryside in autumn at the beginning of the last chapter. But the relationship never grows beyond a somewhat monochromatic wish-fulfillment fantasy—Little Dorrit poor again, in her wretched old dress, nursing Arthur as she once nursed her father, as a prisoner in the Marshalsea.

Everything is imprisoned in the dream concept of the perfectly submis-sive and *dutiful* Victorian woman. There is in the presentation of Little Dorrit none of the capacity to cast a critical eye on such concepts as emerges in Dickens's portrayal of Mrs. General ("a sort of ghoule in gloves").

The absence of all irony goes with a total absence of self-awareness and self-criticism. The prison atmosphere, as we have seen, was very much a part of Dickens's own atmosphere in life: he was fascinated by prisons, Newgate, punishment, crime, and wickedness—much of his creative effort feels as if it were devoted to some kind of expiation of this element in his own life. Perhaps, from his early experiences, he felt it might at any time ruin him?

How could he overcome this possible threat? The answer, I believe, in unconscious fantasy, was by being "good"—making reparation, making it appear to others that he was "good" ("What a good man you must have been to have written that!" as someone wrote him about the death of Little Nell.) This reparative impulse was in considerable conflict with how he actually behaved in life. To save himself from this predicament, he invented Arthur Clennam and Little Dorrit as dramatizations of his own inward life. Both have been severely deprived in their early life. Arthur has a deep sense of deprivation in consequence; he thinks of himself as lacking in feeling and now old and past hope of tender experience. Little Dorrit was actually born in prison, and has been cheated out of her legacy of one thousand guineas by Arthur's supposed mother. Both are ignorant of the real extent of their deprivation, but when it all comes out, of course, they forgive, and they jointly destroy the evidence of Little Dorrit's en-titlement, presumably so that no opprobrium should be cast on Arthur's "mother," who is now dead. (The significance of this act is not quite clear, since Arthur's mother was not his mother, is dead, and so cannot be pained by the recovery of the codicil, while the questions arise as to where the money was, where it is now and who will benefit?)

There is a sense in which all characters in novels are projections from the dynamics of the inner life of an author. But artistic success often depends upon how much the characters are realized "out there," as people in the world. Where an author identifies too closely with a character, he may lose this capacity to make him or her seem real. Dickens's own situation at this time in his life was so painful that he tends, with Arthur and Amy, to idealize them beyond belief. Not only are they fairy tale fantasy figures; they seem to be spun from some desperate devotional belief—that if only one follows Christ's path of love, selflessness, and total devotion to duty, one must triumph. And in this, Little Dorrit, the embodiment of a certain image of idealized woman, becomes virtually the angel who is to lead the deprived victim of life, Arthur, to heavenly bliss.

The language becomes religiose in the extreme, and extravagant in its graveyard fulsomeness: surprise yields

to the feelings which the empty room awakened in Clennam's wounded breast, and to the crowding associations with the one good and gentle creature who had sanctified it. Her absence in his altered fortunes made it, and him in it, so very desolate and so much in need of such a face of love and truth, that he turned against the wall to weep, sobbing out, as his heart relieved itself, "O my Little Dorrit!" (719)

Dickens is here indulging in self-pity, in his identification with Arthur, in his wish-fulfilling fantasy of how a pure and holy woman (a daughter figure of infinite patience) could come to him and save him from deprivation. But the fantasy belongs to childhood, even as Clennam here weeps like a child for his mother: it is only the overall menace of the Marshalsea that persuades us to accept this breakdown into infantile modes of emotion (as it persuades us at the beginning to accept the unacceptability of Amy's scenes with her father).

The Marshalsea represents the inhuman system of "society," and it is the counterpart to the Merdle structure. Neither, however, can really be taken to represent the essence of an industrial-commercial society and its essential inhumanity. Its inhumanity lies in its optimistic indifference to the primary needs of being and to the need for meaning, in the "utilitarian calculus." But this is not the whole story. For one thing, the very prosperity of Victorian industrialism was creating riches that, among other things, had made Dickens and his readership possible. It was also producing that prosperity of which women were demanding their share—an impulse that has led, despite the agonies and anguish of the struggle, to woman's achieve' ment of her independence and freedom, to a great extent. The purchaser of Gad's Hill, and the performer who brought back a fortune of twenty thousand pounds from his American tour, was not unacquainted with the benefits that industrialization can bring to man and society.

The Marshalsea must be seen to be a symbol of another kind: like the dead baby in *Bleak House,* a symbol of elements in the unconscious. It stands for a psychic inheritance of a negative kind that impedes and rots fulfillment, just as Merdle and "the bosom" stand for an attachment to property, to things and "success," which can do nothing for existential needs. Dickens himself was between the devil and the deep blue sea: in his emotional life he must have felt he suffered from the deficiencies of his own inheritance from his parents, not least his mother's shortcomings, which he had projected onto his wife so disastrously. All his success, though it had, as it were, counteracted his own father's fecklessness, only made his emotional life more disastrous. So, the ups and downs of future in *Little Dorrit* are shown to be irrelevant to the life of being in the protagonists.

In Little Dorrit I believe we have something like Shakespeare's quest for a renewed sense of being, through the symbolism of the daughter figures in his late plays, Miranda, Marina, Perdita. It is significant that these are daughters because the problem is to find generosity toward the creative feminine principle of future generations: creative gratitude. And this is bound up with the achievement of an inner faith in one's own being, as manifest in one's feminine element.

But with Little Dorrit, this goes wrong, because the feminine ideal becomes encapsulated too much in the Victorian concept of ideal woman— innocent and submissive*—and is, moreover, falsified by the religious con' notations—falsified because they are not really believed in. I have raised earlier the question of how much the Victorians believed in the angels of dead babies. How much did Dickens believe in the religious precepts (and the domestic virtues that went with them), and how much did he simply reserve them for public presentation?

---

*Shakespeare's young women in the later plays appear in the context of an experienced irony ("O brave new world"): Marina virtually takes on the world of the brothel single'handedly, and wins, but woe betide the reader who doubts this to be possible.

The appearance of Little Dorrit to Arthur after his illness is like a sickly Victorian oleograph: he sees a quiet figure with a black mantle that seems to drop this and become Little Dorrit in her old, worn dress.

It seemed to tremble, and to clasp its hands, and to smile, and to burst into tears. . . .
    . . . her tears dropping on to him as the rain from Heaven had dropped upon the flowers. . . .
    So faithful, tender and unspoiled by Fortune. In the sound of her voice, in the light of her eyes, in the touch of her hands, so Angelically comforting and true! (756)

She draws her arm around his neck, and

nursed him as lovingly, and GOD knows as innocently, as she had nursed her father in that room when she had been but a baby, needing all the care from others that she took of them. (756)

The Euphrasia theme is transferred to Arthur Clennam. The phrase "GOD knows as innocently" is interesting: in what way could her nursing *not* be innocent? Presumably by having some kind of sexual quality or intention? But the emphasis here is on Arthur being nursed like a *baby* by a *mother,* and yet herself being a child, trembling, timid, and above all *innocent*: a child-wife.

So intensely is she an idealized object that, like Estella, she is a star in his life, and even offers him all her money.

There was one bright star shining in the sky. She looked up at it while she spoke, as if it were the fervent purpose of her own heart shining above her. (759)

It may seem somewhat startling for Little Dorrit to offer him her fortune, but in the light of what I have recorded above about Victorian marriage, it was only what every Victorian woman offered when she accepted an offer of marriage. The symbolism of the star becomes quite unreal in Dickens's fervor:

"The star had shone on her face until now, when her face sank upon his hand and her own" (759).

In what possible sense does a star shine on anything? It would be impossible to detect, with the most sensitive instrument, the light from the brightest star ever shining on a face. The image is taken from religious paintings, in which light from the stars is shown to shine on significant personages, and it belongs to the utter unreality of Dickens's idealization.

What do we see when we are told a star might be a woman's heart shining in the sky?

Arthur declares he must never touch her fortune, never; he would see anything like that as disgraceful:

"I am disgraced enough, my Little Dorrit. I must not descend so low as that, and carry you—so dear, so generous, so good—down with me." (760)

Again, it is totally unreal, since, again, to take over a woman's fortune was a normal course of events in marriage, and not disgraceful at all. But Arthur, speaking of his humiliation, now takes her in his arms, "as *if she had been his daughter*" (760).

"You must see me only as I am," declares Arthur. But we have to say that there is something strange about him. Beside William Dorrit, young John, and the other men in the novel, he is a cipher. He is grey and gloomy, conscientious and grave, but also seems at times dull, stupid, and unin-telligent. Who could be so obtuse as Arthur Clennam, who does not realize (or hope) that Little Dorrit was in love with him? The lengths to which poor John Chivery has to go to make him aware of it are absurd. But absurd, too, is the way he allows himself to be made ridiculous by opening the way for Flora's intimacies (though perhaps in this Dickens was cas-tigating himself for making the same mistake over Maria Beadnell). Over business matters with Doyce, Clennam is so ordinary and so lacking in good sense that he is exasperating. He manifests nothing of Pip's self-criticism and development toward maturity, or even Esther's growing good sense. He seems really to represent the dullest and least ebullient dynamic in Dickens—perhaps the most wretched images within his self that he felt he had to drag along with him. Dickens seems to lack *affection* for Arthur Clennam, and he and Amy are a dreary pair, he weeping against the wall and she trembling. No man could be more sexless than Arthur and no woman more sexless than Amy. Between them they represent a relationship devoted to love, fidelity, and care, come what may, but one that is troubled by none of the rich emotional perplexities of passion—because they don't have any. They can therefore offer us no insights into the realities of man-woman relationships.

There is a hint at one point, from Meagles, as to the primary principle behind this relationship in Dickens's mind. He is extolling Little Dorrit's quality to her, in a really rather admonitory way (Tattycoram having had a serious struggle to come home to face the music). Meagles's tone makes one feel there was a good deal in Tattycoram's rebelliousness: "Tattycoram, come to me a moment, my good girl." The sermon is on selflessness:

"If she had constantly thought of herself, and settled with herself that everybody visited this place upon her, turned it against her, and cast it at her, she would have led an irritable and probably a useless existence. Yet I have heard tell, Tattycoram, that her young life has been one of active resignation, goodness, and noble service. Shall I tell you what I consider those eyes of hers that were here just now, to have always looked at, to get that expression?"

"Yes, if you please, sir."

"Duty, Tattycoram. Begin it early, and do it well; and there is no antecedent to it, in any origin or station, that will tell against us with the Almighty, or with ourselves." (812–13)

I must say I find this nauseating. It is evidently addressed to the reader over Tattycoram's head, and is moralizing at the level of an Isaac Watts hymn. It is clear (from biographical accounts of his behavior) that Dickens did not obey the precept, even if, as in his tyrannical procedures at home, he treated his family to a rigamarole of the kind Tattycoram is receiving. But it is not only hypocritical; it cannot be the basis for the discovery of being in the face of society's inhuman system, which Dickens offers, for that system itself depended upon enforcing obedience under the name of "Duty." And as for woman—since *Little Dorrit* is about love and woman— the Victorian world perpetrated monstrous cruelties and forms of unfairness under the banner of "Duty" and the supposition that it was a tribute to the Almighty to spend one's life in servitude.

Little Dorrit's ministrations to her father represent a misconception of duty: acceptance of responsibilities to one's relatives does not require submission to their cruel and insensitive impulses to falsify one's own life and being—does not require the tacit acceptance of misrepresentation, treachery, and meanness. When her sense of duty is transferred to Arthur, one has to insist that to transfer caring affection for a father is not necessarily the best formula for establishing good relations in marriage.

A man does not want a trembling angel, willing to make any sacrifice, innocent and weak. It bodes ill for the future if he envisages a wife as a kind of nurse, offering ministrations suitable for geriatric care. A man wants a woman, not a child, and a good marriage grows out of mutual joy as well as the experience of misery, humiliation, and disgrace.

The end of *Little Dorrit* seems to me artistically very unsatisfactory— the clumsy attempt to introduce comedy with a substantial chunk of Flora;

the religiosity ("they were married, with the sun shining on them through the painted figure of Our Saviour on the window" [825]); and the heavily symbolic burning of the document at the center of the lumbering plot.

Lastly, we may note that Little Dorrit herself virtually proposes to Arthur:

"I have nothing in the world. I am as poor as when I lived here. . . . O my dearest and best, are you quite sure you will not share my future with me now?"

Locked in his arms, held to his heart, with his manly tears upon her own cheek . . . ,

"Never to part, my dearest Arthur; never any more until the last." (817)

It is, really, almost unreadable, deserving some scathing comment such as Huckleberry Finn's on the Victorian pictures. And, as usual, Arthur is pouring out his "manly tears," on whose profusion we might yearn for the comments of a Sam Weller.

The Leavises see *Little Dorrit* as "one of the master's major performances." It is "one of the very greatest of novels," and its omission from any brief list of the great European novels would be "critically indefensible," but this is "not a commonplace" (1970, 213).

It exhibits, says Leavis, "a unifying and controlling life such as only the greatest kind of creative writer can command" (1970, 213). In Little Dorrit, he declares, "the thing is done" (1970, 215).

These claims are, I believe, excessive; and they appear so if we ask, what is the gist of the artistic "life" that the book embodies? Of course, we may agree that Dickens hated the Calvinistic commercialism of the early and middle Victorian age: "the repressiveness towards children, the hard righteousness, the fear of love, the armed vigour in the face of life— he sums up now its hatred of art."

Against Gowan's, we may agree that his concept of art is "essentially Blake's" (1970, 228). We may even agree that the "ethos figured by the Clennam House was the offence against life, the spontaneous, the real, the creative" and that "he represents the creative spirit of life by art."

But where the case sticks lies in the question, must we then take Arthur and Little Dorrit as "life, the spontaneous, the real, the creative," when she is so patently *unreal*, being a figure in a religious oleograph or a fairy in a melodrama, while Arthur displays anything but a perceptive perspective on reality (not in this respect at all like Pip), and both are so dreary, weepy, and grey? They lack the dynamic of the libidinal.

Clennam (as Leavis says) may ask the questions, "what shall I do? What *can* I do? What are the possibilities of life for me. . . . What is life for?" But the answers to these questions do not develop along a substantial path of existential unfolding—again, as Pip's do. It is absurd, as Leavis does, to make an analogy between Clennam's quest and T. S. Eliot's in *Four Quartets:* Clennam simply never rises to the subtlety of that kind of soul searching, and in the end aspires only to accept, weeping, a child-mother woman as nurse. From beginning to end it is just "thinking intelligence" that Clennam does *not* exert: and in many of the dealings with Little Dorrit "thought" is suspended in favor of devotion to the Victorian platitudes: "Duty."

Leavis calls him an "earnest, intelligent, and preeminently civilized man": "we respect him as we respect ourselves" (1970, 219). He differs from Pip in not being the "I" in the novel. But I believe Leavis is misled into this overvaluation of Clennam by his sympathy with Clennam's doubts on the values of Victorian civilization. While Clennam does indeed deserve our respect for that, he is also singularly unsympathetic in his blank and negative response to positive possibilities of joy and fulfillment, or even creative effort in existence (Pip, by contrast, makes some stirring resolutions). Leavis admired controllable women; but his ideal man is controllable, too, the characteristic submissive disciple—and this is the false way in which he takes the dreary Arthur.

"The creative force of life in him has no confident authority," says Leavis (1970, 220). That is just my objection. But, Leavis goes on, this shows that Dickens has transmuted his own experience into someone who doesn't have his own spontaneity, and this shows that his social criticism "has the disinterestedness of spontaneous life, undetermined and undirected and uncontrolled by idea, will and self-insistent ego" (1970, 221). One has a dismal sense that Leavis has become the victim of his own theories: of course, Dickens does at best deal in whole experience and not ideas, but "will" surely shows itself in his deference to Victorian platitudes and concepts of idealized woman. What we complain of is Dickens's failure, in the scenes between Amy and her father and those between Arthur and Amy (one can hardly call them "love" scenes when Arthur is weeping like Mr. Jellyby with his head against the wall), the suspension of *intelligence* and the side-stepping of the reality of passion (as Jane Austen never side-steps it).

Leavis claims that Little Dorrit is "utterly unlike Little Nell" (1970,

225). This is not to "shy away from goodness as Little Dorrit evokes it." I do not balk at what Leavis calls "feminine goodness" (!), but I am questioning whether it is "good" to be, in so many relationships, such a doormat. "Her genius is to be always beyond question genuine—real. She is indefectibly real, and the test of reality for the others" (1970, 226). Can we really find this woman real, with her continual trembling meekness? She is quite clearly an idealized mother:

Clennam, listening to the voice as it read to him, heard in it all that great Nature was doing, heard in it all the soothing songs she sings to men. At no Mother's knee but hers, had he ever dwelt in his youth on hopeful promises, on playful fancies, on the harvests of tenderness and humility that lie hidden in the early-fostered seeds of the imagination; on the oaks of retreat from blighting words, that have their strong roots in nursery acorns. But, in the tones of the voice that read to him, there were memories of an old feeling of such things, and echoes of every merciful and loving whisper that had ever stolen to him in his life. (815)

It is true that Little Dorrit is *meant* to stand for realism in the sense of the "vital core of sincerity" and "the courage of moral-percipience" against "the fantastic play of snobberies, pretences and self-deception" of the Mar-shalsea and the world of society. But to derive from an idealization of motherhood a creature who is so "good" as to give totally self-denying devotion and ministration to others, with a motherlike total capacity to absolve and not to be hurt by their faults, is to fall for Dickens's own falsification of woman.

Little Dorrit does *not* have a "normative bearing," and (as with so many of the things Leavis endorsed) it would be disastrous to live by the "norm" she represents. It is significant that Leavis does not demonstrate Little Dorrit's "reality," but takes refuge in his own theories about Blake and "self-hood" ("The self-hood encloses; it insulates; the closure against the creative flow from below is at the same time a closure against surrounding lives and life" [1970, 230]). It may be true that in Gowan and Mrs. Clennam there is enclosure in egotism. But by contrast one cannot see Little Dorrit and Clennam as representatives of "the creative flow from below": they are, come to think of it, products of the will—not so much of intellectual ideas, but of platitudinous concepts, of "Duty." It can't be said that Little Dorrit represents the "disinterestedness of life" in being "not ego-bound and not slave to a mechanism": she is simply not forceful enough to challenge the attempts made to impose on her, as Pip is. It is not true, as Leavis claims, that "she can bring her father to the point of glimpsing from time to time the reality of what he is and in doing so make him for us something of a tragic figure" (1970, 246).

If we compare the scene with young John discussed above, we can see that this is just what she does *not* do, because she is too much enclosed in concepts from the Victorian melodrama, and Dickens's idealization. Her selflessness is gutless, and this seems no alternative to egoism.

Only at one moment does Leavis note her libidinal deficiency:

> Disinterestedness in her is goodness and love; she differs from Sissy in that, while manifested in scenes of this kind as a decisive presence, she can't be called a challenging one—there are no dark hair and eyes and lustrous gleams (these in *Little Dorrit* belong to Tattycoram). Yet her decisiveness, with its peculiar quality, leaves us in no doubt, it is brought so potently home to us. (1970, 247)

Yes—Little Dorrit is sexless; and it is Tattycoram to whom a sermon is delivered on duty. The lesbian episode with Miss Wade is superbly done, but that, too, suggests that passion is perverted, and that such a claim to passion is neglectful of duty. Little Dorrit, in her passion-killing old frock, is as far from sexual passion as you can get—and so is a split-off, the ideal woman separated disastrously from the libidinal.

Leavis reveals some slight disquiet later on in his essay: surely, if Little Dorrit is so potent as a symbol of spontaneous "life," we shouldn't have these doubts? Little Dorrit (he admits) doesn't represent the whole of Dickens's answer to Henry Gowan (who would have thought her *intended* for that),

> and further . . . her marriage with Arthur Clennam, though (solving the personal problems of each) it may be right and happy, is neither a romantically exalted "happy ending," nor a triumphant upshot of the enquiry, the complex intensity of questioning, that the book so largely is. (1970, 246)

But in what, if not in her devotion to Clennam, her love for him, are her "life" and "creativity" manifest? And as we have seen, it is a relationship conceived in terms of the angelic innocence of a child-mother figure to a man who needs nursing as from a nursing mother: Euphrasia. If the "answer" is not in this, where is it? And isn't it a wrong answer? Dickens, says Leavis,

> is neither a romantic optimist nor a pessimist. . . . And it isn't that Little Dorrit is being *criticized* when we are moved to wish she weren't so docile to Mrs. General. . . . Dickens doesn't simplify . . . he insists that the qualities and energies not represented by Little Dorrit are indispensable too. (1970, 246)

No, alas, Little Dorrit is not sufficiently subject to critical examination. Dickens's insight and intelligence are too easily suspended when she is around—and she is too docile not only to Mrs. General but also to her father, the uppity Fanny, her slothful brother, and Arthur. She doesn't have enough *life* to deal with these people as they need to be dealt with, if she is supposed to love them. And when is an author to be commended for *not* including indispensable elements in his embodiment of "life" (etc.), so as "not to simplify"?

"She is at its centre," says Leavis of the novel. And so bewitched is he by this embodiment of "feminine goodness" that he can say of the very mixed scene from Victorian melodrama, with Dorrit's outbursts of self-pity, that there is "nothing infelicitously theatrical about it"—an astonishing lapse of judgment.

It makes what might otherwise have seemed too challengingly exaggerated in its absurdity, *too* stagey (for William Dorrit is essentially an actor here, playing a role he has cast himself in the play, the histrionic unreality he has made of life in the Marshalsea), wholly acceptable. (1970, 250)

Acceptable on that side—up to a point—but what of Little Dorrit's docile role in it? And her stagey gestures, here and elsewhere? Leavis declares that "our response as to a painful disturbing actuality of life retains its full power" (1970, 250)—but I can never feel this, whenever Little Dorrit appears in this kind of scene: she is a tinsel angel, and the reality of the scene declines in its presence.

Leavis is excellent, of course, on the Merdle world, and on Dickens's passionate defense of humanness against falsification and the effects of the "forms" and varnishing. But, once again, when it comes to the "upshot" of the book, Leavis becomes the victim of his own amateurish philosophical anthropology. We have glanced at his invocation of Blake and "self-hood": he even speaks of Mrs Clennam's "Urizenic domination"!

So we come to Amy Dorrit as disinterestedness—placed by the "creative nisus" at the heart of the novel—and to the principle of "not belonging to oneself." Daniel Doyce is apparently also a manifestation of this recognition. This is Leavis's one religious principle (and has its text in *The Rainbow* in Tom Brangwen's sense that "he knew he did not belong to himself").

Discussing a reference to St. Paul's Cathedral, Leavis says,

It invokes institutional religion, of course, but not in the spirit of satiric irony. The institutional is invoked as representing something more than institution; as representing a reality of the spirit, a testimony, a reality of experience that, although it is a reality of the individual experience or not one at all, is more than the merely personal. (1970, 270)

But what did Leavis believe? He seems to have believed that religious reality lived in the culture, in the language ("the inherited totality of the values"). But when he comes into conflict with T. S. Eliot over *Four Quartets* in *The Living Principle,* he seems to deny the possibility of the existence of a religious reality, as Eliot conceived it. But does he here endorse Dickens's emphasis on the teachings of the New Testament, or is he bending it to suit his own strange philosophical and moral system?

Leavis asks "how Dickens would have replied to theologically Christian questioning" and answers, "who can say?" "The value of Dickens's vindication of the spirit lies in its being a great artist's—as Blake's is" (270). Yes, but. We have seen that Dickens recognized the dangers to humanness of the primitive attitudes of the Old Testament—yet seems strangely equivocal of them around Mrs. Clennam. And where does the stern concept of "Duty" come from? We have seen that he gives tribute to Christ and the Christian virtues, but are the principles that a little child shall lead them and that one should always turn the other cheek really so applicable to adult problems as they are seen to be in *Little Dorrit?*

Dickens's paraphernalia of angels, stars, lights, and the rest are used to give potency to his ideal object: yet, as I believe I have shown, the spiritual qualities Little Dorrit displays spring more from his own desperate need to fantasize a healing kind of "feminine goodness" that involved a massive denial of the true nature of woman.

Leavis would ask, where do we learn the true nature of woman from, if not from the great novelists? But then the question arises, what happens when the great novelists are wrong? Then the answer is to look where Leavis would not look—to the disciplines of philosophical anthropology. There one discovers more adequate answers to the problems of being than the institutionalized religion, or the language art to which Leavis defers.

Leavis is overinsistent about language, as if it were in itself a source of understanding of "life." Of course Dickens's command of language is superb, and it is at its most superb where its "life" is the vehicle of insight and understanding. But the underlying problem is that of consciousness and meaning. We may admit Dickens's engagement with the tragic themes of death and meaning, and his upholding of existential needs against the failings of his time and its inability to provide for the needs of being. But even the "vindicator of the spirit" has his own consciousness to deal with (and its limitations) and his own "psychic tissue." It is true that "Dickens communicates at times a profound insight into human nature, the human situation, and human need." We have no right, says Leavis, to "ask any-thing else of a great artist."

All the same, some of the insights will be wrong. Where love, marriage, and sexuality were concerned, Dickens's insights were seriously limited, by his own inheritance from his mother and by the predominant concepts and attitudes of his time. On the whole he did little to criticize or refresh these concepts and attitudes. In his concern for life and being he does not, in *Little Dorrit*, give us much sense of potentialities in man and woman, in terms of the "being" he sought to uphold. Essentially, he believes in docility for women, believes they should be "little," childlike, helpless, devoted, innocent, and "good"—and it is highly significant that Leavis should find nothing wrong with this. It is much the same with Leavis's attitudes to those novelists like T. F. Powys and D. H. Lawrence who display a strong unconscious inclination to endorse the feeling that love should be under control, and urge that woman must submit—because she is so dangerous.

Leavis's judgment of *Little Dorrit* is very disappointing, not least because he seems to be working not from the text but from his own all-embracing philosophy or psychology of not being "enclosed in the ego"—while yet refusing to have the basis of this philosophical anthropology examined. We have to say that, looked at in the light of psychotherapy and its findings, *Little Dorrit*, despite its excellence, seems a much less successful work, since it fails in the end to uphold life and being in the main protagonists and gives us instead a regression to the unreal child-mother ideogram of Victorian religiosity, in its dread of maturity in equality and freedom between men and women.

Great Expectations: A Radical Ambiguity about What One May Expect

I found myself startled, when I came to work on this book, to discover *Great Expectations* coming so late in the Dickens canon. I suppose because of its similarity in some respects to *David Copperfield,* I had assumed it to be an earlier work. Dickens himself read *David Copperfield* before embarking on *Great Expectations,* to avoid "unconscious repetition," and he reported to Forster that he was affected by it "to a degree you would hardly believe." But on reflection, *Great Expectations* seems a work of maturity, and it is, as Mrs. Q. D. Leavis saw, a very great novel.

The end is significant, whether one takes the sad or the ameliorated conclusion to the book. In trying to explore Dickens's attitude to woman in the present work, I have myself become increasingly sad about Dickens's own predicament: in *Great Expectations,* as the Mackenzies say, it seems that "he had come to accept that he would never know the fulfilment of a true-hearted love" (1979, 331). In the first version of *Great Expectations* Pip is left a wiser man among the complete ruin of his hopes: "His false friends are lost to him, he is poor, he has loved a coldly condescending beauty—the essence of idealized and unawakened womanhood—and he has come to find the only anodyne for his sorrows in work" (1979, 331). In 1861 Bulwer-Lytton suggested that the readers would dislike this end.

Dickens rewrote it to make Pip seem likely to find comfort with Estella in middle age, after a passage of years, and Dickens thought that on the whole this was better.

Great Expectations began to be published in 1860. It was in 1865 that Dickens was involved in a terrible train accident with Ellen Ternan and her mother. In 1867 he records many weekend visits to "N" at "Sl"— Nelly Ternan was living at Elizabeth Cottage in the High Street at Slough, for which Dickens paid the rates under the pseudonym "Charles Tringham." He spent fifty-three nights at Slough between January and July 1867. Although in a footnote in his book on Dickens E. W. F. Tomlin says that the relationship between Dickens and Ellen Ternan has never been proved, the evidence in his pocket book of his visits to Slough seems conclusive. Some believe that he and Ellen Ternan had a child that died in infancy (the Mackenzies note the unexplained word "Arrival" in his diary for 13 April, and references to Ellen being unwell after that date). But it seems that Dickens maintained a kind of "fairy tale" relationship with Ellen, apart from the stresses of normal life.

I mention these biographical details merely to suggest that Dickens had, at the time of writing *Great Expectations* and *Our Mutual Friend,* a secret romantic sexual relationship, and, inevitably in Victorian society, this must have provoked in him much anxiety and guilt (he was for instance very anxious about Ellen's loss of some jewelry in the railway accident, because this might have been brought out in public in any investigation).

Though Pip progresses toward ever-increasing self-awareness and critical "placing" of himself, as Q. D. Leavis points out, the book is pervaded by unconscious preoccupations with woman and murder, and with other dark shadows. There is the blighted Miss Havisham (who could even be taken to symbolize Dickens's own estranged wife), the emotionally bleak but beautiful Estella, the strange murderess woman whom Jaggers has saved from the gallows, and the phantom shadow of the hanged woman whose image recurs in the book. Estella is of course the daughter of the murderess by Magwitch, about whose crimes we know nothing. There are other nightmarish features, such as the sensual boorishness of Bentley Drummle, whom Estella yet chooses to marry—and who beats her. There is the hideous cruelty of Orlick, who makes a murderous attack on Mrs. Gargery, who is struck dumb by his blow, and who tries to kill Pip. There is the furious antagonism between Compeyson and Magwitch and a general feeling of doom and dread—from the convict hulks to the old brewery and the fatal River Thames. (It is followed, we may note, by two other novels about murder and attempted murder, both centering around woman: Lizzie Hexam is brought up amid corpses on the River Thames; and the passions of Bradley Headstone, Neville, and Jasper are murderous due to jealousy over woman.)

What first attracted me to the question of Dickens's attitude to woman was this undercurrent of *murderousness*. It seemed to me to fit in with the problem I had explored in the fantasies of George MacDonald. Why is it that when in these works the protagonist finds the lost phantom woman he is seeking, she turns malevolent? Why so often is the quest for the feminine menaced by death? (I have noted that many women in Victorian literature are waiting, imprisoned, for death.)

Another striking element in *Great Expectations* is the growth of a deep intensity of feeling in Pip for Magwitch, even though the convict has threatened him with inauthenticity, with a false "inheritance": in this I believe the Mackenzies are right to detect deep unconscious feelings about the *father* in Dickens. But how shall we interpret the image of woman? Surely we must relate these to the mother—the abandoned bride, the cold-hearted Estella, the haunting shadow of the murderess? All these figures may be seen in terms of symbols or externalizations of dynamics within Dickens himself, in his unconscious world, around the image of woman in relation to death—in terms of phantoms that he sought energetically to exorcise in order to find his own individuation (to use a Jungian word) through his art. His dangerous obsession with the death of Nancy is a primary clue.

We may begin from a passage at the beginning of the book, an example of the marvelous prose of the art of which this novel is such a superb example:

At the same time, he hugged his shuddering body in both his arms—clasping himself, as if to hold himself together—and limped towards the low church wall. As I saw him go, picking his way among the nettles, and among the brambles that bound the green mounds, he looked in my young eyes as if he were eluding the hands of the dead people, stretching up cautiously out of their graves, to get a twist upon his ankle and pull him in.

When he came to the low church wall, he got over it, like a man whose legs were numbed and stiff, and then turned round to look for me. When I saw him turning, I set my face towards home, and made the best use of my legs. But presently I looked over my shoulder, and saw him going on again towards the river, still hugging himself in both arms, and picking his way with his sore feet among the great stones dropped into the marshes here and there, for stepping-places when the rains were heavy, or the tide was in.

The marshes were just a long black horizontal line then, as I stopped to look after him; and the river was just another horizontal line, not nearly so broad nor yet so black; and the sky was just a row of angry red lines and dense black lines intermixed. On the edge of the river I could faintly make out the only two black things in all the prospect that seemed to be standing upright; one of these was the beacon by which the sailors steered—like an unhooped cask upon a pole—an ugly thing when you were near it; the other a gibbet, with some chains hanging to it which had once held a pirate. The man was limping on towards this latter, as if he were the pirate come to life, and come down, and going back to hook himself up again. It gave me a terrible turn when I thought so; and as I saw the cattle lifting their heads to gaze after him, I wondered whether they thought so too. I looked all round for the horrible young man, and could see no signs of him. But, now I was frightened again, and ran home without stopping. (4–5)

The relationship between the desperate escaped convict and the child is powerfully dramatic—and done imaginatively in such a way that we see things from the child's level (at the very beginning Pip sees everything upside down because Magwitch holds him upside down). The whole of Pip's life is altered because of this chance meeting on the marshes—and what he meets is man reduced to a "poor bare fork'd animal," in desperate straits: "he hugged his shuddering body in both his arms—clasping himself as if to hold himself together." It seems to Pip that the dead people in the graves were "stretching up cautiously out of their graves, to get a twist upon his ankle and to pull him in." Magwitch lives on the verge of death all through the novel, and so presses upon us the problem of "the point of life"—in relation to which question develops the massive falsification of Pip by inauthentic patronage, in reward for the succor he provides for the escapee under duress and threat of execution.

The scene at the end of this chapter has a powerful symbolism, which we may examine in relation to the themes of the novel. Pip "makes the best use" of his legs—he is free—whereas the man limps painfully because he is cold and sore from being in irons—an outcast from the human world, and though "free" as an escapee, hemmed in with threats to that freedom, the right to which he has sacrificed by his criminal acts.

In the scene, there are two "black things"; one is the beacon by which the sailors steered, a cask upon a pole that is an "ugly thing"; the other is the gibbet that once held a corpse. The symbolism seems to convey the impression that the passage through life is painful anyway—even the sign that makes navigation possible is ugly. The other landmark is uglier—the gallows that has held the body of an executed criminal, which has rotted away and toward which the escapee now seems to be moving, to "hook himself up again." Seen as through the child's imagination, the scene seems an allegory of a painful existence that limps between an ugly "true" path, and doom. Magwitch's "young man" is not (yet) Compeyson (though he is on the marshes, too): that fantasy presence gives another touch of mur-derous menace to the scene—and later, of course, Compeyson turns out to be the man who has blighted Miss Havisham's life. Mortality and corruption saturate the atmosphere of this novel from the beginning.

The starkness of the scene thus has an apocalyptic quality:

The marshes were just a long black line then . . . the river was just another horizontal line, not nearly so broad nor yet so black: and the sky was just a row of long angry red lines and dense black lines intermixed. (4)

The angry red lines perhaps evoke a distant image of the weals of whipping and wounds, and the black is the black of death: land, river, and sky are reduced to bleak elemental forms, into which the hunted man looms. The black horizontal lines also evoke the theme of freedom, for as the man limps toward them, he seems to move toward infinite space, and yet to be barred or confined by the dark horizontal lines. We get something of the same effect in Emily Dickinson's poem:

> I'll tell you how the Sun rose—
> A Ribbon at a time—
> The Steeples swam in Amethyst
> . . . .
> Till when they reached the other side
> A Dominie in Gray—
> Put gently up the evening bars—
> And led the flock away.

That is, the sunrise or sunset becomes a *setting*, full of significance, for a human scene in which life becomes a drama.

The drama, with its symbols from the deep unconscious level, acts out deep questions of being. In exploring problems of *expectations* and choice in life, such as Pip engages in, we are involved in questions of existential freedom, and these are inseparable from problems of psychology and models of man. Existential freedom, if it is to be true freedom, cannot be exerted in a superficial way; it needs to take account of the complex nature of humanity, each individual's psychic inheritance, each person's "condition" (in Sartre's sense)—and, ultimately, each person's biological existence, on earth, in time. What is the relation of love to a meaning in the whole life, to man (and woman) as "beings-in-the-world"? How does what happens between man and man, and between man and woman, relate to our life tasks, to the society in which these may be taken up, to our destiny and the meaning of life?

As I have implied in my note on reparation, one important insight here is that our capacities to relate to others are bound up with the development of a special capacity, which is that of *concern*. Concern requires the ex-perience of painful recognition of the possible consequences of one's own hate—a kind of pain that can be a pain of *consciousness*. Love, true love, is only possible through the painful experience of the reality of the "other's being." Here is the vast philosophical problem of "finding" the other, and from this the need for reparation emerges. The painful experiences in *Great Expectations*, like Pip's suffering at Estella's hands, and at Miss Havis-ham's—culminating in Pip saving her from the fire—seem evidently sym-bolic of reparation. And the anguish between Pip and Magwitch, growing into love, seems to belong to a torment of concern, too.

The goal of these ordeals is a sense of wholeness, a sense of being fully human. This is the theme of Dostoevsky's *Crime and Punishment*: to escape from his predicament of not knowing whether he is a man or "vermin," Raskolnikov has to kill the old woman. Dostoevsky himself had to have this painful fantasy in order to try to escape from his own schizoid condition and find love. But the consequent process of experiencing love brings a deep anguish because the adult, his protagonist with whom he identifies, has to go through processes that are normally completed in infancy—but because he is an adult he is aware of the risks as the infant is not. In light of this it is possible to discuss a novel like *Great Expectations* as a dram-atization of intrapsychic dynamics, which is what our dreams are (that is, if we are to believe W. R. D. Fairbairn and others, who explain their significance in this way). Every character can be seen as dynamic of the "I": the art is a quest to bring these disparate energies in the psyche to meaningful reconciliation, and the central theme is the capacity to *find* others and to develop concern: that is, the theme is love, in relation to the problem of being.

There are many Dostoevskyan moments in *Great Expectations*; for ex-ample, the horrible attack by Orlick on Pip's sister, which essentially dehumanizes her, is parallel to Raskolnikov's murder of the old woman. Dostoevskyan too is Orlick's torture of Pip himself and also the ordeals of

Magwitch and the death of Miss Havisham. In these, I believe we may say, Dickens himself, by violent fantasy, is endeavoring to find the capacity for reparation, and then, as I have hinted, to achieve "individuation"—to make whole his divided being. In this process, I believe, the figure of woman is of great significance: she represents the figure of woman in the inner world of the author—his anima, if you like. It is highly significant that by the end of the novel the figure has become by degrees less menacing: Miss Havisham has become repentant, and she and Pip find one another's reality. Estella is refined by suffering and responds sympathetically to him. It is an aspect of the love between Pip and Magwitch that he can tell him he loves his daughter.

The reputation and the quest for integration are noticeably acted out in an atmosphere pervaded with guilt—for guilt is a major harmonic theme in the novel. Behind these problems are those of authenticity—Pip being engaged in a tormented process of seeking to be true to himself, through many diversions.

These are the unconscious themes behind *Great Expectations,* and it is the richness of the symbolism that makes this such a poetic, and such a great book. We have looked at some of Dickens's relational problems, and his difficulties with reality. In several of his biographies, and from his letters, we gather that many felt that these difficulties arose from the very richness of his imaginative life; indeed, in his comments on his wife, it seems that he recognized this himself. But perhaps we may turn the perspective around and say that Dickens, with his imaginative genius, created in his work a fantasy world in which he could live successfully, as he could not in the real world. We have seen that there was a complete contrast between the way he could deal with and organize events in a novel and the way in which he failed to deal with events in life. He kept certain aspects of his life apart, as when he kept "N" to live with in "Sl," and when life became difficult he turned more and more to his dramatic readings and to the response of his audience, seeking approval and réclame there to compensate for the anguish of his difficulties in immediate personal relationships and with his own temperament.

In this conflict, the symbolism of woman was important, and especially the symbolism of woman in relationship to death and woman being abused, threatened, or attacked by man. Why were such fantasies of such importance to Dickens? I believe my references to Dostoevsky's *Crime and Punishment* gives us the clue. The need to fantasy such symbolic attacks on the image of woman reveals a need to reexperience the earliest of infant perplexities about self and not-self; that is, it represents a need to go back to the schizoid stage, what Melanie Klein called the paranoid-schizoid stage, in order to explore the problem of whether *love* is dangerous and is liable to consume the other and annihilate her. In Raskolnikov's urgent need to find out whether he is vermin or human, he has to act out the fantasy of the schizoid problem—or, we can say, Dostoevsky did. Dickens, in his relational difficulties and his problems with reality, had what I believe we must call schizoid problems. Of course, he also tackles depressive prob-lems—problems of a later stage relating to the dangers of hate and the need to make reparation for the possible consequences of hate. But we may take as indicative the recurring problem in Dickens of characters who cannot cope with moral issues in life because of what the psychotherapists call "diminution of affect"—emotional deficiency. Louise and Tom Grad-grind cannot find the capacity for ethical living because they have never had a rich imaginative experience of play, in love. Florence Dombey is threatened with serious emotional damage when her cold father destroys his image in her heart. Estella reveals a schizoid degree of emotional deficiency.

In *Great Expectations* I believe Dickens digs down in his fantasy to the earliest fears of loving and to deep, related schizoid problems of identity. The book is full of images of inner emptiness: Estella warns Pip that she has no heart (and such emotional emptiness could not, in reality, be the product of Miss Havisham's persuasions). Miss Havisham has been blighted emotionally just at the moment of sexual flowering, and her bodily life in an ancient bridal gown symbolizes psychic paralysis. The convicts who are central to the theme of authenticity in the book are outcasts, and have no place in society: Magwitch is desperate to have a real identity and tries to make Pip into his false image of a gentleman. The book is also full of paranoid feelings, starting with the menacing opening that we have looked at: throughout there is a fear of lurking menace, from Compeyson or Orlick, from the punitive authorities who are seeking the convicts, and from the strange murderess lurking in the background, while in the phantom of a hanging woman that Pip sees from time to time there seems to be a more terrible threat from woman. The attack on Pip's sister and Orlick's attack on him are horrible paranoid-schizoid fantasies, while Magwitch's death is dreadful, being a consequence of his impulse to remake a "proper" identity through Pip.

We may link the paranoid-schizoid element with that of inheritance, and with Dickens's own predicament. At this stage in his life he must have felt that his massive imaginative efforts had not solved the existential problems to whose solution they were directed. He had made massive efforts at reparation, yet was still in anguish and chaos in his personal emotional life and family circumstances.

At some level in his psyche he "knew" that this had to do with the psychic inheritance, and so in this work he explores it again. And in this book the image of the father (as the Mackenzies suggest) is as important as that of the mother. There is not in this novel the punitive woman who seeks to promote guilt and to inflict expiation on an infant who thereby inherits disgrace, like Mrs. Clennam and Esther's aunt; Miss Havisham is a pitiable figure whose life has been destroyed by her being jilted. In this book, the father figure is at first terrifying, animal, subhuman, yet also pitiable; then he becomes one who has falsified Pip in his own image of the respectability he does not have. But later he becomes like a father who is loved because of his suffering and is understood even for his false attempts to make "his boy" into the image of his own image of his good self.

The greatest dangers lie in the meeting between male and female: Estella is the daughter of the convict Magwitch and the murderess who lurks in the background of Jaggers's house. Compeyson, who hates Magwitch and seeks his death, has destroyed Miss Havisham, whose teaching has perv-erted Estella. Bentley Drummle is a brutal and coarse husband for Estella. Orlick mutilates and dehumanizes Pip's sister out of jealousy.

How is it possible to triumph over these horrors and the various ways in which they threaten Pip with inauthenticity? The answer is for him not only to gain insight into himself, to mature, but also for him to become capable of love—and the interesting thing about *Great Expectations* is that the love that is gained has strong homosexual elements. Further, this af-fection between man and man (as between Pip and Magwitch, Pip and Joe, and Pip and Herbert) may be seen as symbolic of reconciliation with the dangerous male element within the self. Just as the dangerous woman is mollified, so the dangerous male figure (with nameless crimes in the background) is symbolically embraced. Orlick and Bentley Drummle, Com-peyson and the early Magwitch are frighteningly menacing male figures. Later, Pip's love for Magwitch goes with the process of coming to love himself and of feeling secure in his love for Estella.

This progress we may link with the problem of finding love to be safe.

The schizoid problem is the fear of love, whose (oral) voraciousness is felt to be dangerous, liable to eat the other up. In the primitive unconscious the worst infant fantasy is that of the primal scene: sexual intercourse is felt by the child to be a form of voracious eating, in which the parents may consume one another or, in combination, threaten to turn on the child. I have suggested that some of the menacing elements in Victorian fantasy and around woman in Dickens have their roots in such primitive fantasies. The way in which such fears are alleviated is by mutual "finding"—by finding the reality of the other, and by making good (reparative) relation' ships: by developing love.

In *Great Expectations* there do seem to be recurring fantasies of the primal scene, of sex between father and mother, which is full of danger. (Estella's parents were criminals, one a murderess.) And in general, we might suggest, the intense guilt that surrounded libidinal sexuality in Vic' torian England was bound up with the dread of the primal scene as dan' gerous: one often detects a threat of murder behind Victorian sexuality, and murder certainly pervades this novel in association with sex—with Compeyson, the murderess, Miss Havisham, Orlick, and Bentley Drummle (it is there, too, of course, in the menace of Bradley Headstone in *Our Mutual Friend,* as we shall see).

Dickens's secret sexual relationship with Ellen Ternan and his fear of exposure, as well as his guilt over how he had treated his wife and family, no doubt exacerbated these unconscious fears. His own sexual experiences must have been full of guilt and dread. But we are dealing also with very deep unconscious fears about gender and sexuality, such as we often find in the Victorian consciousness (as, for instance, in the fantasies of George MacDonald and the schizoid flights of fancy of Lewis Carroll). And we may examine it in existentialist terms as the search for a sense of secure being and individuation in relation to sexual perplexity.

As I have suggested in discussing reparation, it is a problem of "concern," of finding the other without eating her up or being eaten, of finding a confidence in encounter in which the other can be allowed to freely exist in her own right. Pip is seeking the capacity successfully to make reparation in the face of the fear of what love might do, and his problem may be associated with unconscious dread of the consequences of loving. I hope such an approach will not be felt to be reductive. It is by no means to reduce Dicken's creative symbolism to say that the murder of Nancy is the "primal scene," any more than I was trying to reduce Mahler when I said that the anguish he suffers from episode to episode in the *Ninth Symphony* has to do with the dread he had as a child of parental sexuality, which seemed to threaten violence and annihilation—even the loss of all meaning to life (see my *Gustav Mahler and the Courage to Be, 1975*). The answer to such terrible fears is to find and establish those forms of love and authenticity that can create meaning. In *Great Expectations* Pip grows to find a love that transcends, in his affection for Joe Gargery and his love for Biddy and in his later affection for Magwitch, but in both of these he allows himself at times to be falsified. He hopes desperately to find love with Estella, but *she* is falsified: she becomes victim of the sensual father figure (Drummle) who destroys *potentia* in her as her cruel husband—yet she is mollified by this terrible experience.

At one point Drummle is said to resemble Orlick, so there is a parallel between Orlick's attack on Mrs. Gargery and Bentley Drummle's on Estella, which we may examine in the light of Bill Sikes's murder of Nancy. All are in a sense references to the primal scene, and we may say that Dickens is finding it difficult to accept the combination of aggression and devotion manifest in parental coition (and so in adult sexuality). Sex perhaps remained in his unconscious mind a kind of *dangerous eating*, as it is to the child, and this is symbolized both by the wedding cake full of mice and spiders and the burning bridal veil that kills Miss Havisham.* With her, sex is death, as it is in other spheres of the symbolism of the novel.

The infantile suspicion that annihilation lurks in sexual love lies behind the recurrent images in *Great Expectations* of the hanging woman and the accompanying shadow of death—which are associated with Magwitch but also with Estella's mother, Miss Havisham, and Estella herself:

It was in this place, and at this moment, that a strange thing happened to my fancy. I thought it a stranger thing long afterwards. I turned my eyes—a little dimmed by looking up at the frosty light—towards a great wooden beam, in a low nook of the building near me on my right hand, and I saw a figure all in yellow white, with but one shoe to the feet, and it hung so, that I could see that the faded trimmings of the dress were like earthy paper, and that the face was Miss Havisham's, with a movement going over the whole countenance as if she were trying to call to me. In the terror of being certain that it had not been there a moment

*He and Wilkie Collins called women of pleasure "periwinkles"—not only flowers but also little things one could eat.

before, I ran at first from it, and then ran towards it. And my terror was greatest of all when I found no figure there. (59)

This is just the kind of nightmare fantasy one might expect a sensitive and imaginative child like Pip to have. But it also belongs to the overall symbolism of the dramatic poem—and in this it is the image of "female element being" gone dead: emotions gone dead, sexuality gone dead, and creativity gone dead. So, it is an image characteristic of the Victorian predicament. The hanging figure Pip sees is the death of *potentia*—in Miss Havisham, in himself, and in Dickens himself. It is the specter of creative being gone dead in a world in which pragmatism, the literal, and the material have triumphed. Sexuality, in the libidinal (Biddy) sense has died; also, in the dimension of whole affectionate friendship (as between men— Joe and Provis), it has died (and has to be resurrected). Significantly, the death images occur in the old decayed brewery, itself symbolizing the decay of good husbandry, and the old ("organic") way of life: so what has died is love-in-community. (Dickens himself has allowed his marriage to die, while his sexuality is in a fairy tale cottage remote from his real life.) But this specter is also a symbol of the damage that the child fears may be done by love, and is a paranoid-schizoid image, the only means of exorcising which is by the achievement of the capacity for reparation through love. And Pip, of course, does such a reparative act when he smothers the flames on Miss Havisham's body, and when he works in the end to save Magwitch.

Significantly, the next time Pip sees this ghost is during a discussion of Estella's own heart:

"You must know," said Estella, condescending to me as a brilliant and beautiful woman might, "that I have no heart—if that has anything to do with my memory."

I got through some jargon to the effect that I took the liberty of doubting that. That I knew better. That there could be no such beauty without it.

"Oh! I have a heart to be stabbed or shot in, I have no doubt," said Estella, "and, of course, if it ceased to beat I should cease to be. But you know what I mean. I have no softness there, no—sympathy, sentiment, nonsense."

What *was* it that was borne in upon my mind when she stood still and looked attentively at me? Anything that I had seen in Miss Havisham? No ... I looked again, and though she was still looking at me, the suggestion was gone.

What *was* it?

"I am serious," said Estella, not so much with a frown (for her brow was smooth) as with a darkening of her face; "if we are to be thrown much together, you had better believe it at once. No!" imperiously stopping me as I opened my lips. "I have not bestowed my tenderness anywhere. I have never had any such thing."

In another moment we were in the brewery so long disused, and she pointed to the high gallery where I had seen her going out on that same first day, and she told me she remembered to have been up there, and to have seen me standing scared below. As my eyes followed her white hand, again the dim suggestion that I could not possibly grasp, crossed me. My involuntary start occasioned her to lay her hand upon my arm. Instantly the ghost passed once more and was gone.

What *was* it? (224–25)

The association between Estella and the ghost is ambiguous. In one sense, Pip is sensing her origins: her mother was the unknown murderess who wished to kill her own child. In the background too is her father Magwitch, the criminal, who believes his child to be dead. The shadow is of murder by the woman murderer and of the child by being abandoned (by the rejecting mother and father).

But there is also a sense in which this ghost stands for something that fascinates Dickens, which leads some people to have the feeling Estella describes, of having a living heart and body but no emotions or tenderness—of being alive but not alive at the same time. This is the schizoid problem with which Dickens often deals, the failure of affect, of appropriate emotions, whose origins are in the failure of "loving communion."* In Pip this failure is represented by the fact that his mother and father are dead; in Estella, by the fact that her mother is unknown, a woman with strong muscles concealed under petiteness and a woman capable of great cruelty and perhaps murder. She is the female annihilating figure Freud called the castrating mother; but Estella is handed over to another such and is brought up by a woman who has deliberately perverted her emotions, devoting herself to this one great vicious intention as an act of vengeance for the destruction of her own emotional life. At the heart of Dickens's fantasy is this preoccupation with the destruction of the creative power of the imagination, of emotion, and so of meaning, by the influence of circumstances and especially by inheritance and upbringing. This aspect of his own psychological condition he turned into a fundamental (and valid) criticism of nineteenth-century industrial society, and utilitarianism.

*This emotional failure is there in Gradgrind, Dombey, Murdstone, and Lady Dedlock, the names being often indicative of a petrified state of heart: Gradgrind a grindstone, Dombey a tomb of dead emotions, Murdstone "inner contents" turned to stone, Lady Dedlock's emotions in rigor mortis.

Pip, brought up by Mrs. Gargery, who is also cruel and cold, has been brought up, we might say, by the experience of "pseudo-male doing": rather like Sartre and Genet, he has had to "make himself." Yet in his experience of Joe's kindness ("What larks!"), there is enough love to give Pip potentialities from which a vital self can grow, while in Miss Havisham's care for Estella, however evil in intention, there is just enough affection to make it possible for Estella, at the end, to be redeemed for love by suffering. Bitterly, Pip and Estella struggle through to the capacity for reparation, but the ambiguous end reveals an uncertainty as to whether love and meaning are really achieved. The ambivalence surely reflects Dicken's own unhappy situation in love?

Dickens's insights into the schizoid problem are confirmed by recent psychoanalytical thought, except that we have today traced a closer connection between very early processes and schizoid disabilities. Miss Havisham could not really have generated such dire heartlessness in Estella. But it is likely that such a tragic infancy as Estella's could well have left her a schizoid person—and then, certainly, a woman like Miss Havisham, impelled by such bitterness and envy, could exploit the potentialities in her. Certainly Pip, in his heartless disregard of his relationship with Joe, shows schizoid tendencies—but again, his growing recognition of his failings here, and his pain, show that his schizoid proclivities are the common ones with which we have to struggle in order to find our humanness and warm-hearted responsibilities. Dickens, like Dostoevsky, was schizoid enough himself to be aware of such terrible possibilities of the death of the potentialities of one's being: for the ghost that haunts *Great Expectations* is the ghost of the schizoid atrophy of the self due to emotional and creative ignorance. By "ignorance" here I mean the failure to experience those forms of care by which alone we can make our way to the "significant other" and thus to a world full of meaning and a sense of a meaningful self. Since (as Winnicott and Masud Khan have argued) the act of realization of the self is an imaginative one between mother and infant, itself a dynamic of "female element being," this self-fulfillment could be particularly inhibited by a utilitarian, mechanical age—so Dickens turns the schizoid problem and the discovery of concern and love into a philosophical and political attitude, embodied in his art. Being must be redeemed from extinction by love. It is because of this need for imaginative, loving, meaning redemption that he is so dedicated to Christ's example and teaching.

Love is called out by one person from another, as the mother calls it out in her infant (a process hallowed in the image of the Virgin and Child). Estella says that Pip can call out nothing in her:

"It seems," said Estella, very calmly, "that there are sentiments, fancies—I don't know how to call them—which I am not able to comprehend. When you say you love me, I know what you mean, as a form of words; but nothing more. You address nothing in my breast, you touch nothing there. I don't care for what you say at all." (343)

We recall Louisa, the product of Mr. Gradgrind's upbringing and educa-tion, talking thus to her father in *Hard Times*. Dickens is making a radical criticism of a society that breeds such alienation. Louisa cannot deal with the world because failure of imaginative experience has left her ignorant of the truths of the heart: she has no moral capacity because she has been starved of those sources of sympathy, play, and poetry.

Compeyson, who is a swindler, confidence trickster, and crook, is a characteristic product of a materialistic, acquisitive society, as is also the less fortunate Magwitch (less fortunate because less cunningly intelligent and "charming," a more *feeling*, body-life person). It is Compeyson who has ruined Miss Havisham emotionally, and Estella, whose life began among those whom society reduces to its dregs, was left affectless by the emotional dearth of her infancy and disturbed upbringing. She, too, is the victim of Compeyson's coldness, of the "icy water" of his "egoistical cal-culation" (to borrow phrases from Karl Marx).

Yet, with his characteristic and marvelous belief in human creativity and vision, Dickens makes Estella an inspiration for Pip. Although she cannot yet understand, and seems untouched by, the reparative impulse (the caring impulse, which, through its suffering, can cure schizoid alien-ation), she gives Pip's world meaning. She comes along the passages like a star: she is the *Stella maris*. The passage in which he speaks of this reminds us of the passage in *Wuthering Heights* in which Cathy cries, "Nelly—I *am* Heathcliff!"

"You will get me out of your thoughts in a week."

"Out of my thoughts! You are part of my existence, part of myself. You have been in every line I have ever read, since I first came here, the rough common boy whose poor heart you wounded even then. You have been in every prospect I have ever seen since—on the river, on the sails of the ships, on the marshes, in the clouds, in the light, in the darkness, in the wind, in the woods, in the sea, in the streets. You have been the embodiment of every graceful fancy that my mind had ever become acquainted with. The stone of which the strongest London buildings are made, are not more real, or more impossible to be displaced by your hands, than your presence and influence have been to me, there and everywhere, and will be. Estella, to the last hour of my life, you cannot choose but remain part of my character, part of the little good in me, part of the evil. But, in this separa-tion I associate you only with the good and I will faithfully hold you to that always." (345)

"The rhapsody," says Pip, "welled up within me, like blood from an inward wound, and gushed out." This is a strong metaphor and obviously springs from the unconscious depths of the fantasy. The images of blood and an inward wound belong to fantasies of "concern" and reparation, and there is a sense in which the outburst refers to feelings about the mother, such as we experience in infantile fantasy and body-feeling. Dick-ens is writing about feelings toward the mother, and while Estella is in a sense his Madonna, in the "Holy Mary Complex," she is by degrees, and by suffering, repaired as a female image in the fantasy, by Pip's love: at the end of the novel we feel at least a potential real and equal relationship between them.

In the symbolism of the novel, Estella represents the capacity in the "object" to inspire us. As Goethe said, "Woman lifts us up." It is a principle of object-relations psychoanalytical theory and of the "new" existentialism that our perception of the world and our capacities to deal creatively with it are bound up with our experience of loving encounter, between ourselves and the mother, and ourselves and the "significant other." It is this that Pip realizes in his love for Estella. His long path through all manner of suffering and self-doubt leads Pip to find the true self and true love, so he can ask, what is authenticity? What is most valuable in life? What is freedom? What is fulfilled being? Moreover, Pip embodies imaginative transcendence. All these qualities in the work come from the vision that Estella, as a star, calls out in him. Of course, we must say, it was Dickens who had the vision! But he identifies so closely with his protagonists that we can say that through Pip he experiences the power of the imagination to enable a man to find his true path, under the inspiration of love, both for woman and man. Pip's redemption comes by acts of imagination—by gradually coming, for example, to be able to imagine what Joe is suffering: and then by being confronted with the reality of Joe as he comes out of his illness in a state of delirium: this is itself a crisis of the imagination freeing itself to perceive a shocking truth. When Pip speaks of the marshes in the passage quoted below, he speaks as much of the marshes, the darkness, and evil, as he does of graceful fancy and light. He speaks, too, of how love is more real than the stones of London, and in this we see those Blakean impulses in Dickens to assert that human love and vision are more significant than any material reality, or a comfortable career as a gentleman.

The quest for meaning in *Great Expectations* makes it a book of more than mere "social" or "political" relevance: *Great Expectations* is a work of art very much concerned with freedom as an inward condition of spirit, in the pursuit of authenticity. Of course, "society" in *Great Expectations* is a society of injustice, and this is physically manifest in the recurrent symbolism of *being manacled*—while some of the characters like Magwitch and Estella's mother bear the scars and mannerisms of the convict all through their lives. The hulks, out beyond the marshes, symbolize the way in which society puts beyond its bounds the creatures it has brought down by its own darkness and moral miasma. These characters have forfeited their freedom, or have had it destroyed (which is why Magwitch wants to enshrine freedom in Pip but gets it wrong).

Throughout the book Pip fears the loss of freedom and authenticity as a death; it is the death that this society threatens one with, the death of one's *potentia*. Estella says, "I must be taken *as I have been made*," and this relates to the central theme of the "natural heart." The heart might be said to be a beacon, and the alternative a gallows: throughout Pip has a recurrent image of a *suspended death* such as is symbolized in those opening passages of poetic prose that we have examined.

Pip is threatened throughout the book with contamination from this world of the criminal, which is the menace (as I would put it) of "false solutions"—the false solutions of hate, violence, and murder but also of money and "manners makyth man" in the wrong and superficial sense. Of course, Pip is not likely to fall into crime, but he suffers from the defects of those *who ruin other people's lives* as a consequence of their own false solutions.

At the end of chapter 22 Pip feels this contamination, as Wemmick shows him Newgate:

I consumed the whole time in thinking how strange it was that I should be encompassed by all this taint of prison and crime; that in my childhood on our lonely marshes on a winter evening I should have first encountered it; that, it should have reappeared on two occasions, standing out like a stain that was faded and not gone; that, it should in this new way pervade my fortune and advancement.

While my mind was thus engaged, I thought of the beautiful young Estella, proud
and refined, coming towards me and I thought with absolute abhorrence of the
contrast between the jail and her. I wished that . . . I might not have had Newgate
in my breath and on my clothes. I beat the prison dust off my feet as I sauntered
to and fro and I shook it out of my dress, and I exhaled its air from my lungs. So
contaminated did I feel . . . that . . . I was not yet free from the soiling consciousness
. . . when I saw her face. . . .

What *was* the nameless shadow which again in that one instance had passed?
(249–50)

Of course Pip has the shadow of Newgate on him, and Estella is the
daughter of a criminal woman and Pip's criminal patron. But at another
level revealed by the psychoanalytical analysis of symbolism, I believe we
can say that there is a sense in which the "shadow" is the shadow in Pip
of his own male libidinousness, his sexual assertiveness, which he also
recognizes to be potentially there in Estella (and which she fulfills in her
sadomasochistic marriage to Bentley Drummle). In his quest for meaning
Dickens involves the search for sexual wholeness, libidinal and ideal united,
and while in life he failed to find this fulfillment, he comes near to realizing
a love of equality and mutual respect in Pip and Estella.

There are two aspects of the libidinal that are especially explored in
this book. One is the natural (sexual) heart represented by Biddy, whose
name surely means "the libidinal." Of course, Freud devised the term long
after Dickens wrote, but the word "biddy" for a libidinal girl is found in
Twelfth Night ("Ay, Biddy, come with me," "biddy" here meaning a
chicken, with a sense of "poule"). When Pip decides to go and propose
to Biddy, despite the inauthenticity of such a choice (for he has not courted
her and merely assumes—arrogantly—that she is "available"), this is a
stage in his acceptance of his libidinal dynamics, and also in his becoming
able to distinguish between true "being" love and "willed" love.

The other aspect of the libidinal is the problem of homosexuality—or,
to put it in a more meaningful way, Pip's acceptance of the male element
as well as the female, in its tender proclivities. The relationship between
Pip and Joe Gargery is homosexual in this sense: "What larks!" exlaims
Joe, whose delight in Pip seems to belong almost to the stage of play
between adolescents of the same sex, which everyone goes through in
normal development. There are also strong homosexual elements in Pip's
relationship with Magwitch—"homosexual" in that they are like the deep
feelings between father and son—and the last tenderness of Pip to Magwitch as he is dying is that of homosexual love, in this sense. In the pattern

of intrapsychic dynamics, we may speak of Dickens learning to love his maleness, which one might say (as with Mahler) is loving the father in oneself as a stage in the development toward sexual and emotional wholeness.

Between Joe and Pip, and Magwitch and Pip—even between Jaggers, Wemmick and Herbert, and Pip—this homosexual element is positive and enriching. With Orlick and Bentley Drummle there is a false "manliness" that impels them toward sadistic cruelty. It often seems that Dickens's fear of the libidinal aspects of woman was associated with a fear of male proclivities that he was equally afraid of in himself, and in this book he seeks to come to terms with them all, to find unity.

These sexual elements may be linked with the essential theme of the book, which is that of existential freedom and self-realization. The "upshot" seems to be this: it is possible for the natural heart to be influenced by both male and female, by both mother and father, in such ways as to resist the imposition of inauthenticity upon oneself by society or by people with false ideas, in order to find the true self. One needs, like Pip, to find one's manhood. But in realizing "true self-being," the exploration of the image of woman is crucial: her capacity to inspire, her libidinal potentialities, the dark side of her nature, and her capacity for care.

The engagement with the figure of woman in *Great Expectations* is as intense as that "gush of blood" in Pip's speech above. Consider the intensity of feeling in the visions of Joe's sister, of Miss Havisham, of Biddy in her honesty and sympathetic devotion, and in the entrancing image of Estella, the murderess, and her hanging shadow. In these Dickens shows himself intensely engaged in an imaginative engagement with the anima—with the woman of infantile and unconscious fantasy. And these explorations of the nature of being male and being female are held together by the central figure of Pip, who tells the story as the "I" who pursues the existential quest in a great novel.

I haven't perhaps in the space available been able to draw the reader's attention to the richness of Dicken's language, in the way it serves his symbolic purpose. If I were to try to exemplify this, I might take this passage:

Next day the clothes I had ordered all came home, and he put them on. Whatever he put on, became him less (it dismally seemed to me) than what he had worn before. To my thinking there was something in him that made it hopeless to attempt to disguise him. The more I dressed him, and the better I dressed him, the more he looked like the slouching fugitive on the marshes. This effect on my anxious fancy was partly referable, no doubt, to his old face and manner growing more familiar to me; but I believed too that he dragged one of his legs as if there were still a weight of iron on it, and that from head to foot there was Convict in the very grain of the man.

The influences of his solitary hut-life were upon him besides, and gave him a savage air that no dress could tame; added to these were the influences of his subsequent branded life among men, and crowning all, his consciousness that he was dodging and hiding now. In all his ways of sitting and standing, and eating and drinking—of brooding about, in a high-shouldered reluctant style—of taking out his great horn-handled jack-knife and wiping it on his legs and cutting his food—of lifting light glasses and cups to his lips, as if they were clumsy pannikins—of chopping a wedge off his bread, and soaking up with it the last fragments of gravy round and round his plate, as if to make the most of an allowance, and then drying his fingers on it, and then swallowing it—in those ways and a thousand other small nameless instances arising every minute in the day, there was Prisoner, Felon, Bondsman, plain as plain could be.

It had been his own idea to wear that touch of powder, and I conceded the powder after overcoming the shorts. But I can compare the effect of it, when on, to nothing but the probable effect of rouge upon the dead; so awful was the manner in which everything in him that it was most desirable to repress, started through that thin layer of pretence, and seemed to come blazing out at the crown of his head. It was abandoned as soon as tried, and he wore his grizzled hair cut short. (318–19)

Every vivid element in the description enhances the awful sense of falsity that Pip perceives in Magwitch and Magwitch's idea of a "gentleman"—the image into which the convict has tried to mold him.

The passage is a marvelous example of Dickens's awareness of what today we would call "body language." The harsh life to which Magwitch has been exposed is now integral with his whole bearing: the way he treats his knife and his plate, soaking up with his bread the last fragments of gravy as if "to make the most of an allowance," speaks of his existence. The "touch of powder" speaks of his yearning to be a gentleman, or at least of his concept of gentility, and it exacerbates the deathliness of his predicament—because if he is taken as a returned felon he will be hanged. The description is not merely to give us the vivid presence of Magwitch, however, but to symbolize the moral horror Pip feels because he is trapped into hiding this man, whose concept of a gentleman has been forced upon Pip by deceit, so that he feels his own life to be corrupted, existentially, by a false idea—itself based on crimes of which he does not know the nature. Yet at the same time, clearly, from the description itself, he sympathizes deeply with the harshness to which the felon has been subjected by a punitive society. The moral complexities of such a scene can be recognized as standing behind (say) Joseph Conrad's power of portraying moral isolation, as in *Under Western Eyes,* and one could trace in Conrad both Dickens's existential themes and the realization that the way he uses language makes possible.

CHAPTER SIX

Finding One Another's Reality:
Lizzie Hexam and Her Love Story in
Our Mutual Friend

It was a remark of Merryn Williams's that sent me back to *Our Mutual Friend*, to appreciate the great strength of Dickens's portrayal of Lizzie Hexam: "Lizzie Hexam and Helena Landless are both strong, responsible women . . . with no charm or playfulness" (87). I had always been fascinated by the portrayal of Bradley Headstone, the compulsively jealous idolizer of Lizzie, as an acute psychological study. But I have always found the James Harmon/Rokesmith plot daunting, the transformations of Boffin incredible, and the Wegg business unreadable. More recently, I found Ian Robinson's comments on the meaning of Eugene Wrayburn's violation fascinating from a phenomenological point of view; it is as if Dickens could only allow a fulfillment between lovers when the man has been virtually castrated, in the psychoanalytical sense of being annihilated.

But a further reading of the novel, after this book was virtually complete, seemed to me to put a new light on the relationship. Merryn Williams is quite right: Lizzie is a very strong woman—the obverse, one might say, of the "fallen" woman. Lizzie is not going to be fallen, and Eugene Wrayburn, although he is to a degree the Steerforth type, is to be redeemed from the carnal and unthinking involvement of the playboy. Steerforth occasionally voices regrets in the presence of David; with Wrayburn, from the first, a real apprehension of the reality of the woman begins to operate on his effete and dehumanized attitude to life, to generate in him a new sense of authentic existence. Lizzie's formidable strength is an important contribution to this redemption of the man.

Lizzie is brought up by a father who salvages dead bodies from the Thames, and who is accused by Rogue Riderhood of murder. Riderhood himself is possibly guilty of murder, or at least connivance in manslaughter, and Lizzie's greatest distress centers on her desire to clear her father's name. She is no stranger to death, and she is fostered on the money salvaged from the pockets of drowned corpses. On the one hand, as "society" observes at the end of the novel after her marriage to Wrayburn, no woman could have been raised in less propitious circumstances: no one could be more tainted by association with a dreadful trade. With Lizzie we see Dicken's most genuine concern to follow the teachings of Jesus and find the most positive stirrings of the human spirit in the lowliest. For Lizzie from the beginning is torn between love for her father and distress over his trade. From the first page there is a look with a "touch of dread or horror" in her face as she watches his face earnestly. She cannot sit near the corpse they "catch," but when her father reminds her that the very basket that she slept in as an infant was washed up ashore, while the very rockers her father made to put it upon to make a cradle of it were cut from a piece of driftwood, she kisses her hand "and for a moment held it out lovingly towards him." When a notice is put up saying that the corpse had nothing significant in its pockets, Lizzie knows her father has robbed the corpse and has lied to conceal this, and so, fearing that doubts about this will be seen in her face by Lightfoot or Wrayburn, she goes out; as she explains to her brother, "I was afraid he might know what my face meant."

But, phenomenologically speaking, Lizzie's acquaintance with the corpses of suicides, drunks, fallen women, and other derelicts, in the mythical river of Dickens's London, is also an acquaintance with the ultimate questions of existence: the river here bears a symbolic resemblance to Lear's heath and the storm. It is also an acquaintance with the unconscious, and the darker aspects of being of which the river is a symbol. Just as Mark Twain drew an existential strength from the Mississippi River and so a strong moral power (the pilot who was not committed and responsible would perish), and Conrad drew his existential vision from the merchant navy and the exigencies of sea navigation, so Dickens draws his strength, as a questioner of being, from the somber presence of the Thames in his grim London. So, Lizzie's skill and strength, in rescuing the unconscious, battered body of Eugene from the river at the end is a manifestation of her moral strength—which is the strength of love. So, the symbolism of murder and death turns to a theme that "love is as strong as death": in lifting Wrayburn into the boat and taking him to the surgeons, Lizzie finds superhuman strength in, at last, total commitment to her future with this man, even though he seems at the time unlikely to survive.

In its power the moment is as redolent of complex tragic meaning as (say) Heyst's last moments in *Victory,* for what we draw from it is a sense of the strength of love: even in the face of oblivion, even in the toils of fate, mere death seems insignificant, as it does to Lear and Cordelia when, as birds in the cage, they become "God's spies."

The conversations that lead up to this triumphant conclusion have a strength and maturity, in the realization of character that rise to the level of George Eliot's greatest moments. And in these it is the strength of being in Lizzie Hexam that is made real to us.

The drama of the relationship between Wrayburn and Lizzie is in the depth of her appeal to him. He is a shallow, drifting man from the rich classes, like Steerforth, liable to fall into trouble from sheer aimlessness and boredom. He could easily have wandered into the seduction of a girl of less mettle than Lizzie, and caused ruin. But from the beginning his fascination for Lizzie has a real quality that is almost too strong for such a vague personality to deal with.

Eugene is with Lightwood when the latter questions Lizzie's father, during which interrogation she goes out to hide her face, while Wrayburn is looking hard at her. The room is seen with particular intensity:

The low building had the look of once being a mill. There was a rotten wart of wood upon its forehead that seemed to indicate where the sails had been, but the whole was very indistinctly seen in the obscurity of the night. The boy lifted the latch of the door, and they passed at once into a low circular room, where a man stood before a red fire, looking down into it, and a girl sat engaged in needlework. The fire was in a rusty brazier, not fitted to the hearth; and a common lamp, shaped like a hyacinth-root, smoked and flared in the neck of a stone bottle on the table ...roof, and walls, and floor, alike abounding in old smears of flour, red-lead (or some such stains which it had probably acquired in warehousing), and damp, alike had a look of decomposition. (21)

There could be no less prepossessing setting for the discovery of a heroine. Lizzie is barely literate, though she can read pictures in that red fire and clearly has an imaginative spirit. Her brother says of her, "if she knows her letters it's the most she does—and them I learned her." It is of course one of the major problems of class division that we find it difficult to grasp: a girl, however beautiful, was impossible to think of as a companion for a man out of her class, because she was uneducated. Even Dick Swiveller in *The Old Curiosity Shop* has to get the Marchioness educated before he can marry her—even though she saves his life by her devotion.

The gap is huge and seemingly unbridgeable between indolent lawyer Wrayburn and the daughter of a scavenger. In the normal everyday world of Victorian England, the likely relationship would be a seduction, like one of "Walter's," followed by the woman's ruin, a disastrous pregnancy, after which she would be on the streets to survive. If the interest Eugene feels in Lizzie was not to result in such a disaster, what else could ensue? He could perhaps aspire to make her his mistress, but this might well ruin his reputation in "society," as well as hers: later, of course, his marriage to her ruins him for "society," but he defies them and doesn't care.

This is why he regards his own fascination with foreboding:

"that lovely girl with the dark hair runs in my head. It was little more than a glimpse we had of her that last time and yet I almost see her waiting by the fire tonight. Do you feel like a dark combination of traitor and pickpocket when you think of that girl?"
"Rather," returned Lightwood. "Do you?"
"Very much so." (162)

Wrayburn is already compelled to seek her:

He could see the light of the fire shining through the window. Perhaps it drew him on to look in. Perhaps he had come out with the express intention...(163)

He climbs a bank to look in through the window:

She had no other light than the light of the fire. The unkindled lamp stood on the table. She sat on the ground, looking at the brazier, with her face leaning on her hand. There was a kind of film or flicker on her face, which at first he took to be the fitful firelight; but, on a second look, he saw that she was weeping. A sad and solitary spectacle, as shown by the rising and falling of the fire. (163)

He sees the bills posted up around the room respecting drowned people:

But he glanced slightly at them, though he looked long and steadily at her. A deep rich piece of colour, with the brown flush of her cheek and the shining lustre of her hair, though sad and solitary, weeping by the rising and the falling of the fire. (164)

Lightwood and Wrayburn are, of course, involved in an investigation, and are pursuing the question of Hexam being accused of murder. But their investigations are brought to a halt by Hexam's death, caused by an ac-cident with his own lines in attempting to recover another corpse.

Wrayburn has seen Lizzie start up and call for her father. When they find the body of Hexam "soaking into this filthy ground," and while the inspector is demonstrating how he died, Eugene slips away to fetch Abbey Potterson to convey the news to Lizzie that her father is dead. He is motivated by compassion for the lonely girl and realizes that she will need a woman to counsel her, in her grief. We learn this later from Charley.

"He brought the news home to my sister early in the morning, and brought Miss Abbey Potterson, a neighbour, to help break it to her. He was mooning about the house when I was fetched home in the afternoon—they didn't know where to find me till my sister could be brought round sufficiently to tell them—and then he mooned away." (230)

"Mooning" is a good description of Wrayburn's manner, for he behaves in such circumstances somewhat like a sleepwalker: he doesn't know why he allows himself to be involved, and he hides his concern from Lightwood, saying only, "I also felt I had committed every crime in the Newgate Calendar. So, for mingled considerations of friendship and felony, I took a walk." (177)

It gradually emerges that Wrayburn continues to visit Lizzie. She finds a temporary lodging, soon after her father's death, working as a needle-woman and keeping the stockroom of a seaman's outfitter. She shares a lodging with the Doll's Dressmaker ("a child—a dwarf—a something"), who is a cripple: "The queer little figure, and the queer but not ugly face, with its bright grey eyes, were so sharp, that the sharpness of the manner seemed unavoidable" (222). This creation of Dickens's is one of his triumphs—like Miss Mowcher in *David Copperfield*. Jenny Wren, with her alcoholic father, her industrious application, and her capacity for de-votion and love, even in her state of severe handicap, but with her beautiful hair, is completely convincing (as little Nell is not). Her real name is Fanny Cleaver; the appellation Jenny Wren was one she bestowed on herself.

She has shrewdness, intelligence, and (like Miss Mowcher, who is badly hurt capturing Littimer) a profound moral sense combined with wit. She is one of those representatives of the world of serious play, like the people of Sleary's circus, who embody a kind of warm-hearted folk wisdom. With great delicacy and tact Dickens hints at the end that she may form a relationship with the boy Sloppy—he takes it no further, being evidently aware that even to hint of a sexual relationship with this deformed child would be tasteless. But Jenny is the embodiment of the feminine virtues of sympathetic response, and of caring for the needs of being—divorced from the libidinal problem. Like Lizzie she loves a father who, like little Nell's, deceives and betrays her: another version of the Euphrasia theme. But the portrayal of her dealings with this drunkard are devoid of the exaggerations of melodrama and are totally unsentimental.

Jenny Wren becomes a necessary companion to Lizzie, and later, of course, a nurse for Wrayburn. She embodies a woman's understanding of the needs of those in difficulty. From the beginning, for instance, she recognizes that Lizzie has a need for privacy, when visited by Wrayburn:

"And she always has the use of this room for visitors," said the person of the house, screwing up one of her little bony fists, like an opera-glass, and looking through it, with her eyes and her chin in quaint accordance. "Always this room for visitors; haven't you, Lizzie dear?" (226)

Bradley Headstone notices "a very slight action of Lizzie Hexam's hand, as though it checked the doll's dressmaker"—for Lizzie does not wish her brother or the schoolmaster to know she receives visits from Eugene Wrayburn.

Lizzie's concern, of course, is to preserve her good name. So, Wrayburn's visits are made in the presence of Jenny Wren. Eugene's main concern at the beginning is to offer Lizzie education; in this he is showing, perhaps in spite of himself, an intention to try to bring her within the circumference of a woman who might be thought of as real to him. On her part, she is doubtful because to accept would put her under an obligation to him.

Lizzie sat so still, that one could not have said wherein the fact of her manner being troubled was expressed; and yet one could not have doubted it. Eugene was as easy as ever; but perhaps as she sat with her eyes cast down, it might have been rather more perceptible that his attention was concentrated upon her for certain moments than its concentration upon any subject for any short time ever was, elsewhere. (235)

Lizzie is turning Eugene, despite himself, into a serious person. He is trying with Lightwood to clear Hexam's name. But he confesses to Jenny he is an "idle dog" because "there is nobody who makes it worth while" for him to reform.

We have a man here, like Fred Vincy, who needs a good woman to make a man of him. His impulse to educate Lizzie is the first gesture he has ever made to going outward from his own listless egoism toward another:

"The thing is worth nothing in itself. The thing is worth nothing to me. What can it be worth to me? You know the most I make of it. I propose to be of some use to somebody—which I never was in this world, and shall never be on any other occasion—. . . . If I proposed to be the teacher, or to attend the lessons— obviously incongruous—but as to that I might as well be on the other side of the globe or not on the globe at all." (235–36)

His final touch is to imply that her refusal does wrong to her dead father (who was hostile to "learning"):

"By perpetuating the consequences of his ignorant and blind obstinacy. By resolving not to set right the wrong he did you. By determining that the deprivation to which he condemned you, and which he forced upon you, shall always rest upon his head." (236)

"It chanced to be a subtle string to sound," says Dickens: and it is. Lizzie perceives "the passing appearance of earnestness, complete conviction, injured resentment of suspicion, generous and unselfish interest."

All these qualities, in him usually so light and careless, she felt to be inseparable from some touch of their opposites in her own breast. She thought, had she, so far below him and so different, rejected this disinterestedness because of some vain misgiving that he sought her out, or headed any personal attractions that he might descry in her? (236)

Eugene is genuinely disappointed, and his arguments continue to work with force upon her. They are conveyed in writing that is at times so subtle as to be difficult to follow, and, to our satisfaction, we feel as if we might be following human dialogue of the seriousness (say) of that between characters in Jane Austen or George Eliot; as, say, between Elizabeth and Darcy, or between Dorothea and Will or Grandcourt and Mrs. Glasher. That is, we are following dialogue between a real man in all his complexity and a real woman. There is great depth in the exchanges, because Wrayburn is taking Lizzie seriously to a degree he does not realize, which is a new capacity drawn out by her: he loves her (we perceive) although he has as yet no clear inkling of the fact. On her part, beneath her strong commonsense resolution not to be toyed with by a man far outside her class and circumstance, she is drawn to him by the very seriousness she perceives she is capable of arousing in him.

"It's not easy for me to talk to you," returned Lizzie, in some confusion, "for you see all the consequences of what I say, as soon as I say it."

"Take all the consequences," laughed Eugene, "and take away my disappoint-ment. Lizzie Hexam, as I am your friend and a poor devil of a gentleman, I protest I don't even now understand why you hesitate."

There was an appearance of openness, trustfulness, unsuspecting generosity, in his words and manner, that won the poor girl over; and not only won her over, but again caused her to feel as though she had been influenced by the opposite qualities, with vanity at their head. (337–38)

Wrayburn is emerging not only as a serious person but also a subtle one—as when he is shocked by the possibility (after a careless remark) that he might be thought to be trifling with Jenny's infirmity. But he is as yet far from sensitive understanding, as the gulf between himself and Jenny is shown, by her fantasy of the children who made her "light." To this fantasy he refers, later, when he is thought to be dying.

One might surmise that it is the very reality of Eugene Wrayburn and Lizzie Hexam that means they had to face the grueling experience of his near-murder. The underlying currents of their relationship are extremely powerful, and the intense compulsions of Bradley Headstone reveal how destructive the power of passion can be. This realm of the deeper levels of human love was very disturbing, it would seem, to the Victorian mind: in Lewis Carroll and Ruskin we find different forms of dread of mature sexual responsiveness. The intense daughter-father relationship, the Eu-phrasia syndrome, is one way of escaping the power of mature love—and this is why the Little Dorrit-Clennam relationship is so unsatisfactory: it seems to perpetuate something of a father-daughter devotion, without phys-ical fulfillment: it is nonlibidinal. The Wrayburn-Lizzie relationship is powerfully libidinal.

Eugene and Lizzie face impossible barriers; yet their mutual attraction generates a profound respect for one another, and they interact as man and woman on equal terms as beings, making choices of integrity, in com-mitment. To a Victorian consciousness there seemed something terrible about this, and Wrayburn's near-destruction seems almost a baptism or a rite of passion, rather than a castration.

One element in this matter is surely the difficulty a writer must have in allowing his characters to reach a fulfillment he has never known himself. An obvious case here is Thomas Hardy: Tess can only find sexual fulfillment with Angel once she is condemned to death. But the novel during the nineteenth century largely became a vehicle of nonfulfillment—as it is often, for instance, in Henry James and Edith Wharton. In *Jane Eyre*, Jane can only marry Rochester after his maiming and blinding. Murder, as I have said, hovers in the background between Pip and Estella, and the end is equivocal.

In *Our Mutual Friend* the context of the lovers' relationship is death from beginning to end and so imbued with a certain solemn gravity. Around Lizzie Hexam the deepest fears of the unconscious are explored: she grows up in the presence of death and the daily destructiveness of the fatal river (in which the mysterious focus of the mystery story, John Harmon, is supposed to have perished). She is nourished on death, and her acquaintance with the management of corpses on the river equips her to save her lover when he is virtually reduced to a corpse in the river.

The complement to Wrayburn's strangely unwilling involvement with Lizzie is Bradley Headstone's psychological involvement and his fanatical jealousy. He is increasingly the living embodiment of envy, and we feel in the end that his hate is directed at love itself. The reluctance of the nineteenth-century novelist to portray sexual fulfillment may have behind it a dread of envy, perhaps an unconscious fear of sex as a form of eating, in which (in childhood fantasy) the mother and father might eat one another up, or even turn on the child (the primal scene and the fantasy of the combined parents). The intensity of such fears associated with sex suggests some deep disturbance at the level of infantile fantasy, associated perhaps with experiences of the breast and of being weaned (experiences that certainly lie behind George MacDonald's fantasies). Bradley Headstone's murderous rages and fits are perhaps a dramatic embodiment of the threats felt to be latent in sexual passion—and so Headstone ends in the river, too, killing himself and Rogue Riderhood, on whom he tried to pin his own murder (while Riderhood is possibly a murderer, too).

What Eugene Wrayburn undergoes is, by contrast, a death and resurrection. He has to suffer and virtually die to become fit to marry Lizzie. And on her part she has to make an extreme reparation to become ready to commit herself to this man. For both, I believe we may say, phenome-nologically, these experiences are necessary to make them "safe" to enter the dangerous realms of sexual fulfillment, just as Tess has to be condemned to death before she can enjoy her brief spell of sexual love with Angel.

The river, as I have said, is the river of the unconscious and primal passion. It is in this dark river of the unconscious that one encounters the ultimate existential challenge—and it is from immersion in this river that Lizzie fulfills her marvelous moral integrity and Eugene finds himself as a real man.

This is to look at the matter more positively than Ian Robinson, who sees the hero as having to be maimed before fulfillment. The development of their love can flower only when the proximity to death has removed completely the possibility of the marriage being consummated for the time being—for they are married when Wrayburn is physically prostrate and only half-aware in consciousness. This one might interpret as a kind of castration, but there is no suggestion that the marriage isn't consummated later. What the murderous theme makes possible is a concentration on the deep underlying love that is stronger than death, without any possibility of physical communion, but yet a love that can confront and transcend mortality—in a tragic way.

They have to suffer to come through to love and meaning—and then passion can be fulfilled. But first what must be established is the kind of mutual respect—despite the daunting differences in condition of life—that is a quality of true love, as it is between, say, Darcy and Elizabeth or Emma and Mr. Knightley. It is perhaps worth remarking that there is never any problem with Jane Austen of her heroes and heroines being libidinal, and there is in her novels no embarrassment about passion and its conse-quences: Colonel Brandon has a natural daughter, Wickham has seduced a woman, Harriet is a natural daughter, and Henry Crawford is an adul-terer. The social and moral consequences are severely examined, but there is no coyness or dread about sexual experience, however firmly misde-meanors are placed.

Wrayburn's enigma is that he respects Lizzie from the start:

"Don't mistake the situation. There is no better girl in all this London than Lizzie Hexam. There is no better among my people at home; no better among your people."(294)

But when Lightwood asks, "What follows?" Wrayburn has no answer, because it is still a riddle to him, which he has given up.

> "Eugene, do you design to capture and desert this girl?"
> "My dear fellow, no."
> "Do you design to marry her?"
> "My dear fellow, no."
> "Do you design to pursue her?"
> "My dear fellow, I don't design anything. I have no design whatever."(294)

Mortimer, however, persists in asking, "Then what is to come of it? What are you doing? Where are you going?"

Wrayburn's willingness to drift with the experience is in danger, clearly, of doing great harm, as Harold Skimpole's egoistic irresponsibility does. But we suspect (because of his occasional outbursts of seriousness) that he is more in love than he realizes. Lizzie is definitely in love with Eugene, though she has a strong realism about the impossible gulf between them. Jenny Wren is used as a choric interrogator, to get so much out of her. The Doll's Dressmaker invites her to look into the fire again, into the "hollow down by the flare," and dream of being a lady—what then would she think of Eugene Wrayburn?

> "She is glad, glad to be beautiful, that he may be proud of her. Her poor heart... is given him, with all its love and truth. She would joyfully die with him, or, better than that, die for him. She knows he has failings, but she thinks they have grown up through his being like one cast away, for the want of something to trust in, and care for, and think well of. And she says, that lady rich and beautiful that I can never come near, 'only put me in that empty place, only try how little I mind myself, only prove what a world of things I will do and bear for you, and I hope that you might even come to be much better than you are, through me who am so much worse, and hardly worth the thinking of beside you'."(349)

Jenny Wren gazes at her with "something like alarm"—for, with her sympathetic worldly wisdom, she realizes that this girl, by being in love with a gentleman, is exposed to serious emotional damage, since she can never hope to marry him.

The fact that she is in love with Wrayburn helps her to repulse Bradley Headstone, though she is also strongly aware that the man is a dangerous egoist. She protests to him when he declares himself; when repulsed, Head-stone menaces Wrayburn, and she tells him that Wrayburn has merely been most considerate, in connection with the death and with the memory of her poor father.

"He is nothing to you, I think," said Lizzie, with an indignation she could not repress. (399)

Headstone abuses Wrayburn as a rival, and Lizzie is strong in her reply.

"Mr. Headstone," returned Lizzie, with a burning face, "it is cowardly in you to speak to me in this way. But it makes me able to tell you that I do not like you, and that I never have liked you from the first, and that no other living creature has anything to do with the effect you have produced upon me for yourself."(399)

The language, we may note, has all the elegance of the language used by Jane Austen's characters, and it has the same strength, showing human beings dealing courageously with hate. Yet she is at the same time "compassionating the bitter struggle he could not conceal, almost as much as she was repelled and alarmed by it."

A short scene follows this bitter trial, and it is done with great subtlety. Lizzie is being escorted home by Aaron, who refuses to leave her to be escorted by Wrayburn. Wrayburn and Aaron see her home together, the former baffled—learning that her brother has been cruel and the schoolmaster menacing. But while Lizzie is distressed and resolute in her determination not to be left alone with him, even his light-heartedness entrances her, contrasting as it does with the brooding selfish petulance of Headstone:

so faithful to her, as it seemed, when her own stock was faithless; what an immense advantage, what an overpowering influence were his that night! . . . his occasional tones of serious interest (setting off his carelessness, as if it were assumed to calm her), . . . his lightest touch, his lightest look, his very presence beside her in the dark common street, were like glimpses of an enchanted world. (406)

Wrayburn repeats Lightwood's questions and declares, "we shall soon know now, Ah!" with a heavy sigh.

Lizzie hides away in isolation. Later she has an intimate exchange with Bella Wilfer, who suggests she is trying to wear out her weakness for the gentleman who admires her. Wouldn't it be better to lead a natural life and not be shut out from "your natural and wholesome prospects . . . would that be no gain?" "Does a woman's heart that—that has that weakness . . . seek to gain anything?" (627). Bella is chastened by this reply, and of course it relates to the riches versus integrity theme of the rest of the novel.

Lizzie's love is a hopeless and gainless one. What would she lose, if she came out of hiding?

"I should lose some of the best recollections, best encouragements, and best objects, that I carry through my daily life. I should lose my belief that if I had been his equal, and he had loved me, I should have tried with all my might to make him happier and happier, as he would have made me. I should lose almost all the value that I put upon the little learning I have, which is all owing to him. . . . I should lose a kind of picture of him . . . which I somehow feel I could not do a mean or a wrong thing before. I should leave off prizing the remembrance that he has done me nothing but good since I have known him, and that he has made a change within me, like—like the change in the grain of these hands, which were coarse, and cracked, and hard, and brown when I rowed on the river with father, and are softened and made supple by this new work as you see them now."
They trembled, but with no weakness, as the showed them. (527)

She has never dreamed of the possibility of being his wife.

"And yet I love him. I love him so much and so dearly, that when I sometimes think my life may be but a weary one, I am proud of it and glad of it. I am proud and glad to suffer something for him, even though it is of no service to him, and he will never know of it or care for it." (528)

The exchange is there to show Bella what an "unselfish passion" is like, but in itself it belongs to a powerful love story.

Wrayburn is not yet redeemed; though he regards Jenny's father with some compassion, "he was sorry, but his sympathy did not move his care-lessness to do anything but feel sorry." When challenged by Lightwood, he tentatively admits he is more serious about Lizzie than he is taken to be.

"And yet, Eugene, you know you do not really care for her."
. . . After a prolonged pause, he replied: "I don't know that. I must ask you not to say that, as if we took it for granted." (536)

And yet, as the old questions arise, he is flippant, and says icily, "What do I mean now? But it would be premature in this stage, and it's not the character of my mind." Lizzie is being brought gradually from the realm of a remote object of fascination and possible seduction, to that of the real woman. And her realness is powerfully before us, in the marvelous con-versation by the river just before the attempted murder.
He has at last found Lizzie, and they meet as equal man and woman.

She is solemn and her eyes are downcast: "He put her hand to his lips, and she quietly drew it away."

"Will you walk beside me, Mr. Wrayburn, and not touch me?" For, his arm was already stealing round her waist. (691)

The gestures are of course intensified for us, because they are also being watched by Bradley Headstone.

She challenges him as to whether he found her by chance (as he has said) or design. He admits design. He challenges her to admit she left London to get rid of him.

"How could you be so cruel?"

"Oh, Mr. Wrayburn," she answered, suddenly breaking into tears, "is the cruelty on my side? Oh, Mr. Wrayburn, Mr. Wrayburn, is there no cruelty in your being here tonight?"

"In the name of all that's good—and that is not conjuring you in my own name—for Heaven knows I am not good"—said Eugene, "don't be distressed."(692)

Her distress, however, is a tacit admittance of her tormented love.

"What else can I be, when I know the distance and the difference between us? What else can I be, when to tell me why you came here, is to put me to shame!" said Lizzie, covering her face. (692)

By this, she reveals that his presence can only put before her impossibilities, which can only humiliate her. He seems to be moved in a new way.

He looked at her with a real sentiment of remorseful tenderness and pity. It was not strong enough to impel him to sacrifice himself to spare her, but it was a strong emotion. (692)

He has at last "found" her.

"Lizzie! I never thought before that there was a woman in the world who could affect me so much by saying so little. But don't be hard in your construction of me. You don't know what my state of mind towards you is. You don't know how you haunt me and bewilder me. You don't know how the cursed carelessness that is over-officious in helping me at every other turning of my life, WON'T help me here. You have struck it dead, I think, and I sometimes wish you had struck me dead along with it." (692)

The words are ominous in the circumstances; but at last she has made him a serious person.

She had not been prepared for such passionate expressions, and they awakened some natural sparks of feminine pride and joy in her breast. To consider, wrong as he was, that he could care so much for her, and that she had the power to move him so! (692–93)

The conversation is so powerful because the two people move closer to each other's reality. She begs him to think of her, though she is a working girl, as if she were a lady, and to respect her rights. He is genuinely anxious when he asks, "Have I injured you much, Lizzie?" She asks him to leave her alone, and not drive her away. He seeks to force her to disclose her heart:

"Lizzie! . . . Answer what I ask you. If I had not been what you call removed from you and cut off from you, would you have made this appeal to me to leave you?"

"I don't know, I don't know. Don't ask me Mr. Wrayburn. . . . "

"If I had not been what you made me out to be . . . would you still have hated me?"

"O Mr. Wrayburn," she replied appealingly, and weeping, "you know me better than to think I do."

"If I had not been what you make me out to be, Lizzie, would you still have been indifferent to me?"

"O Mr. Wrayburn," she answered as before, "you know me better than that too!"

There was something in the attitude of her whole figure as he supported it, and she hung her head, which besought him to be merciful and not force her to disclose her heart. He was not merciful with her, and he made her do it. (694–95)

But she can only proclaim their situation "so endless, so hopeless" and asks, "Spare me." Until tonight, she declares, she never supposed he "needed to be thought for":

"If you do truly feel at heart that you have indeed been towards me what you have called yourself tonight, and that there is nothing for us in this life but separation, then Heaven help you, and Heaven bless you." (695)

(He has called himself her lover.)

The purity with which in these words she expressed something of her own love and her own suffering, made a deep impression on him for the passing time. He held her, almost as if she were sanctified to him by death, and kissed her, once, almost as he might have kissed the dead. (695–96)

At last, he has found her reality, and to himself, at the level of ego, he is surprised: "Can I even believe it myself?" He even finds, "in the appeal and in the confession of weakness, a little fear" (696). Dickens realizes the painfulness of commitment, and the fear of dependence, while Wrayburn reflects with a new realism on the truth of their natures: "She must go through with her nature, and I must go through with mine."

"I should like to see the fellow...who would undertake to tell me that this was not a real sentiment on my part, won out of me by her beauty and her worth, in spite of myself, and that I would not be true to her." (697)

"The rippling of the river seemed to cause a corresponding stir in his uneasy reflections." The challenge from the deep river reveals "parts of his thoughts" for their "wickedness."

"Out of the question to marry her," said Eugene, "and out of the question to leave her. The crisis!" (698)

The crisis is solved by the massive act of reparation that follows, as Lizzie hears his cries as he is stricken, and applies herself, from her early training, to rescuing this body from the river. As she bends over to secure a line, she recognizes the victim, and "the river and its shores rang to the terrible cry she uttered."

She is possessed of supernatural spirit and strength, and realizes that "if she lost distinctness of intention, all was lost and gone." Indeed, she has the strength of a working girl—for none of Jane Austen's heroines, or any "lady," would have been likely to have performed her life-saving task. Her strength is the reality of knowing what to do in a dire catastrophe. She kisses the mutilated face,

and blessed and forgave him, "if she had anything to forgive." It was only in that instant that she thought of herself, and then she thought of her self only for him. (701)

The murder attempt has brought home the full discovery of their reality to one another, even on the brink of death.

The Wrayburn who drifts in and out of consciousness is a Wrayburn of a new gravity. It is a master stroke of Dickens's, to get Lightwood to fetch Jenny Wren, to nurse Wrayburn, and to make her play such a significant part in his recovery: it is she who suggests the word "wife" as the clue to his recovery from brain damage.

The wedding ceremony, performed in the presence of death, takes nothing from melodrama or that kind of morbidity. Deeply moved, we follow the ceremony, "So rarely associated with the shadow of death; so insep-arable in the mind from a flush of life and gaiety and hope and health and joy" (752)—but not, of course, at the unconscious level. For unconscious reasons, the wedding ceremony is traditionally, in folklore, associated with menace—the bridesmaids being brides in disguise to deceive the evil spirits, for instance. But on the other side of the resurrection Wrayburn and Lizzie are free to meet at the level of beings, untrammeled by social divisions and the haunting fears of the dark river of the unconscious.

"Ah, my beloved Lizzie!" he said faintly. "How shall I ever pay all I owe you, if I recover.... It would require a life, Lizzie, to pay all; more than a life." (753)

She on her part is anxious never to discredit him: he on his, hopes he may put his "trifling, wasted" youth behind him and fears he may disappoint her good opinion if he does live. But we have no such fears, because of the strength they have found in their discovery of one another.

The only limitation, perhaps, is that the wife is portrayed in the role of nurse; but there is no indication that the marriage is not to be fulfilled, even though at first Eugene is a "shattered graceless fellow" and he bravely challenges "society" with this wife at his side.

But this marriage is no father-daughter situation nor a man's liaison with a child-wife, nor with an idealized angel-Agnes figure—nor is the wife a devoted custodian with her little basket of keys. Lizzie Hexam is a strong and capable woman, fully and passionately loving, and Wrayburn is at depth serious and sensitive, despite his origins. It is not too fanciful to compare them with Benedict and Beatrice or Elizabeth and Darcy, as tangible lovers who discover their possibilities for freedom and equality in their mutual plight.

CHAPTER SEVEN

Dickens's Own Relationships with Women

Toward the end of his life, Dickens was a rich man: he left some ninety-three thousand pounds.* His worldwide reputation was secure. He had difficulties with his children, and his marriage had been at an end for some time ("That figure is out of my life for evermore [except to darken it]"). He had the clandestine relationship with Ellen Ternan, and seems to have kept this secret from his adoring public. Some people who knew him well knew of his worst offenses; for instance, when one of his sons died he did not even write to his estranged wife, and a friend of hers, Sir William Hardman, wrote that this sank Dickens in his esteem to the lowest depths: "As a writer I admire him; as a man, I despise him." But as for Dickens, whatever distresses he was in, the "personal affection," as he called it, of his public consoled him, and he needed this acclaim more and more.

In the end he virtually killed himself by his obsessional need to indulge in public his fantasy of the murder of Nancy by Bill Sikes. Great artist in the novel as he was, Dickens suffered from that strange and corrupt morbidity that afflicted the Victorians: he was fascinated by public executions, and reflected a great deal on the shapes of the corpses of the Mannings,

*The equivalent of almost six million dollars today.

who were hanged for murder—the man's clothes looking like something on a scarecrow, the woman's form remaining clear and fine. He spoke of the "terrible impression" of

"the two forms dangling on top of the entrance gateway—the man's, a limp, loose suit of clothes as if the man had gone out of them; the woman's a fine shape, so elaborately corseted and artfully dressed, that it was quite unchanged in its trim appearance as it slowly swung from side to side." (quoted in Mackenzie, 218)

The fascination with the gallows, murder, prisons, and instruments of torture might well have been seen as part of the novelist's preoccupation with human reality in all its ranges. But the obsession with the murder of Nancy seems to reveal something more: "I have been trying, alone by myself, the *Oliver Twist* murder, but have got something so horrible out of it that I am afraid to try it in public" (quoted in Mackenzie, 373). Five years later he worked again on this text: "It is very horrible but very dramatic" (Mackenzie, 373).

He was, say the Mackenzies, more and more attracted to the idea of a new reading that would satisfy his need for a sensational climax. Of note are his doubts about using the murder of Nancy for this effect:

I have no doubt that I could perfectly petrify an audience by carrying out the notion I have of the way of rendering it.... But whether the impression would not be so horrible as to keep them away another time, is what I cannot satisfy myself upon. What do you think? (Quoted in Mackenzie, 374)

He admitted that the murder scene drove all the breath out of his body— and Dickens at this time was suffering from sleeplessness and sickness.

Yet he must try the reading on an invited audience with oysters and champagne afterwards: Yates wrote,

[As he] flung aside his book and acted the scene of the murder, shrieked the terrific pleadings of the girl, growled the brutal savagery of the murderer, brought looks, tones, gestures simultaneously into play to illustrate his meaning there was not one . . . but was astonished at the power and versatility of his genius. (Quoted in Mackenzie, 374)

Dickens noticed that his listeners were "unmistakeably pale and had horror-stricken faces." One physician present warned Dickens against promoting mass hysteria (and Dickens had an astonishing electrifying effect on his audiences). The Shakespearean scholar William Harness wrote that "I had an almost irresistible impulse upon me to *scream,* and that, if anyone had cried out, I am certain I should have followed" (Quoted in Mackenzie, 374).

When he invited the painter W. P. Frith to the first public reading, Dickens said, "It is horribly like, I am afraid. . . . I have a vague sensation of being '*wanted*' as I walk about the streets" (Mackenzie, 375). Yet he now added the hunt for Sikes and his final death, being hanged by accident. He was now "trying it daily with the object of rising from that blank state of horror into a fierce and passionate rush at the end" (Mackenzie, 375).

Sikes, say the Mackenzies, was a "diabolic embodiment of his own darkest feelings," which felt a murderous rage against Nancy. The Duke of Argyll declared that Dickens had the faculty that other great actors have of "getting rid of their own physical identity, and appearing with a wholly different face and a wholly different voice." This power in Dickens was astonishing.

These reading tours were making Dickens seriously ill; yet when Dolby urged him to choose "less stressful items," Dickens became angry, smashing a plate and shouting at his agent for his "infernal caution," (Mackenzie, 377), then relenting and embracing him tearfully, admitting "there was a little too much 'murder' in our arrangement." Yet, as he went ahead, he "looked desperately aged and worn; the lines in his cheeks were now deep furrows; there was a weariness in his gaze and a general air of fatigue and depression about him": his "extraordinary elasticity of spirits" seemed to have left him (Mackenzie, 377).

All this is strange; but it especially illuminates Dickens's problem with woman. There was within him some intense need to repeat compulsively that intense fantasy of an attack on the libidinal woman who has acted out of sympathy and love for a child but who has betrayed her brutal lover. He was angry with those who suggested that this obsession with acting out this fantasy might seriously damage his health. One might even say that his addiction to this horrific, sadistic fantasy of the assault on the phantom woman of the unconscious killed him.

The compulsion surely also has sexual connotations. It is clear from the descriptions of the hanged corpses of the Mannings above, from the murder scene in *Oliver Twist,* and from other images in Dickens that the shadowy fantasy in which woman is associated with murder is the primal scene: a haunted fantasy of parental sexual intercourse conceived of, as by a dis-turbed child, as a kind of murder, or an activity involving the possibility of annihilation. Murder lurks behind sexuality in the later novels, as I have shown. Sexuality can only be exorcised of this threat by prodigious suffering and reparation, beyond the murderous moment, as with Eugene Wrayburn and Lizzie Hexam. Throughout there is an urge to mold woman into a sexless role, as by creating her in the image of a daughter, or a certain Euphrasia role of a kind of childlike sexlessness, as with Little Dorrit (whose partner regards himself as beyond "that tender aspect of life," as in Arthur Clennam).

The power Dickens had to assume a "different" face and voice may be linked with the "double" theme in his work by which an individual often turns out to be somebody else—as with John Harmon in *Our Mutual Friend*—or there is a switch, as with John Jarndyce's transformation from husband to father. In *Edwin Drood* Jasper is evidently a split character. These oddly evasive manifestations may be associated with schizoid elements in Dickens, which occasionally affect his work. One cannot escape the persistent sense of dread that lurks behind his creative impulse to avoid certain realities, with an urgent need to keep certain things apart—his characteristic attachment to compartmentalization. Biographers of Dickens speak of a "deep-seated but inexplicable malaise," and of his frequent depressions. Dickens's mode of driving himself furiously into all kinds of public activities is clearly manic; but there lurks something more terrible behind his life—what biographers call "the darker side of Dickens." Moreover, it must not be forgotten how terrible was his sense of failure over his marriage:

It is all despairingly over. A dismal failure has to be borne.... What a blighted and wasted life my marriage has been. (Mackenzie, 299)

And yet this marriage had gone through fifteen pregnancies before its end—five miscarriages and ten children in twenty-two years. Yet, like George MacDonald, while he knew woman in the flesh, he spent a lifetime trying to "find" her in art.

There are many indications of the strange fantasy splits in Dickens's relationship to woman in life as well as in his art. His wife seems to have been in youth plump, spoiled, and self-indulgent, but he found her childishness and passivity appealing. The Mackenzies believe that she provided "the necessary antithesis to his dominating vigour." But after the end of his marriage he said of her, "she never presented herself before (the children) in the aspect of a mother.... It is her misery to live in some fatal atmosphere which slays everyone to whom she should be dearest." If, as some psychotherapists believe, in marriage "psychopathology plays a part on both sides," there was a deadly kind of compulsive incompatibility between them: this constantly pregnant wife never seems to have enjoyed motherhood, while she was jealous of Dickens's creative work and could not cope with his fame. His work is full of dark phrases that have a ring of sorrow about the failure to find a harmony of shared interests and a true mutuality.

Dickens's attitude to woman was compartmentalized in several ways, as I have suggested. The disillusioned view, formed around his own mother, was split off from the vision of the "angel," ideal woman. During his courtship with his wife, Mary Hogarth, who was then fifteen, acted as chaperone, and in the early years of his marriage she was worshipped by him as the epitome of ideal womanhood. Throughout his life he seemed to need to idolize this kind of devoted sister figure like Agnes in *David Copperfield* and Rose Maylie in *Oliver Twist*—angelically beautiful, devoted, inspiring, and the object of pure admiration. Astonishingly, when Mary died, Dickens bought a double plot in Kensal Green cemetery, hoping to be buried alongside her when he died; he said, "I have never had her ring off my finger." Little Nell was spun out of memories of Mary. Later, when a brother died, he sold the burial plot, but had to visit it when Mary's coffin was uncovered; inevitably, all his feelings for her were revived. It is difficult to imagine what the feelings of the wife must have been (though in the earlier years of their marriage Mary shared their life closely, to the pleasure of all three). The death of Little Nell is the death of Mary Hogarth.

Georgina Hogarth later entered the Dickens household in much the same way—as a self-sacrificing sister in a sexless relationship who took Dickens's part in the breakup of his marriage and declared that "a man of genius ought not to be judged with the common herd." Her dutiful, pure devotion was perhaps the inspiration for Little Dorrit, the child-wife and daughter-slave.

Dickens had other "inspirational" feelings for other women: Christiana Weller (a woman of "wonderful endowments") and Mrs. de la Rue, whom he sought to treat by mesmerism, finding himself in doing so in combat with some dark masculine ghost in her psyche.

Finally, there was the relationship with Ellen Ternan, who belonged to his stage world and with whom he acted the scenes of an older man in relation to a girl, and whom he later kept in the fairy tale house in Slough, totally apart from his real life.

And then there was the humiliating experience when he became sentimental over his memories of Maria Beadnell, and wrote to her: "You ask me to treasure what you tell me, in my heart of hearts. . . . O see what I have cherished there, through all this time and all these changes." When he met her, it was a terrible shock: she had become fat, giggling, and verbose, and her "intimate manner had become an embarrassing familiarity" (Mackenzie, 270–71). It was, indeed, exactly like Arthur Clennam revisiting Flora: painfully awful.

The compartmentalization that afflicted Dickens seems to belong to a general problem of the Victorian male. The Mackenzies have a most insightful paragraph on this. (Interestingly, this follows immediately after an account of what a tyrant Dickens was in the house, inspecting the children's rooms every morning, keeping everything under strict control: daughter Kate said, "My poor mother was afraid of my father . . . she was never allowed to express an opinion—never allowed to say what she felt"):

Georgina gradually assumed all the functions of a wife, except those of sexual partner, although the wife herself was still alive and well and living in her own home. The Victorian conventions made many men ambivalent about their sexuality; physical passion seemed a hidden and shaming thing, and in public they idealized womanhood and extolled chastity. One means of coping with this contradiction was the double standard, which made mistresses and prostitutes the price of domestic virtue. Dickens apparently found a different solution, which was echoed in one novel after another, and harked back to the triangular relationships of the short-lived idyll in Furnival's Inn—and possibly even to complex childhood feelings towards his mother and his sister Fanny. During the first year of his marriage his powerful attachment to Mary Hogarth enabled him to polarize his emotions. He was physically attracted to Catherine whereas young Mary became the epitome of innocence. Her death not only shocked him, it also destroyed the balance of his emotional needs. He later declared that his troubles with Catherine began soon afterwards. . . . After Georgina joined the family . . . the balance was to some extent restored.(245–46)

The compartmentalization that the MacKenzies call "polarisation" was so intense that Dickens, who wore Mary's ring, wanted to be buried with her. He did not want to be buried with the woman with whom he shared physical passion. That desire to be buried has an important symbolism: it is surely the desire to be merged with another, in that eternal ultimate way the infant is merged, or desires to be merged, with the mother in the "oceanic feeling" of baby-mother union? Dickens's ideal women therefore tend to be "little mothers," but also (because sexless) *sisters*. As we have seen, there are many moments in Dickens's novels in which the intensest man-woman relationships are those between brother and sister, as with Tom Pinch and his sister.

As with the problems of Lewis Carroll and Ruskin, it seems clear that it is sexual maturity in the woman that is dangerous. It is adult sexuality that is the menace, threatening murder and confusion, because out of this dark, unconscious realm arise the fantasies of infant fears of dangerous voracious appetite.

This takes us back to the Victorian attitude to babies, and especially dead babies, discussed at the beginning. The baby was adored because of its innocence: if only it were possible for it not to be the product of the shameful physical passion of its parents, their "wrath"!

Again, the Mackenzies, in their life of Dickens, have an insightful paragraph in their discussion of the original title of *Little Dorrit*: "Nobody's Fault." Dickens felt that "everyone within the system . . . is in some way a prisoner." In *Little Dorrit* the characters cannot escape their roles, except for Little Dorrit. And this may be linked with Dickens's preoccupation with inheritance, and his own feeling that his early life had borne upon him harshly and cripplingly:

Childhood is the only phase of life on which the shades of the prison house have not closed and its innocence is embodied in her unsullied goodness. Unlike Little Nell she (Little Dorrit) has survived into adult life, caring for her selfish father like a child-wife. Disappointment had led Dickens to idealize women more strongly than ever; and for him *innocence remained the clue to perfection*. (Mackenzie, 278; my italics)

So, we may link the preoccupation with innocence and the idealized sister-wife or child-wife relationship to Dickens's nostalgia for childhood. His concern for the child, and his defense of the child against brutality and oppression was, of course, one of his major creative themes—and it represents a defense of being against a brutal world. It is one of the great themes of his art, and F. R. Leavis was right to applaud and endorse it.

But in the realm of adult sexuality, and the quest for truth and freedom in the relationship between man and woman, it will not do to hanker after adult versions of child relationships, based on a concept of "childhood innocence."

It is valuable to see Oliver Twist as the victim both of a harsh society and of the new poor laws inflicted by utilitarian economics. It is valuable to see Louisa Gradgrind as lacking in moral sense because the "childhood of the mind" has been deliberately neglected in her upbringing, while she has been starved of play, imagination, and love. It is valuable in Dickens's novels to follow Oliver Twist in becoming at last a child who comes into his own inheritance; to follow Pip in overcoming a falsifying inheritance that is a legacy of chance in early childhood; to follow David Copperfield as he progresses to manhood through tremendous deprivations in child-hood. It was valuable for Dickens's art that every now and then he recalled with dread his own catastrophes in childhood—"I forget that I am a man and wander desolately back to that time of my life" (Mackenzie, 213)—because it thrust upon him the need to tackle the deepest problems of authenticity and fulfillment. At times, of course, his solutions to these could be themselves too much like childhood dreams—magical solutions that depend upon fairy godmothers and godfathers. As the Mackenzies say, his

adult will to forgiveness was not sufficient to dispose of the deeply ingraved feelings of self-pity and injustice, nor the fantasies of revenge that lay behind them.... To make human kindness prevail, when innocence was so weak and villainy so pow-erful, he had to resort to such tricks as changes of heart, quirks of fate, and the avuncular figures, uncorrupted despite their wealth, who cast a glow of goodwill and gold over so many of his closing pages ... something like a transformation scene at the end of a pantomime was always needed to get the clowns and devils off the stage and to bring on the final tableau of familial bliss.

Such a fantasy solution—the domestic paradise regained—was essentially Uto-pian, and like all Utopias it lay beyond the border of magic. (212)

They go on to say, "The problems of adult life cannot be properly stated let alone understood and solved, even by the cleverest child."

And even the cleverest adult cannot cope with them, maturely, when his vision of the world is shaped by the perspectives of childhood and coloured by its enduring resentments. (212)

It is a considerable critical task to try to say which "solutions" in Dickens's novels are "beyond magic" and which are not.

But the sexual solutions, and the problems of love, are those that are least successful, because they are shaped by the perspectives of childhood— and by a wishful desire to return to the childhood state of innocence before the development of adult sexuality, because adult sexuality (the primal scene) threatens death.*

I have tried to pursue this study in the spirit of my assertion that English is a Humanities subject: it belongs to the pursuit of truth such as was initiated in Greek antiquity and the *telos* of that movement. The value of this pursuit of truth is that it may promote self-realization and the achievement of a sense of meaning.

In those pursuits, questions of gender and sex are obviously important: as Lawrence saw, the problem of relationships between man and woman is at the heart of the search for "spontaneous-creative fullness of being."

As Leavis saw, Dickens was concerned to uphold "being" against a society that threatened it, with its attachment to money and industry, and its utilitarian philosophies. But as we have seen, when it came to the problems of man-woman relationship, he was seriously hampered, not only by the attitudes of his age but also by his own emotional makeup and psychic pattern.

Dickens was obviously a deeply disturbed man, whose restless energy and creative effort was devoted to holding his world together and warding off depression—and something deeper, a sense of dread and fear of chaos, with schizoid elements. He believed consciously in love, charity, and forgiveness, but even here there was a deep division between art and life. If he asked, like David Copperfield, "whether I shall turn out to be the hero of my own life," it is clear that in life he often behaved like one of his own villains rather than a hero. To say as much does not invalidate his insights or even his moral didacticism. But it does mean that we must be careful when we consider his "solutions" to the problem of life, not least when they are sicklied o'er with the false ideals and moral precepts of the audience he tried to satisfy.

Philosophical anthropology seems to imply that the fundamental problem in our lives is that of authenticity—of seeking to become that which we feel we have it in ourselves to be. Only if we fulfill that potential true self can we hope to find meaning in our lives. This theme is often struck in Dickens, as with Pip; and when William Dorrit is released from the

---

*We have not escaped this problem: the obsession of our age with pornography is an obsession with the primal scene and death, too.

Marshalsea, Little Dorrit's joy is that now she will see him as he really is, or was meant to be. But how do we extend this concept of fulfillment and authenticity into man-woman relationships, into the realm of sexual love?

Here Dickens had an intense personal problem. Just at the age when the world began to unfold to him and he was hoping for an education, his father made a mess of the family budget and was imprisoned in the Marshalsea. Dickens was sent to work on a tedious job, pasting labels on blacking bottles, and felt humiliated by the incarceration. Worse than that, when things improved and he had escaped for a while, he found that his mother, for the sake of a few shillings, wanted to send him back. This seemed to him, when he contemplated that awful time, an attack on his authenticity and self-realization from the one person who was supposed to be the fount of life, the mother. At that time, he said, books "kept alive my fancy and my hope of something beyond that place and time," so books became for him the clue to the solution to the problem of life, to a creative future.

That the mother could be so insensitive seems to indicate deeper deficiencies in her, in her capacity to "be for" her child, which left Dickens with a deep feeling of threat to his state of being even from the mother, and a consequent dread of woman that lurked in his unconscious mind. In his obsession with the murder of Nancy it could be that he was indulging in a fantasy of putting to death the witch-woman who had blighted his emotional life. Another possible way of interpreting his compulsion is to see Nancy as a figure in fantasy likely to be emerging from her role as libidinal woman into the role of the mother, because of her maternal feelings for Oliver. The murder so frequently associated with the phantom woman could symbolize the dread that libidinal woman, if she gets out of hand, could destroy that "purity" that belongs to mother. But the intensity of the obsession suggests a deep fear of harm from woman. Again, as we have seen, a constant theme of his novels is the individual whose emotional life has been blighted—Estella, Louisa Gradgrind, Florence Dombey—and there are in general many themes having to do with disinheritance and neglect.

Money, as we have also seen, is an important symbol in these themes: it is suddenly lost (as with Little Dorrit, David Copperfield) or is a suddenly and magically restored (as to William Dorrit, Pip, Aunt Trotwood); it consumes people (like Richard Carson) or deadens them (Dombey, Lady Dedlock, Merdle), though some can both have money and be loving and

generous (Mr. Jarndyce, the Cheeryble brothers). The problem of money
was again clearly central in Dickens's life: his mother's father had been an
embezzler stealing thousands from the post office; his father was a Micawber who continued to scrounge on Dickens all his life. The way in which
loss of money blighted his own life led to his studies of individuals who
are caught up in the possession or pursuit of money, and the ruthlessness
that went with it, which hardened hearts and destroyed lives. Men especially seem in his novels to be affected by attachments to money: Dorrit,
Dombey, Merdle, Micawber, Magwitch—all emerge clearly from his experience of his father and his money problems. And with money, many of
his solutions are manic, such as a child in distress might invent in a situation
that he knows about but feels powerless to alter. Moreover, money as a
symbol must be related to "inner contents."* When it comes to authenticity, we may find in Mrs. Gaskell a much more realistic attitude to money:
in her novels, there has to be much more effort made to rescue and redeem
oneself. By contrast, Dickens's solutions are too often only magical, and,
despite his valid criticism of a material society (as with Merdle), depend
themselves on a sentimental view of benevolent patronage.

The same kind of objection may be made to many of his "solutions" to
the problem of relationships between man and woman. There are women
in Dickens who are seeking fulfillment, like Esther, Lizzie Hexam, Bella
Wilfer, even Estella at the end. But there is great reluctance to celebrate
sexual fulfillment. There is not one fully realized happy sexual relationship
in the whole of Dickens, and the best he can do is offer us the equivocal
end of *Great Expectations,* and the wounded—if promising—marriage of
the Wrayburns. After much suffering and penitence, as with Esther, Pip,
David, and Eugene, the upshot seems to be that there is perhaps a chance
of sexual fulfillment. But Little Dorrit, having been a child-daughter-wife
to her father, becomes a child-daughter-wife to Arthur Clenham, and this
couple—whom Leavis saw as the epitome of married togetherness—feel
sexless.

For unconscious reasons, the woman in Dickens had to be kept under
severe control, because she was so dangerous. The dread of this danger-

---

*Here the names are indicative: *Dorrit* echoes *d'or* (gold), while *Merdle* contains the word
merde (Fr. faeces). As Freud pointed out, gold is "inner contents." In *Merdle* and *Murdstone*
we have also echoes of the word *murder*: this is the male danger.

ousness prompts his attention to the punishment that follows any unac-
ceptable indulgence of the passionate life: then she has to die, or at least
(like Little Emily) go abroad. In his home for fallen women that he set up
with Angela Coutts, the inmates had to accept their charity in penitence:
they must be reeducated and then sent to emigrate—which was a kind of
death. In his novels, woman—whether sinful, born in sin, or born in
prison—has to make immense reparation, like Lady Dedlock, or spend a
life in duty and toil, like Esther, who became "Dame Durden,"* and Little
Dorrit, in order to gain our sympathetic respect. His world is heavily loaded
against woman, and in part this is due to his own inclinations.

While Dickens as an author was on the side of the outcast, the victim
of society, the poor and deprived, he was in his private life something of
a tryant and certainly authoritarian, as we have seen. This impulse to
control others extended to woman. When a girl sauced him in the street
and swore at him, he insisted that she be arrested, went home to get his
legal manual to show why, and made sure she was fined. While Dickens
is regarded by many as a radical, he was not a political radical. Of course,
he was appalled at the idea of revolution or class warfare, as *Hard Times*
and *A Tale of Two Cities* show. But if one compares him with nineteenth-
century women writers like Mrs. Gaskell and Mrs. Humphrey Ward, one
sees that his attitudes to women show no glimmer of leaning toward
celebrating the possibilities of social and political equality of the sexes.

And as for his morality, it is clear from the biographies that he was not
altogether respectful of his marriage vows, and often failed to respect the
legal and moral obligations of his relations with publishers. Moreover, there
is often a feeling with Dickens that the purpose of his moral fervor is to
gain that "personal affection" from his public, to boost his ego. As someone
said of the death of Little Nell, "what a good man you must be to have
written that!" So, often, when one is reading Dickens, one finds oneself
involved in fierce moral indignation against wickedness—and then (as with
the death of Nancy) drawn into strangely false emotions, as with the
thrashing of Squeers, or even the ducking of Mr. Stiggins. As in the murder
scene of Nancy and the death of Sikes, there are moments in Dickens that
must make us uncomfortable for the intensely righteous feelings they in-
duce, which are nearly sadistic. The reader is too often involved in a

---

*Dame Durden is perhaps one who accepts the *burden* of *Duty*.

perverse enjoyment of a sense of outrage, in which one is all too likely to fail to give the victim sympathetic understanding, while gloating on his punishment or death (Quilp, Squeers, Fagin, Headstone, Sikes).

So when it comes to the problem of woman, I believe we have to ask about *freedom*. The real clue to solutions of the problem of relationships between man and woman is that of freedom: the need for mutual regard and respect—the capacity to let one another go, in terms of the life solutions of each. Here, the deep unconscious fear of woman is the enemy, not least when, as for Dickens, a dread of sexuality in woman impels the need to control woman, and to oblige her to seek "repentance," to make massive reparation and be submissive. The idealization of woman, requiring her to be "pure," "innocent," and submissive, were weapons in this, as was the compartmentalization, which kept ideal woman apart from the libidinal and sexual one.

The themes of prison and release in *Little Dorrit* are clearly meant to relate to themes of freedom and self-realization. But Little Dorrit's reduction to a pure, all-good, submissive, ideal child-wife requires a parallel reduction in the hero to sexless, past-the-tender-stage-of-life, paternalistic "caring": in this image of man-woman relationship, Dickens falls a long way short of anything we can accept as a definition of love or even good relationships. Only perhaps with the strong character Lizzie Hexam did he in a sense meet his match, for she, although she is very womanly in feeling and devotion, and conscious of her low social status, has an independence and dignity that enables her to deal with a great many trials and temptations, while showing, as at the great crisis of her life, the murder attempt on her lover, the capacity to act and deal with reality on equal terms with any man.

Bibliography

Psychology and Philosophy

Bowlby, John. *Attachment and Loss*. London, 1969.
——. *Child Care and the Growth of Love*. Harmondsworth, 1953.
Brink, Andrew. *Creativity as Repair*. Hamilton, Ontario, 1982.
——. *Loss and Symbolic Repair*. Hamilton, Ontario, 1977.
Fairbairn, W. R. D. *Psychoanalytical Studies of the Personality*. London, 1952.
Freud, Sigmund. *The Interpretation of Dreams*. London, 1900.
Klein, Melanie. *Envy and Gratitude*. London, 1957.
——. *Our Adult Society and Its Roots in Infancy*. London, 1963.
Klein, Melanie, and Joan Riviere. *Love, Hate, and Reparation*. London, 1967.
May, Rollo. *Love and Will*. New York, 1969.
May, Rollo, with Ernest Angel and Henri F. Ellenberger. *Existence: A New Dimension in Psychiatry*. New York, 1958.
Milner, Marion. *The Hands of the Living God*. London, 1969.
Naevestad, Marie von. *The Colours of Rage and Love*. Oslo, 1979.
Stern, Karl. *The Flight from Woman*. London, 1968.
Straus, Erwin. *The Primary World of the Senses*. Glencoe, Ill., 1963.
Suttie, Ian D. *The Origins of Love and Hate*. London, 1935.
Ulanov, Ann Belford. *Receiving Woman*. Philadelphia, 1981.
Ulanov, Ann, and Barry Ulanov. *The Witch and the Clown*. Wilmette, Ill., 1987.

Winnicott, D. W. *Collected Papers: Through Pediatrics to Psychoanalysis*. London, 1958.
———. *The Maturational Processes and the Facilitating Environment*. London. 1965.
———. *Playing and Reality*. London, 1971.

Literary and Historical Works

All references to the works of Dickens are to the *New Oxford Illustrated Dickens*.
Brewer, Derek. *Symbolic Stories*. Woodbridge, England, 1980.
Forster, John. *The Life of Charles Dickens*. London, 1872.
Frank, Lawrence. *Charles Dickens and the Romantic Self*. Lincoln, Nebr., 1984.
Guerard, Albert J. *The Triumph of the Novel: Dickens, Dostoevsky, Faulkner*. New York, 1976.
Harrison, Fraser. *The Dark Angel: Aspects of Victorian Sexuality*. London, 1977.
Hogarth, Georgina, and Mary Dickens. *Letters of Charles Dickens*. London, 1882.
Holloway, John. Preface and notes. *Little Dorrit*. Penguin edition. Harmondsworth, 1967.
House, M., and G. Storey. *The Letters of Charles Dickens*. 12 vols. Oxford, 1965.
Johnson, Wendell Stacey. *Living in Sin: The Victorian Sexual Revolution*. Chicago, 1980.
Johnston, Edgar. *The Heart of Charles Dickens*. New York, 1952.
Klingopulos, R. On the Victorian Scene in *The Pelican Guide to Literature*. Ed. Boris Ford. Vol. 6. Harmondsworth, 1982.
Leavis, F. R. *The Great Tradition*. London, 1950.
Leavis, F. R., with Q. D. Leavis. *Dickens the Novelist*. London, 1970.
Leavis, Q. D. *Collected Essays*. Vol. 1, *The Englishness of the English Novel*. Cambridge, 1983.
Mackenzie, Norman, and Jeanne Mackenzie. *Dickens: A Life*. Oxford, 1979.
Marcus, Steven. *Dickens: From Pickwick to Dombey*. London, 1965.
Mill, John Stuart. *The Subjection of Women*. London, 1869.
Neff, W. F. *Victorian Working Women*. London, 1929.
Nisbet, Ada. *Dickens and Ellen Ternan*. Berkeley, 1952.
Patmore, Coventry. *The Angel in the House*. London, 1854–56.
Patterson, R. W. K. *The Nihilistic Egoist: Max Stirner*. Oxford, 1971.
Petrie, Sir Charles. *The Victorians*. London, 1969.
Rotkin, Charlotte. *Deception in Little Dorrit*. New York, 1989.
Rubenius, Aina. *The Woman Question in Mrs. Gaskell's Life and Work*. Upsala, Sweden, 1950.
Slater, Michael. *Dickens and Women*. London, 1983.
Stopes, Marie. *Married Love*. London, 1918.
Storey, Gladys. *Dickens and Daughter*. London, 1939.
Thompson, E. P. *The Making of the English Working Class*. London, 1963.

Tomalin, Claire. *The Invisible Woman: The Story of Nelly Ternan and Charles Dickens.* New York, 1990.

Welsh, Alexander. *The City of Dickens.* Oxford, 1971.

Williams, Merryn. *Women in the English Novel, 1800–1900.* London, 1984.

Yates, Edmund. *Recollections and Experiences.* London, 1884.

Zwerdling, Alex. "Esther Summerson Rehabilitated." *PMLA* 88 (1973): 429

Index

181